MARXISM AND CHRISTIANITY

MARXISM
AND
CHRISTIANITY

Giulio Girardi

TRANSLATED BY *KEVIN TRAYNOR*

THE MACMILLAN COMPANY
New York

Library of Congress Catalog Card Number: 68-31277

FIRST AMERICAN EDITION

First published in English in 1968 by
M. H. Gill and Son Limited, Dublin

Originally published as *Marxismo e Cristianesimo*
by Cittadella Editrice, Assisi

The Macmillan Company, New York
Collier-Macmillan Canada Ltd., Toronto, Ontario

Printed in the United States of America

50,499

Contents

INTRODUCTION   vii

AUTHOR'S PREFACE   ix

MARXIST HUMANISM AND CHRISTIAN
HUMANISM   I
MARXIST HUMANISM AND CHRISTIANITY   13
CHRISTIAN HUMANISM FACE TO FACE WITH MARXISM   73

MARXIST SOLIDARITY AND CHRISTIAN
SOLIDARITY   140
MARXIST SOLIDARITY   143
CHRISTIAN SOLIDARITY   157

MARXISM AND INTEGRALISM   173
FIRST ANTINOMY   : INDIVIDUAL-HISTORY   181
SECOND ANTINOMY   : BASE-SUPERSTRUCTURE   185
THIRD ANTINOMY   : CLASS-MANKIND   193
FOURTH ANTINOMY   : PERSON-INSTITUTION   196
CONCLUSION   202

PEACE AND REVOLUTION   205

THE PROBLEM   205

THE CAUSES OF WAR   218

THE IDEAL OF PEACE   222

ACTION TOWARDS PEACE   243

A HISTORICAL PERSPECTIVE   254

CONCLUSION   262

Introduction

Giulio Girardi, author of the present volume, has become widely known, even outside Italy, as a result of his participation in the convention organized by the *Paulusgesellschaft* in the Spring of 1966 at Chiemsee (Bavaria). This convention brought together representatives of Christian culture and Marxist Communism, and at it the author furnished a report and contributed to the discussions. On that occasion, before eminent scholars, he distinguished himself as a leading expert on Marxism, both in its history and in its contemporary forms. He clearly enumerated the essential starting-points of any dialogue between Christianity and Marxism.

In the spirit of the task entrusted by the Holy Father to the Secretariat for Non-Believers, the author sets out in this book to specify what presuppositions are necessary, from the point of view of Christianity, for meetings and discussions with philosophical and militant atheism. There are undoubtedly many amateurs at work in this very difficult and topical field. They venture to the table of dialogue without adequate preparation, and do more harm than good. This is the case above all, when such dialogue comes to be transferred indiscriminately to the political plane. For this reason, it is also a particular merit of this outstanding specialist that he has placed at our disposal a sound knowledge of those elements which form the necessary background to such dialogue, and that he has distinguished between what is essential and what is incidental to it.

In order that it should be possible for dialogue, whether oral or written, to be conducted along sound lines, good will alone is not enough: it must be accompanied by a very exact knowledge of the opposing position. Since atheism directs its attacks, in the name of man, against the alienation of man from his own potentialities and purposes, it constitutes, for that reason, the greatest challenge to Christianity in our times. It has been rightly pointed out that this challenge could help to purify our descriptions, both of God and of Christianity, of all that is too human in them. Rather than have recourse to an unproductive apologetics when faced with contemporary atheism, we ought to concern ourselves with weeding out from Christianity what is not authentic, and we should even be grateful to atheism for the purifying function which it performs in this way. Eighteen years ago, in his volume *La Signification de l'Athéisme Contemporain*, Jacques Maritain was already drawing attention to the positive function of this spiritual movement of our times. Of course, this positive function of atheism is sometimes too highly valued, and this attitude is no less false than a purely negative resistance.

To what extent Marxism is, by its nature, bound up with atheism, ought to be deduced, not only from an analysis of Marxism itself, but also very largely from the evolution of Marxist states in the political sphere. It is a particular merit of Girardi to have posed this question with great accuracy. One of the tragic aspects of the whole problem is constituted by the fact that Marxist humanism is seen, in practice, to differ from its theory. Real life, then, will give us an answer which the theory is unable to provide.

CARDINAL FRANZISCUS KOENIG,
Archbishop of Vienna,
President of the Secretariat
for Non-Believers.

Author's Preface

In this volume I am gathering together some articles on the theme of Marxism and Christianity, namely 'Marxist Humanism and Christian Humanism', 'Marxist Solidarity and Christian Solidarity', 'Marxism and Integralism' and 'Christians and Marxists Face to Face on Peace.'

These are certainly not intended to replace the numerous historical studies of Marxism which already exist, and which are rich in analysis and erudition. My concern has been primarily theoretical (in the sense, of course, of 'theory' that is bound up with existence and history). It is to be understood, in other words, as a process of singling out the various basic themes around which doctrinal dialogue with Marxism ought to be built, the convergences and divergences that it reveals, and the directives according to which inspired Christian philosophical reflection ought to be conducted. This naturally presupposed an effort at interpretation and understanding. In making it, I am principally concerned with extracting the central motives and aspirations of Marxist philosophy. It was not my intention, in the section expounding Marxism, to write a purely historical study. At times, indeed, moving from within the system, I have sought to point to possible lines of development, while remaining faithful to the original inspirations.

Although each of these articles, taken broadly, has an object and character of its own, numerous interconnections and even repetitions will be observed. 'Marxist Solidarity and Christian Solidarity,' for instance, takes up again the paragraphs dedicated to communal humanism in 'Marxist Humanism and Christian Humanism', while developing them considerably. 'The last chapter, 'Peace and Revolution' develops principally the sections dealing with revolutionary humanism and economic humanism. More numerous are the interconnections between the first and third essays, both of which are attempts at an integral interpretation of Marxism, and which might seem, at first sight, to contradict each other on some points. In actual fact there is a difference of object between them which it is important to keep in mind. 'Marxist Humanism and Christian Humanism', while it refers to the thought of Marx and of contemporary Western Marxists, is principally concerned, nevertheless, with the Soviet type of Marxism. In 'Marxism and Integralism', on the other hand, the possibility of an internal re-thinking of Marxism itself is outlined, and a new 'model', inspired directly by Marx and by his most advanced contemporary disciples, is sketched out. Regarding the last two chapters, originally presented as contributions to the Congresses of Marxists and Christians held at Herrenchiemsee in West Germany, and at Marianske Lazne in Czechoslovakia respectively, I think it is important to mention that they are the fruit of prolonged discussions held in Rome with restricted groups of Marxist and Christian intellectuals, as well as of personal reflection. Thus they also reflect the considerable convergence of views achieved there.

Recalling the predominantly theoretical character of this enquiry, I should like to exclude from it, in fact, any concrete political design whatever. I would have neither the authority nor the competence necessary for such a task. When I speak of dialogue with Marxism, therefore, I am affirming the urgency of it and trying, for my part, to make a beginning. I have in mind a more brotherly human coexistence, with mutual understanding at the doctrinal level as an essential component.

'For our part, the desire for such dialogue, which can lead to truth through love alone, excludes no one, though an appropriate measure of prudence must undoubtedly be exercised. We include those who cultivate beautiful qualities of the human spirit, but do not yet acknowledge the Source of these qualities.

'We include those who oppress the Church and harass her in manifold ways. Since God the Father is the origin and purpose of all men, we are all called to be brothers. There-fore, if we have been summoned to the same destiny, which is both human and divine, we can and we should work together without violence and deceit in order to build up the world in genuine peace' (Pastoral Constitution on the Church in the Modern World, no. 92).

Even though I can see how immense such a project is, or rather, precisely because I can see it, I can also see quite well how modest is the contribution which the present small volume can make towards its realization. Many Catholic and Marxist friends have told me of their conviction that these essays could be of some use, even in their embryonic form. I was weak enough to be persuaded. I promise, however, to return to the subject with a wider and more profound treat-ment.

I hope that these pages will contribute, in some measure, to the increase of mutual understanding. When men love each other truly, God is present among them, even if they do not know it.

GIULIO GIRARDI.

Rome, 22 August 1966.

MARXISM AND CHRISTIANITY

CHAPTER I

Marxist Humanism and Christian Humanism

Christianity Face to Face with Marxist Atheism

One of the most significant aspects of the contemporary situation is the fact that the alternative of choosing a religious or irreligious perspective has become a radical alternative.

At the beginning of the modern age, the Protestant Reformation posed the problem of a choice for or against Catholicism; the French Revolution, proposing the ideal of a natural religion, raised the question of a choice for or against Christianity; the Soviet revolution and others inspired by it, e.g., the Chinese and Cuban revolutions, call for a stand to be taken up for or against God.

Atheism, which had an exceptional and clandestine character in the past, is today becoming a mass phenomenon and expressing itself in militant movements. It constitutes the official ideology of immense states, which propagate it with all the force of their totalitarian apparatus. Besides affecting philosophical doctrine, it penetrates into literature, the cinema and the interpretation of psychology, sociology, religious and civil history, art, etc., to the point of forming an atmosphere of culture and of life. 'This', writes Paul VI in his encyclical *Ecclesiam Suam*, 'is the most serious problem of our time'.[1]

This atmosphere forms the context of the new Christian

---

[1] *Op. cit.* E. tr., London 1964, 36. Cf. *A.A.S.* 1964, 651.

presence in the world. For the Church, it is no longer solely a question of announcing the gospel to men of other religions, but of announcing it to men who have no religion of any kind. Moreover, since there are irreligious zones right in the very heart of the traditionally Christian nations, the whole Church is put in a 'state of mission'. The problems arising out of this concern not only atheists, but believers too, who find themselves having to live out their faith in a *diaspora* situation, i.e., in continuous confrontation with atheism and with the objective conditions that have provoked it. These problems, then, are not unique to atheism. When examined with due care they are seen to be the great problems of the modern world become radical; or, more precisely, the eternal problems of man relived in the context of modern sensibility. If, therefore, atheism is limited as a fact, it is universal as a pressure and a risk; it is universal as a problem. As a result of this new situation a profound re-thinking is required both of philosophical and theological doctrine, and of pastoral, catechetical, pedagogical and ascetical methods.

Naturally, the first step in this re-thinking should consist of reflection on the nature of atheism, with the intention of extracting the problems which it raises for the Christian conscience.

Many see in atheism only an error, the most dangerous error in history; they find its roots in moral deviation, and their prime concern is to proclaim its condemnation. This way of approaching atheism is inspired by an anxiety for clarity and fidelity, but when it becomes exclusive it is both historically inadequate and pastorally sterile.

It is historically inadequate because it does not allow the actual subjective significance of atheism, or what it means for the atheist himself, to be grasped from within. This subjective significance can emerge, in fact, only insofar as the system is placed in its theoretical and lived context. Since man is fundamentally orientated towards truth and authentic values, it is to be expected that, for the atheist himself, the meaning of atheism consists more in the truths which it involves than in the errors in which it finds expression; more in the real values which it affirms than in those it denies. To understand atheism means, therefore, to ask what are the truths which the atheist intends to affirm and the values to which he intends to adhere when he denies God.

The method of condemnation is also fruitless from a pastoral point of view, because it precludes any possibility whatever of dialogue, and prevents the apostle from transmitting his message on the receiver's wavelength.

On the other hand, however, some Christians, animated by this desire for dialogue, affirm that atheism can be reduced to the rejection of a deformed image of God and of religion, and they lay the responsibility for this image on believers. They are thus compelled, unconsciously as it were, towards a paradoxical conclusion: since, in the last analysis, the atheistic denial is directed at a falsely-conceived God, atheism is not in fact error, but truth.

This, however, is no longer dialogue, but abdication. Dialogue with atheism involves, on the part of the believer, an acute and balanced power of discrimination, equidistant from either a global condemnation or a global acceptance. Atheism may not be reduced either to its errors or to its truths. It results from both.

The encyclical *Ecclesiam Suam* seems to indicate this attitude when it says: 'But though we must speak firmly and clearly in declaring and defending religion and the human values which it proclaims and upholds, we are moved by our pastoral office to seek in the heart of the modern atheist the motives of his turmoil and denial'.[2]

---

[2]*Ibid.*, 37—38. Cf. *A.A.S.* (*loc. cit.*), 652.

Even within the prescribed limits, the effort to understand the atheistic vision and experience remains of fundamental importance to the Christian. It is a delicate and complex task inasmuch as the psychological distance (to say nothing of the doctrinal differences) between the worlds of atheist and believer is greater than it is thought to be. And the Christian, especially if he has been formed in a totally Christian environment, and is accustomed to accept his faith and his system of values as beyond discussion and to see them accepted as such, will find it very difficult to become aware of difficulties and aversions towards them on the part of others. The task must be confronted with this awareness of its urgency and complexity.

The Marxist form of contemporary atheism is the most massive and spectacular of its kind. In facing up to it, it is more difficult to assume an attitude of dialogue than it might be in other cases, since, in this case, ideological differences are intertwined with political conflicts, both national and international, and with social and economic battles; and since the limits imposed on religious and all other liberties in the countries where it is the reigning power lead one to doubt the sincerity with which dialogue (the outstretched hand) is welcomed, or even offered. 'Dialogue in such conditions', writes the Pope, 'is very difficult, not to say impossible, although, even today, we have no preconceived intention of excluding the persons who profess these systems and belong to these regimes. For the lover of truth discussion is always possible'.[3]

In spite of these difficulties, which might induce greater precautions, the attitude of the Christian, even in confrontation with Marxism, should not be merely one of condemnation, but should include the effort to understand, of

[3]*Ibid.*, 37. Cf. *A.A.S.* (*loc. cit.*), 651.

which I spoke earlier. The success of Marxism in today's world is undeniable and clamours for attention. It attracts the masses and the intellectuals, the rich and the poor, the peoples of ancient culture and the new peoples alike. It has its convinced militants, impassioned and generous, its heroes and its martyrs.

Cardinal Suenens writes about it:

> Communism arouses in its millions of followers a faith, a fanaticism and an enthusiasm that are not produced by command alone. It is undoubtedly true—and to forget it would be to distort the situation—that the success of Communism is due, in great measure, to the material poverty of the masses, which is still serious today, especially in the underdeveloped countries, where people live in conditions that are scarcely, if at all, human. The hunger which grips about sixty per cent of the world's population is in itself a call to social revolution. At the same time Communism uses means, such as totalitarian government and unscrupulous propaganda, that no Christian could ever use. But when all this has been said, we must recognize that it has in its favour many undeniably positive elements. There is a Communist asceticism, a Communist mysticism and a spirit of total sacrifice to the cause, which Pius XII underlined in his 1954 Christmas message, and which partly explains its power to seduce. There is also a gigantic effort at persuasion and teaching that it would be dangerous to underestimate, and whose secret we must penetrate.[4]

Pius XII referred to it as follows in his 1954 Christmas message:

> Though illusory, this idea (the Marxist idea of a terrestrial

---

[4] Cardinal Suenens, *La Chiesa in stato di missione*, Rome 1956, 20—21.

paradise) has succeeded in creating, at least outwardly, a compact and hard unity, and in being accepted by the uninformed masses. It knows how to inspire its members to action and voluntarily to make sacrifices. The same idea, within the political framework that expresses it, gives to its directors a strong capacity for seduction, and to the adept the audacity to penetrate as an advance guard even into the ranks of the other side. Europe, on the other hand, still awaits the re-awakening of her own consciousness.[5]

Doubtless it is the positive aspects of this doctrine and movement that constitute its exalted significance for the Communists themselves. Testimonials to this effect abound, and are to be found throughout the literature inspired by the Marxist ideal. This is true, above all, in Western countries, where there is no reason to doubt their sincerity.

I shall give some examples at random. In Kravchenko's book, *I Chose Freedom*[6], we read:

Now my life had for me an urgency, a purpose, a new and thrilling dimension of dedication to a cause. I was one of the *élite*, chosen by History to lead my country and the whole world out of darkness into the socialist light. . . .

My privileges, as one of the elect, were to work harder, to disdain money and forswear personal ambitions. 1 must never forget that I am a Comsomol first, a person second. . . .

There was no longer much margin of time for petty amusements. Life was filled with duties—lectures, theatricals for the miners, Party 'theses' to be studied and

[5]*Op. cit.*, (E. tr. *I.E.R.* LXXXIII 1955, 137).
[6]*Op. cit.*, London 1947.

discussed. We were aware always that from our midst must come the Lenins and Bukharins of tomorrow. We were perfecting ourselves for the vocation of leadership; we were the acolytes of a sort of materialist religion.[7]

In the middle of 1929 I was admitted to the Party. It seemed to me the greatest event in my life. It made me one of the *élite* of the new Russia. I was no longer an individual with a free choice of friends, interests, views. I was dedicated forever to an idea and a cause.[8]

Another testimonial is that of Han Suyn, a Chinese writer who went from Catholicism to Communism:

When I feel that I am one of the many who are working in this renewal of honesty, enthusiasm and faith, I am happy. Many of us are greater than before, because we now have an aim in life. Each of us is dedicated to the reconstruction of China . . . .

It bears religious emotion and faith in man. It is intolerant and fanatical like all new faiths. It has come to clothe the poor, to feed the hungry, to render justice to the oppressed. It has its zealots, its soldiers and its saints. It has come to re-awaken the most beautiful things in the human soul. It calls for zeal, the desire for purity, singleness of mind and abnegation.[9]

Reading these testimonials, and, above all, meeting the enthusiastic and generous figure of the militant Marxist in

[7]*Op. cit.*, 38.

[8]*Ibid.*, 55.

[9]Han Suyn, *L'amore è una cose meravigliosa*, Milan 1957, 327—328. Among the many other testimonials it would be possible to mention we might single out the following: I. Lepp, *Psychanalyse de l'athéisme*, Paris 1961; H. Prauss, *Eppure non era la verità*, II ed. Rome 1962; D. Hyde, *I Believed*, London 1951.

real life, we are taken by surprise, for he does not correspond to the oversimplified pattern which we had made for him. We are perhaps overtaken by a certain uneasiness when we compare this figure with that of many a 'practising' Catholic, formalist in religion and egoist in life. What is it, then, that gives the Marxist ideal such power to fascinate the contemporary soul?

The Problem of Values in the Marxist System

I propose to describe the Marxist system of values. What position does this problem occupy in the system as a whole?

Anyone who has been trained in the atmosphere of scholastic philosophy will be used to thinking about the problem of God within the framework of discussions on the proofs of his existence. Discovering the existence of atheists, he is led to see them essentially as those who deny the validity of the classical demonstrations, to ask what difficulties they may have with these procedures, and to maintain that the debate should be centred on these themes.

Undoubtedly, he who denies the existence of God denies also the proofs leading thereto, and the examination of these proofs remains of the greatest importance, therefore, in discussion with atheism. On approaching atheistic literature, however, one is astounded at the sparse treatment given to the said proofs. It rather seems as though, amid the diverse forms of contemporary atheism, indifference towards discussion of the proofs emerges as a common characteristic.

Now our first concern, in the effort to understand atheism, should be to single out, with all possible precision, its problems and the motives inspiring it. In our discussion with atheists, it is only thus that we can respond (or hope to respond) to their problems and not to our own. In this way alone can we avoid discussions in a vacuum.

Scanning the history of atheism, one is struck by the

extreme variety of forms which it assumes. This fact makes us very wary of proposing general characterizations. It is more a question of discovering the 'inspiring motives', which, though they give the phenomenon a certain unity, can be expressed, nevertheless, in a wide variety of forms and even of principles.

Even with these precautions, however, it seems possible to speak of a positive characteristic common to all forms of contemporary atheism: its central perspective always leads to man, not to God. Atheism shares the reflex, anthropological character of all modern thought. It poses, in its negative stage, more as a critique of religion than as a critique of God. God is thus considered primarily in relation to man. This relationship is not seen from God's point of view, however, as it was in classical theodicy, but from man's point of view.[10] Consequently, the philosophy of religion comes notably to the fore.

While lived atheism may be a primitive phenomenon, philosophical atheism is always a post-religious phenomenon: this means that it must be understood dialectically, as a critique of religion. The values which it intends to affirm relate to, and are in contrast with, religion. Besides, although it is a critique of religion as such, atheism is really concerned with religion in its historical, psychological and sociological manifestations. That is why Western atheism is originally a post-Christian phenomenon, why it poses, that is, as a critique of the Christian religion. It is largely the work of theologians. In the East is assumes various forms, depending on the positive religion which it is presently criticizing (thus

[10]Cf. A. Dondeyne, 'L'athéisme contemporain et le problème des attributs de Dieu', in *Ephemerides Theologicae Lovanienses* (XXXVII) 1961, 462–480. For the opposite point of view cf. R. Verneaux, *Leçons sur l'athéisme contemporain*, Paris 1964, 25.

we expect to find atheism that is post-Jewish, post-Islamic, post-Buddhistic, post-Confucian, post-Hindu, etc.).

Man can focus his reflective power on two aspects of his conscious life, namely, his knowledge and his vital dynamism. By 'vital dynamism' I mean here the appetitive life of man, the total movement of the person towards the actualization of values: this is a generic formula, to be rendered specific according to the various forms which it assumes. Let us call the first viewpoint 'gnoseological', the second 'axiological'. These two viewpoints, which are central in modern thought and give it its great inspiring motives, are central also to the characterization of atheism.

In the gnoseological viewpoint is expressed the 'critical instance', i.e., the necessity of affirming only what has been vigorously tested. Axiological reflection, on the other hand, can lead in various directions, depending on whether one concentrates on the inevitability of evil or on the actualization of values. In the first case will emerge the 'tragic instance', in the second, the 'humanistic instance'.

The critical and humanistic instances are both present in Marxism, and both are essential to its characterization: in fact it insists, on the one hand, on its 'scientific' basis, and, on the other hand, presents itself as a 'philosophy of *praxis*'. But if we are seeking the most unifying characterization of the system that is possible, then it must be situated in the area of *praxis*. Only when this has been done can the gnoseological problem be faced.

This characterization does not emerge from the current presentations of Marxism–Leninism, which perhaps on account of the need for clarity and popularization, strike off from an exposition of the metaphysics of dialectical materialism. Arising from this is the impression that the various parts of the system (historical materialism in particular) are applications of metaphysical principles. The end-result of all this is that Marxism loses a great deal of its originality and presents a structure that is abstract and, in the main, easily crumbled.[11]

This foundation is alien to Marx's own thought, however, since he had not even completed the extension of materialism and of the dialectic from the world of history to that of nature; this transition was to be the work of Engels, and later of Lenin. Consequently it would be difficult to see in a general theory of reality the central inspiration of the system without creating a serious rift between Marxism and Leninism. On the other hand, Leninism, notwithstanding its didactic form of presentation, remains faithful to the principle of *praxis* as the criterion of truth. But this is enough to make possible the deduction that the concept of *praxis*, with all its implications, is the soul of the system.

Our presentation of Marxism will not be simply exegetical, therefore, but will rather be an attempt at reconstruction. The intention will be to point up the coherence and solidity of the system as much as possible. In disputed matters, whenever the interpretation of a text seemed uncertain, I have chosen the interpretation that gave the most coherence and

---

[11]The French Marxist H. Lefèvre's judgement of official Leninism is quite severe, and I agree with it only partially: 'From the Marxist viewpoint, this philosophy is completely desiccated, schematized, dogmatized and reduced to a number of "points", which are always the same. It is no longer a propaedeutic to the sciences of nature or of society. The dialectic is taught formally, in rules or laws, stripped of all content, considered arbitrarily (contrary to the dialectical method itself), like eternal truths. To the abstract formalism of the majority of "non-Marxist dialecticians" there corresponds the formalism of Marxists. Humanism, and the connection of integral humanism with the dialectical method and materialistic theory, far from constituting the core of doctrine, have almost fallen silent. A deepened discussion of alienation and the meaning of this concept has never taken place. The works of Marx's youth continue to be distrusted.' (*Le matérialisme dialectique*, Paris 1957, IV ed., 11–12).

solidity to the system. By adopting this historiographical criterion, I have been able to counter many of the customary objections to Marxism on grounds of internal inconsistency, which sometimes cause it to undergo a summary justice. It seemed to me that by doing this I was fulfilling a duty of objectivity and honesty. The Christian often laments the fact that at the root of many criticisms of him, including those by Marxists, lies a deformed image of the Church, its message and its mission. These deformations are illicit, whether used against Christians or by them. By adopting this criterion I have, naturally, made the task of criticism a more wearying one. But perhaps it will make it possible to structure the debate on the truly central problems and the really decisive differences.

The soul of the system, then, lies in a problem that is neither gnoseological nor ontological, but axiological. Consequently, when we face up to the problem of values, we are not answering questions of a socio-psychological nature alone, about the reasons for the attraction exercised by Marxism on the masses. Rather, we are placing ourselves, from the logical point of view, right at the centre of the system.

The solidarity of theory and practice in Marxism means, among other things, that it is at once a system and an experience. Thus it can be understood as a logically coherent system only insofar as it is understood as an experience, as a system of lived values. We ought to try, therefore, to confront it with that 'methodological sympathy, which, conversely, we should like to see applied by Communist intellectuals towards the Christian attitude.'[12]

Consequently, we shall pose two orders of problems:

1. What is the system of human values from which the Marxist draws his inspiration, and which gives him

[12]J. Lacroix, *Marxisme, existentialisme, personnalisme*, Paris 1960, IV ed., 6.

such great powers of seduction? Why does he maintain that adherence to these values imposes the rejection of Christianity?

2. What alternative to this system of values is offered by Christianity?

We shall examine in succession, therefore, the topics: 'Marxist Humanism and Christianity'; 'Christian Humanism and Marxism'.

MARXIST HUMANISM AND CHRISTIANITY

Before proceeding to examine Marxist humanism and its religious implications, it seems necessary to posit two orders of premises: the first aimed at specifying the general meaning of Marxism as a philosophy of *praxis*, the second aimed at establishing a more proximate basis for the problem of the relationship between Marxism and atheism.

Marxism as a Philosophy of Praxis

A deepening of the concept of philosophy of *praxis* will enable us, on the one hand, better to justify the point of view we have adopted, and on the other hand, to appreciate how it points up the originality of the Marxist system.

When Marxism is defined as a philosophy of *praxis*, this is intended as an affirmation of the fact that its content is shot through with vitality and involvement. More precisely, it is intended as an affirmation of the fact that Marxism is bound up with the concept of action, and as an explanation of the role which this concept plays within the system. *Praxis*, for the Marxist, is concrete, effective action accomplished by the proletariat. Its aim is to transform the world, be it nature or society, and to render it worthy of man. As transformer of nature it consists in production, labour and technology; as transformer of society it consists in political action that is militant and revolutionary. Making a first approximation, we may say that the function of *praxis* in the system resides in the fact that it is taken as the criterion of truth and value. What contributes to the success of *praxis* is true and valuable; what hinders this success is false and evil. In this sense Marxism is a pragmatic system. It is not a form of pragmatism, however, for it remains faithful to the absoluteness of truth, whereas pragmatism, in current usage, is relativistic. In fact, *praxis* itself demands objectivity if it is to abide by reality.

But we must further clarify the pragmatic significance of Marxist philosophy. If the system is examined from close quarters, while *praxis* emerges as a criterion of truth and value, it also emerges that it is not the only criterion. This is so, first of all because the success of *praxis* must be accounted for scientifically in its turn and therefore implies the criterion of evidence, and more generally, because Marxism grants validity to scientific and historical experience, which are difficult to reduce to *praxis* in the Marxist sense.

Above all, however, the concept of *praxis* itself gives way to another, more fundamental one. An action is successful if it reaches that towards which it is tending. This presupposes a value to which it is orientated, a value to be realized, an ideal. The concept of *praxis* is defined in relation to an ideal of humanity, namely, liberty in the ethical and economic sense. This is really the ultimate criterion of value and truth, and the key to the whole system.

Finally, the same criterion of *praxis* cannot be adequately justified from *praxis* itself, nor from experience in general. It implies, in fact, a faith in the final success of history, in the realizability of the ideal, which experience may confirm and verify, but which remains anterior to experience. Its validity is grasped in the concreteness of history, but more by intuition than by induction. At the root of the Marxist system, therefore, lies an axiological affirmation that lays hold, simultaneously, of man's ideal and its attainability through the medium of *praxis*. This faith in man, in an ideal, in history, is the soul of the system, and, at the same time, the cause of its active and revolutionary commitment.

The Marxist ideal is not a purely abstract one, a piece of wishful moralizing, or the object of sterile contemplation or vague aspirations. It is an ideal inscribed in reality and in history, and it gives them a direction and meaning that must be followed by *praxis*.

The entire system may be understood in the light of this basic tenet. Reality is structured in such a way that liberty is attainable, and its final triumph possible, through human action, which, for its part, must be organized into a liberating force. The procedure, therefore, is not from a vision of reality to the affirmation of values, but vice versa, from the affirmation of values to a vision of reality which renders them attainable. This procedure is sometimes called postulatory; it is quite widespread in modern thought, and is common to various forms of contemporary atheism.

At first sight it seems an arbitrary procedure, and, indeed, by qualifying atheism, and particularly Marxism, with the term 'postulatory', it is often intended to give it an anti-intellectual interpretation. Besides being an interpretation, it is also an evaluation, in that it reduces the fundamental standpoint of the system to a simple question of choice, an 'option'. So, from the very start, every pretence of these philosophies to give a 'critical' foundation to their system is rejected; simultaneously, the road to doctrinal dialogue is closed, given that, in the last analysis, the position in question is held to be, not a doctrine, but a free act.

However, this interpretation seems to have an inadequate basis. For my part, I prefer to avoid the ambiguous term 'postulatory' in describing this procedure, and to use instead the term 'axiological'. This means assuming an attitude widespread among theists and even among the scholastics. The affirmation of some moral values as absolute is quite frequently considered to be a first principle in the practical order, one which it does not owe to being founded on the ontological order. From the absoluteness of moral principles, or of conscience, many thinkers proceed to affirm the existence of God. There is a transition, therefore, from the order of values to the order of reality. The atheistic humanist uses the same type of argument to the opposite effect. Whereas for the theist the affirmed values demanded the existence of God, for the atheistic humanist they demand his non-existence. On the positive side, they demand an ontological structure that will permit the realization of values. This is a procedure of debatable validity. Nevertheless, it cannot be considered atheoretical, much less arbitrary. In Marxism, as has already been said, axiological intuition is never separated from historical experience; at the same time, it is not, in my judgement, reducible to it.

The pragmatic outlook, which lies at the basis of Marxism, characterizes, not only its content, but also the nature of its philosophizing. Philosophy is not a purely speculative activity for the Marxist, but is essentially orientated towards *praxis*. This is not an extrinsic, subjective orientation, a *finis operantis*, but an essential disposition, a *finis operis*. Of course, philosophy as a purely speculative science remains possible. It contemplates the universe and interprets it without being concerned to transform it. It is the philosophy of professors. This conception has dominated the history of thought. Hegel and Feuerbach remained faithful to it. It is content with overcoming the contradictions, the 'alienations' at the level of theory, and it leaves intact the contradictions that rend the concrete order.

Thus understood, philosophy makes no contribution to *praxis*. Rather, it distracts attention from it, giving rise to the conclusion that the problems have been solved because a theoretical answer has been given to them. Pure ideology, even if materialistic like that of Feuerbach, is an alienation, an estrangement from reality, because it distracts man from *praxis*. Philosophical alienation must be overcome through the fulfilment of philosophy. The fulfilment of philosophy consists in its suppression (as pure philosophy); and its suppression (as pure philosophy) is its fulfilment.

In order to pin down the function of value-judgements in the Marxist system more precisely, it seems necessary to distinguish in it (without wishing to be exhaustive) four stages, namely, the axiological, the ontological, the critico-historical and the methodological. I refer to them as stages, as though they were distinct, but in the construction of the system they are essentially united, and so none of them can be understood and justified except in relation to all the others. They are stages in the sense of integral components.

In the 'axiological' stage, Marxism elaborates a model of man and of the community, which can be summarized by the term 'liberty'. In the 'ontological' stage, it elaborates a vision of reality, and of human history in particular, which renders the ideal attainable. In the 'critico-historical' stage, it analyses past and present historical situations in the light of the ideal. We would say nowadays that it accomplishes a 'revision of life' on a worldwide scale (this is a process of seeing history, judging it, and acting accordingly). The balance-sheet for this stage is negative. History may be decidedly orientated towards the liberation of man, but it is still a long way from its goal, and, for the moment, man finds himself governed by alienation at various levels. These three stages are essentially directed towards *praxis*. Nevertheless, in order that *praxis* should be possible and scientific, they require that a 'methodology' be worked out that can proximately regulate this liberating action.

The solidarity of these stages is one of the reasons for the originality and influence of Marxism. It gives a concrete character to the ideal perspectives, incarnating them in history and action. On the other hand, it enlivens concrete analyses with a breath of idealism, projecting them onto a vast horizon of truth and values. In comparison with abstract ideologies, Marxism emerges as a vision that is committed and effective. In comparison with political and economic 'praxologies', it emerges as a world-view capable of conferring a profound and unifying significance on the immediate data.

Moreover, the link with *praxis* imposes on Marxist doctrine a continual renewal in the light of historical evaluation, which, without putting the fundamental theses of the system in question (this would be revisionism), preserves it, nevertheless, from doctrinal immobility or dogmatism.

Finally, the characterization of Marxism as a philosophy of *praxis* remains fully valid. This means, first of all, that *praxis* is the sole criterion of truth on the methodological plane: this, however, is not a characteristically Marxist stand-point. It also means that, on the axiological and ontological planes, *praxis* is the counterproof of theses established in other ways. It is a criterion of truth, therefore, but not the only one. Above all, however, Marxism is a philosophy of *praxis* because it is essentially directed towards *praxis* in its various parts, and, even more radically, because it is based on the affirmation of a supreme and unifying ideal, believed to be attainable with certainty through the medium of *praxis*.

Marxism and Atheism

Our approach to Marxism in this section will be concerned

with understanding its attitudes to religion, particularly Christianity.

The atheistic character of Marxism is not questioned by any serious scholar. Where divergences of interpretation exist, they concern the question of the *nexus* between atheism and the system as a whole.

The first question to be asked is whether, in Marxism, atheism is derived from political, economic, or social doctrine, or is independent of these.

If the former is true, it may be further asked whether atheism, for the Marxist, is a purely historical and political attitude, based on the (condemned) historical alliance between the Church and capitalist regimes, or, rather, an ideological thesis transcending the various historical situations.

For those who understand Marxism as pure methodology, the historico-political interpretation of atheism is beyond doubt. On the other hand, for those who see Marxism as a philosophy—and they form the majority of its interpreters— it is still possible to ask whether atheism is a part of the philosophy or of the methodology.

The importance of this problem is easily grasped: were atheism merely a component of Marxist methodology, it would be dependent on a determinate historical situation, and could be abandoned as the situation evolved; if, on the other hand, it were a philosophical thesis, it could not be altered without a profound revision of the system.

It should be noted, however, that these divergences of interpretation concern Marxism only, and not Leninism, about whose philosophical character it is difficult to raise doubts. More precisely, they concern the mature Marx, since the ideological character of his youthful period, which inspired in great measure by Hegel and Feuerbach, seems also beyond doubt.

My exposition, while naturally taking notable account

of Marx's own thought, will refer expressly to the Leninist interpretation, which is being defended and spread today by official Soviet thinking and by those throughout the world who are inspired by it.

But one cannot deal with Marxism nowadays, especially on the matter of religion, without examining the revisionist movement, which, for some years, has been making headway in Italy and France.

It remains true to the atheistic character of the system, but takes another look at certain theses of considerable importance, such as those concerning the concept of religion as the 'opium of the people', and the question of religious intolerance.

The developments in this field are unforeseeable, but they might assume decisive importance in the history of international Communism and, therefore, of the world. From the doctrinal point of view, they demand a probing of the connections between Marxism and atheism. In fact, it is only on the basis of a precise determination of the meaning of atheism within the system that it can be decided how far revisionism can be pushed without compromising internal cohesion and putting the fundamental theses in jeopardy. The possibility of dialogue with revisionist Marxism is closely connected with such problems.

Like other forms of contemporary atheism, Marxism is a post-Christian system. This attribute is not just significant chronologically. It is pivotal for an understanding of the system. Marxism stands at the end of a critique of Christianity that spans a great part of modern thought and has found in Hegel and Feuerbach two of its principal exponents.

Consequently, in order to understand the attitude taken up by Marxism towards Christianity, it is necessary to reconstruct the image of Christianity which it has formed. On the one hand, such a reconstruction will inform us of what type of

Christianity or religiosity is being criticized by Marxism; on the other hand, it will reveal the Christian origin of many of the themes inherited by Marx from the laicized theology of Hegel, and even of Feuerbach. In the course of my exposition, I will recall various features of this interpretation of Christianity. For the present, it will suffice to remember that Hegel, Feuerbach and Marx knew Christianity in its Lutheran form, which is inspired (or is intended to be), in its turn, by Ockham and St Augustine. Let it be added that Marx, Lenin and the Leninists are quite well aware of the significance of the Church as an historical institution, and of the effective *rapport* which it maintained, and still maintains, with temporal, political and economic regimes. Their ideological interpretation of Christianity is greatly influenced by their interpretation of its actual historical function.

As I have already shown, our theme demands that we answer two questions of interpretation. First, what motives inspire Marxist humanism? Second, why are these motives developed in an atheistic, anti-religious, anti-Christian direction? Now the second question is no less important than the first, and, in order to answer it, we must reconstruct, at every stage, the image of Christianity that is criticized by Marxism.

Marxism is a Humanism

We shall now examine the Marxist system of values in more detail. It presents itself primarily as a humanism. By humanism is meant (as an initial approximation) a doctrine that affirms the value and dignity of man. It takes on a more precise meaning inasmuch as it affirms that man is an end in himself, and that he consequently rejects any form of servitude that would reduce him to a means at the hands of an owner.

This is the basic meaning of the liberty or autonomy claimed by modern man: it has a certain quality of axiological absoluteness.

Directly, therefore, it signifies neither free will nor the power to choose, much less the rejection of every moral imperative. What follows will further clarify this.

The concept of liberty, which Marx inherited from modern thought through Hegel, is of capital importance in Marx's system. It is asserted, sometimes as a natural aspiration built into man, sometimes as an ideal expressed in the human calling.

The liberty of man is not yet an accomplished fact, however, and the historical critique reveals how dramatically it falls short of the ideal. In the concrete, man is deprived of liberty, enslaved, made an instrument. Consequently, the history of man is an unceasing process of liberation or humanization. The history of man is the history of salvation. Marxism is a soteriology.

At the root of the Marxist system, alongside the positive theme of liberty, it is necessary to place the negative theme of servitude, which is inseparable from it. The theme of alienation is the negative pole of the Marxist system, just as the theme of liberty is its positive pole. Just as liberty is the supreme good, so alienation is the supreme evil. The liberating movement is a battle between good and evil: it is the soul of history. In these general terms, however, both themes are common to various forms of humanism. We must move on and see what characteristic shape they assume within Marxism.

The term 'alienation', so widely used in Marxist philosophy, is rich in acceptations that are distinct though connected in various ways. In the concrete, it is sometimes one, sometimes another of these that is accentuated, according to the type of alienation being examined. This will also be seen in the course of the exposition. By way of introduction, here is a synthetic presentation of the fundamental usages of the term.

Alienation is defined with reference to the ideal, complete man, man as he ought to be—man as free. That man is alienated means, more precisely:

(a) That he is not what he ought to be. Something that ought to be there is missing. Alienation is an impoverishment, a 'privation'.

(b) That there is lacking in him something of his very self, of his ideal essence. Alienation is a 'mutilation'.

(c) That the part of him of which he is deprived is somehow outside of him, commandeered by others. His ideal essence has been torn away from his real essence; he has been dispossessed of it; he has become a stranger to himself. This projection of man outside of himself is unreal, imaginary. By it, in other words, man is estranged from himself and from reality. In either case alienation is an 'estrangement'.

(d) That the imaginary existence which man has projected outside of himself generates in him the illusion that he possesses in reality what in fact he possesses only ideally. He 'identifies' himself psychologically with this imaginary existence, which thus becomes a substitute for reality. Alienation is an 'identification'.

(e) That this part of man which exists outside of him turns against him, so that man is torn by a conflict between his real essence and his ideal essence. Alienation is a 'contradiction'.

(f) That man's ideal essence is defined by liberty, by his being an end. Consequently, alienation consists in his being reduced to a means, to slavery. Alienation is an 'enslavement'.

The process of overcoming alienation is the process through which man becomes what he ought to be, attains his ideal essence, seeks and again finds himself, repossesses that part of himself which had been seized from him, resolves the contradiction within him and reaches liberty.

Man's historical commitment to liberty is animated by certainty: certainty that the liberation of man will be achieved, that the alienations will be overcome, and that the final triumph in the historical battle will belong to the good. Every human event is orientated to this final success, which will give it meaning. The whole of history is traversed by this eschatological hope. In fact, Marxism carries on a polemic against the various forms of pessimism. In particular, it is distinguished from tragic atheism of the Nietzschean or existentialist type. Its intention is to restore man's faith in mankind; to announce to man that life has a meaning and is worth living.

In this way, the Marxist dialectic affirms the essentially dynamic and progressive character of reality, and, before it is yet a scientific datum, this fundamental thesis is an axiological requirement. Not only is the history of man spanned by this perspective, but, in a reflex manner, so also is the history of nature, which is interpreted as an evolutionary process ascending from matter in chaos to ever more perfect forms of reality, and ultimately to man. Ontological progressivism is demanded by practical progressivism, and, in turn, justifies it.

But who is this 'man' whose greatness Marxism proclaims? Is it individual or collective man? We are touching here on one of the most delicate points of the system. Undoubtedly, however, it is not permissible at once to identify Marxist 'man' with the collectivity, be it humanity, class or party. For Marxism, isolated man is an abstraction. As we shall see, man is essentially relative to society (as well as to nature). But this ontological relationship is not equivalent to axiological subordination. History is orientated towards a type of society where there will be no class, party or state, and where each individual will be fulfilled as an end in the fulness of liberty. The perfect society is characterized by this harmonizing of liberties.

Meanwhile, man goes through a period of transition, and an emergency regime is in force. Under this regime the requirements of the common good are not fully in harmony with those of the individual, and the common good may often demand renouncement from the individual, even the sacrifice of life. But already in this phase individual needs must be respected as far as possible. Marxism does this by proclaiming the principle that all men are equal, and by acting so that this principle may take flesh in reality; for while one man is enslaved, mankind is not free. The position of the community tends to become identified with that of the person.

In virtue of its affirmation of the dignity of every man, Marxist humanism is distinguished from the Nietzschean kind, to which Nazism, and to some extent fascism, owed their inspiration. In the Nietzschean view the greatness of man is embodied in one category, the superman. The inferior brand of men are, by their nature, destined to serve the superman, and might, where necessary, be sacrificed for his sake. Thus racism, the privileged cult of one race and the extermination of inferior races, is explained. It is an aristocratic egoistic humanism. From the Marxist point of view, the fundamental form of egoistic humanism is capitalism, in which a minority of proprietors dominate great masses of workers.

One might be led to think that Marxism substitutes for the exclusivism of race that of the proletarian class, and for the ascendancy of one aristocracy, that of money, the ascendancy of another aristocracy, that of the workers. As we shall see, however, division of society into antagonistic classes is provisional according to Marxism. It is destined to disappear in the final phase of history.

The proletariat is a class, therefore, but its mission is universal. It combats the capitalist class, not in order to enslave it in turn, but in order to eliminate it as a class, and to create a new society that will include the members of that class, a society of free and equal men.

It is on the level of objectives that the radical conflict between Marxism and Christianity is to be found. According to Marx, the essence of religion is the affirmation of man's total dependence on God, the total enslavement of man by God. Following Hegel, he identifies the religious relationship with that between master and slave. Now the slave is his master's possession, and as such he has no finality, no value of his own. Under these conditions the relationship between man's greatness and God's greatness is presented as an alternative. Between God and man there is axiological rivalry: a choice is necessary. Marxism chooses man. The denial of God is a condition of the very possibility of the affirmation of man.

In the sense indicated above, therefore, religion is a form of alienation. Through it, man is deprived of his fundamental right to be an absolute value, to be his own master. This right is usurped by God.

The argument is clearly impeccable if one accepts this concept of religion. Undoubtedly there exists a concept of religion that so stresses the theme of God's glory, of God's dominion over the world, as to reduce all other realities, including man, to the status of slaves—slaves in the sense of instruments in the glorification of God. This mentality finds expression e.g. in the thesis of the damnation of infants who die unbaptized (attributed to St Augustine), or the thesis of damnation *ante praevisa merita* (of Calvinist theology). More generally, this theocentric exclusivism seems to pervade the Lutheran vision of religion, as also the Ockhamist and Augustinian views by which it was inspired. Divine voluntarism is its most radical and consequent expression. God may do what he likes as there are no essences, no values which could oppose his will. He is an absolute, tyrannical monarch who, according to the requirements of his glory, saves whom he wishes to save and damns whom he wishes to damn.

There is a conception of religion, Augustinian in inspiration, which, without reaching these extreme forms, tends, nevertheless, to view the relationship between God and man in terms of rivalry. At its root lies, at least implicitly, an exclusivist idea of the glory of God, of God's 'jealousy'.

With this conception of religion it is not easy to escape the logic of the Marxist argument: if man must be sacrificed in order to affirm God, then God must be sacrificed in order to affirm man.

Marxist humanism consists, not only in the fact that, for man, man is the supreme being, the supreme value, in other words God, but in the fact that man becomes the ultimate *raison d'être* of all reality. In its development, reality is ordered, in fact, to increasingly higher stages, and the summit of this development is man. Every stage of this development is necessary, particularly the presence of man. Even if the individual man is contingent, humanity as such is necessary. It was impossible for it not to have come to be, and it would be impossible for it to cease to be. The necessity which religion attributes to God has been restored, therefore, to the universe, and in particular to man. The ontological argument in proof of the existence of a necessary being has given way to the axiological argument. Since the whole of reality is orientated towards man as towards its supreme stage, man becomes the ultimate *raison d'être*, the foundation of being on the level of finality. The heavens no longer proclaim the glory of God; they proclaim the glory of man.

Marxism is an Ethical Humanism

The liberating movement that we call history is pervaded by a powerful ethical force for change. This statement may astonish those who are used to thinking of the denial of God as though it were equivalent to the denial of morality ('if there is no God, then everything is permissible'), and to the idea that the ultimate explanation of atheism is to be found precisely in this desire to be free of every moral bond. In Marxism, particularly, many see the denial of all morality and the subordination of all other values to economic and political values.

The question is really much more complex. As far as atheism in general is concerned, if, in certain cases, it appears to be immoral and to have psychological roots in a desire to be free of the chains of morality, it is illicit, nevertheless, to generalize on this basis.

'Sometimes, too,' writes Paul VI, 'the atheist is spurred on by noble sentiments and by impatience with the mediocrity and self-seeking of so many contemporary settings'.[13]

There are certainly atheists whose lives are highminded and generous; there are versions of atheism that defend the autonomous consistency of moral values. More basically, atheism is often a justification of the denial of God in the name of moral values themselves. In the history of modern atheism, the problem of the relationship between morality and religion is very much in the foreground; and the conflict of which I have spoken, the conflict between the value of man and the value of God, often emerges as a conflict between morality and religion. In other words, religion comes into opposition to morality in the measure in which it dehumanizes man.

Historically, much immorality has been justified in the name of religion, e.g., the violation of liberty of conscience, persecutions, 'holy' wars, human sacrifice and sacred prostitution. The alliance between throne and altar confers the seal of religion on the whims of governments and canonizes

[13]Op. cit., 38. Cf. A.A.S. (loc. cit.), 652–653.

injustice and established disorder. In the last analysis, a voluntaristic theology negatives all absolute morality: what God wills is good and what he does not will is evil.

It is understandable, therefore, that many atheists believe they must reject religion in order to be faithful to morality— a morality consisting precisely in the affirmation of the dignity of man as an absolute value, and rejecting anything that might compromise it. The first commandment of this morality could be formulated, following Kant, as follows: 'Act in such a way as to consider the person always as an end, never as a means'.

With regard to Marxism in particular, the immoralist interpretation might seem, at first sight, to be confirmed by its many apparently heavily critical utterances in relation to morality.

But in reality these take a certain type of morality as their target, the conservative, immobilistic, defeatist, eschatological, heteronomous, 'middle-class' type. This morality is replaced by another, whose content must be specified as we go along, but of which we can remark, at this stage, that its fundamental principle is precisely the absolute value of man. Liberty is the supreme value, both ontologically and morally; alienation is the supreme moral and ontological evil. 'Sin' is not the offending of God but the offending of man and of his liberty. The struggle between good and evil, which animates history, is also a moral struggle. The requirements of this struggle are of the highest order: it imposes on its militants a total dedication to the cause and can even reach the point of asking them for the sacrifice of life.

The fundamental principle of Marxist ethics is really the principle behind the whole system, therefore. It follows that the specific content of this morality can only be known at the end of the system; it follows, above all, that the ethical outlook will pervade the system from beginning to end.

Marxism is a Demiurgic Humanism

Man cannot be his own end unless he is author of his own history and master of his destiny. This reflects the idealist (and especially the Hegelian) theme of man creating himself by means of his activity or work. Besides, this liberty is an incessant conquest and an ethical commitment: for Marx, as for Hegel, liberty is liberation; for Marx, as for Hegel, it is man who liberates man, who is his own messiah, his own redeemer.

But the effectiveness of man's construction of history is incompatible with the affirmation of God. Here we come up against a new aspect of the rivalry between man and God. The author of history is either man or God. If it is God, then it remains for man simply to abandon himself passively to God's action and to execute his infallible eternal designs; he would become a spectator of history, a simple pawn on a vast chessboard in God's game. 'Man proposes and God disposes.' If God is master, in other words, then man can only be slave. Once more, it is a question of choosing between man and God, between reliance on man and reliance on God. Marxism chooses man; it reclaims for itself the autonomy which had been alienated and projected onto God. It undertakes the construction of history without awaiting help from on high, counting only on its own forces and with full confidence in itself.

In this manner Marxism, like other forms of atheistic humanism, brings up again the classical and most serious problem of the relationship between human action and divine action. But whereas in the classical context this problem arose in the guise of the problem of the coexistence of finite and infinite as soon as the existence of God had been proved, in atheistic humanism, on the other hand, the problem appears prior to the affirmation of God, as a condition of his possibility. God does not exist because, if he did, it would be impossible for man to act. The problem can be stated more neatly on the level of values, however. It is a question of the coexistence, not just of two actions, but of the value of man and the value of God, and their respective value is expressed in their actions.

Again, the argument may be understood in the light of a totalitarian conception of God's dominion, which cannot be affirmed without destroying man's initiative. This reconstruction does not lack foundation. In a religious vision inspired by Augustine, and especially by Ockham, God's glory must be affirmed by attributing to him the greatest possible activity of being, thereby reducing that of the creature as much as possible. According to occasionalism, the creature becomes, in the end, a mere occasion for divine action. On the supernatural plane, these ideas are encountered in the Lutheran interpretation of original sin and its consequences, which reduces man to absolute helplessness in the moral sphere. His salvation is thus accomplished independently of his works, by virtue of the extrinsic application of the merits of Jesus Christ. It is understandable that in such a view the relationship between divine and human action is necessarily formulated as an alternative.

Religion, therefore, is a personification in the ideal world of the real forces which dominate human life. Its purpose is to overcome with heavenly aid the sense of insecurity experienced by man in the face of forces which dominate him. Thus religion is the illusory answer to a real problem.

At this point a serious internal difficulty arises in the Marxist system: how to reconcile the certainty that history proceeds according to the necessary laws of the dialectic towards an inevitable final success, with the affirmation of an autonomous and effective human initiative. If determinism is chosen there can be no room left for liberty, and man, though free from God, is reduced, nevertheless, to being a pawn on the chessboard of history. This difficulty is frequently urged against Marxism, but it does not seem impossible to answer it.

A first reply to the theist questioner might be as follows: Marxist man finds himself up against history in conditions analogous to those of the Christian man faced with the 'providential plan' of God. They struggle with very similar difficulties, even if their outlook differs profoundly. Each must reconcile the claims of a movement that proceeds infallibly towards its end with the free initiative of the men who actualize that movement. But this is only a comparison. It is made in order that the theist critic may not hasten to denounce absurdities in the system which he is opposing, without being aware that he must face an analogous problem himself.

The comparison is inadequate, however, since objective historical laws are immanent in history, whereas the providential plan is distinct from it. Marxism defends freedom of choice, therefore, insofar as it is compatible with historical and sociological laws (which, as we shall see, are founded on the laws of economic development, according to the Marxist). It excludes as unreal the conception of liberty that would have it independent with respect to objective laws. But what margin do these laws allow to liberty? In Marxism, they are laws which, though historical, have the absolute quality of ontological laws. They are valid, however, only for extended periods of history and for the great masses. They allow a margin of contingency and initiative to single historical moments and individuals. Within these limits, everyone can move either with the direction of history or contrary to it, retarding or accelerating its course. But no one can prevent these laws from being actualized throughout evolution as a whole. So the problem of the coexistence of personal liberty with historical and sociological laws is undoubtedly quite a

serious one. It arises, however, not only for the Marxist.
but for anyone who proposes liberty in concrete terms,
inserting it into the fabric of social and economic conditions.

Autonomy in the area of finality and autonomy in the
area of efficacy: these are the fundamental and correlative
aspects of the concept of liberty which lies at the root of
Marxist humanism. The conflict that makes opponents out
of liberty, thus understood, and religion, gives way to the
fundamental problem—a problem rarely faced in a direct
manner by atheistic humanism—of the coexistence of infinite and finite on the level of being. The problem of humanism leads back to the metaphysical problem of participation.

In the perspective of atheistic humanism it is impossible
to affirm that God is all without deducing from this that man
is nothing: rivalry between man and God in the realm of
values involves rivalry in the realm of being. Taking up
Feuerbach's theme 'the poor man creates the rich man',
Marx affirms that 'the more reality man gives to God the
less he has left for himself'. The same presupposition that leads
the pantheist to deny the distinctness of man in order to
affirm God, brings the atheistic humanist to a denial of God
in order to affirm man. The Platonic and Augustinian mentality implicitly or explicitly accepts this presupposition,
though without drawing out all its consequences. It tends to
belittle sensible reality, to give it a shadowy, non-authentic
being, in order to exalt super-sensible reality, the authentic
being, God.

At the heart of the humanist critique of Christianity and
of religion in general, therefore, lies an interpretation of it in
Platonic terms. As Nietzsche would say, Christianity is the
people's Platonism. But this identification is already present
and operative in Marx's thought.

There is an historical and theoretical affinity between
Platonism and voluntarism. This will seem paradoxical at

first sight, since the central concern of Platonism is with the absolute and eternal quality of truth, which is contested by voluntarism. But by situating eternal truth outside history, by founding it on a transcendent world, Platonism really robs the sensible world of all necessity and consistency, thus preparing it to become the free field of action for divine omnipotence, and, eventually, for divine will.

Marxism is a Terrestrial Humanism

The Marxist wants to be faithful to the earth, to actualize secular values in all their requirements by dedicating himself fully to them and by respecting their autonomy. Earth, for him, is not a period of exile or a 'vale of tears', but the fatherland. A finite and temporal being, he aspires naturally to finite and temporal goods, which are capable, in consequence, of satisfying his expectations in full. His innate anxiety does not demand that the finite be transcended with a view to the infinite, nor that time be transcended with a view to eternity. Rather, it impels him to indefinite progress in the finite realm, to an incessant transcending of the present with a view to the future.

It would be inaccurate to say that Marxism claims autonomy for each sphere of values in relation to the others. On the contrary, any such fragmentation of values would clash with the profound inspiration that leads it to unify the personality around *praxis* and as a consequence, to subordinate every other sphere to the requirements of *praxis*. But terrestrial values, or secular values in their entirety, demand an autonomy that excludes all extraneous interference.

It is in the name of earthly values, of fidelity to the earth, that Marxism rejects the religious vision of the earth. By outlining the prospect of a future life, not only does religion attribute aspirations to man which in fact he has not got, but above all, by disclosing this prospect to him, it comes into conflict with the demands of fidelity to the earth. Indeed, by orientating man towards an ultra-mundane happiness, religion distracts him from his earthly commitments and creates in him the psychology of the exile, leading him to accept the want, the injustice and the oppression of earth as inevitable or insignificant. The true life is another life, which man cannot construct, but must await. Religious preaching ends up by fostering immobilism or conservatism, when it does not actually consecrate unjust and oppressive regimes with the chrism of legality or of downright divine investiture, thus becoming their accomplice. In this sense religion is a drug, a narcotic that paralyzes at the outset every serious desire to transform and liberate. It is an alienation, insofar as it projects the true life into another world, effecting a split between real life and ideal life. In his struggle against servitude on earth, man is inhibited, indeed paralyzed, by his religious outlook; religious alienation is reflected onto secular alienations and tends to consolidate them.

In Marxism, these statements are significant both philosophically and historically: it is asserted that the Christian religion has obstructed, and still obstructs, man's progress, through the institution in which it is embodied in history. But it is also a necessity, part of man's very nature, and part of the nature of the religious phenomenon. The historical forms may change, therefore, but the essence of religion is present in all its forms. This continuity between historical and philosophical analysis is the more understandable in Marxism in view of the fact that historical development is seen as regulated by necessary laws.

Here, too, one may ask whether the Marxist image of religion, and of Christianity in particular, is entirely without historical foundation. Contempt of the body, of the world and its vanities, the monastic ideal of the *fuga saeculi*, the theme of detachment from created goods, of terrestrial exile, of the vale of tears, the *quod aeternum non est nihil est*, etc—these are to be found in certain presentations of Christianity (one thinks of St Peter Damian), which are so anxious to prove the primacy of spirit that they justify the belief that the consistent Christian is a man lost to earthly life.

On the other hand, there is a way of conceiving the promotion of secular values by religion that makes these values instrumental to the affirmation of religious values. As a result, secular institutions, principally the state, are subordinated to the Church and deprived of their autonomy. The primacy of the spiritual over the temporal leads to the affirmation of the subordination of temporal institutions to the Church. The principle of the direct power of the pope over sovereigns constitutes the theory behind this attitude. It is to be found in many treatises inspired by the Augustinian mentality, and is described as 'political Augustinianism'.

The clerical mentality, even if it is not formulated in such precise juridical terms, persists where the cleric becomes involved in spheres of value which transcend his competence, and, in a more general way, where the *consecratio mundi* is understood as the utilization of the secular sphere for religious purposes. The same principle is implied in 'monastic' flight from the world and in the consecration of the world understood in terms of clericalism—the principle that the secular sphere as such has no value.

Once again, therefore, the problem is posed in terms of rivalry between the secular and religious spheres, or between earth and heaven. The Marxist chooses earth. On earth he will build his paradise. In opposition to heavenly messianism he sets up a terrestrial messianism; in opposition to the fruitless expectation of the heavenly city he proposes an effective effort to construct the earthly city.

Since man is essentially a secular being, his liberation should be carried out essentially in the secular sphere. It is there that the fundamental alienations, the real servitudes, are found. In the religious sphere man enslaves himself in an ideal manner —ideal because his master does not exist. In the secular sphere, however, man is really enslaved to man. Basically, alienation is the expression of an interpersonal relationship that violates man's liberty on the political, social and economic planes. Genuine liberty exists only when these alienations have been overcome. As has already been remarked, human anxiety reveals a need, not of God and of another life, but of a better humanity and of indefinite progress.

The ideal alienations, i.e., those that are religious and philosophical, are derived from real alienations by psychological mechanisms whose nature must be determined in the light of economic science.

Let it suffice for the present to point out that we are dealing with mechanisms of a defensive kind, through which man seeks the answers, in a world of illusory values, to problems that he has failed to solve in the real world. These take the form of a placation of frustrated tendencies, or a consolation prize that will enable him to resign himself more easily to defeat. Religion originates as a kind of compensation or evasion. Man has no natural religious anxiety: it is merely the product of historical vicissitudes, an acquired need. It is an abnormal, not a normal phenomenon; the reflection of other, more profound anomalies. The religious world is not authentic but, rather is a surrogate of reality. To conclude, it is not God who creates man, but man who creates God.

The liberty and happiness towards which man is moving are not only possible; they are possible on this earth. He seeks, not eternal salvation, but temporal salvation. For Communism, as for ancient Israel, the messianic era must be attained on earth by means of a profound transformation of the actual situation. But Marxist man does not await the

liberation of earth by God or by his envoy: he himself is the
messiah.

The ideal epoch to which history is tending by an infallible movement is the translation of the ancient Christian
paradise into terrestrial terms: a fraternal and happy society
of free and divinized men, classless and without laws; a
paradise without God, where eternity becomes the future,
the 'tomorrow that sings'. Meta-history is absorbed in history.

The terrestrial character of the Marxist vision of man is
also expressed in the certainty that man's existence on earth
will never end. There is no 'end of the world'. Matter and man
are necessary. Eternity is reduced to endless temporal succession, the immortality of the individual to the immortality
of humanity as a whole.

I should like to draw attention to the moral content of
this terrestrial conception of existence. Its result is not to
liberate man from moral duty but rather to re-create it for
him. In fact, whereas the eschatological view of life, by
estranging man from the present life, allows him to escape
the exigencies of the struggle against injustice, to take refuge
in the comfortable ethics of resignation, and to postpone the
solution of problems and the final triumph of the good until
the 'beyond', the terrestrial conception, on the other hand,
is a vigorous summons to the immediate task of transforming
the world.

The terrestrial concept of life has another important im-
plication for morality, namely, that while the believer's moral
zeal is never disinterested, is never an act of pure generosity
(since he always awaits recompense for his act in another
life), the moral zeal of the Marxist must often be absolutely
disinterested, inspired by free dedication to the cause. He must
renounce immediate benefits for the sake of very remote
achievements, which will probably belong only to the
humanity of tomorrow. Death ends the path of the individual,

even if something remains of him in the collective history that he has helped to build.

The highest expression of this generosity is the sacrifice of life freely given. This is very frequent in the various Marxist struggles and revolutions and is often prepared for by terrible tortures undergone in order not to betray companions or the cause.

Ernest Bloch, the Communist writer, has celebrated the solitude of the Red hero in Nazi-fascist prisons:

> They all bear with them to the tomb the one-time flowers, some of which have withered or have become unrecognizable. Only one category of men goes to death destitute, as it were, of the traditional consolation: the Red hero. Professing until death the cause for which he has lived, he advances definitely, coldly, towards the void in which he has been taught to believe as a free spirit.
>
> Hence his sacrifice differs from that of the ancient martyrs: they died, almost without exception, with a prayer on their lips, believing thus to have gained heaven, whereas the Communist hero, under the tzars, under Hitler, or under some other regime, gives himself without hope of resurrection. His Good Friday is not softened, or simply suppressed, by any Easter Sunday—a Sunday when he would return personally to life. The heaven towards which the martyrs stretched their arms in the midst of flame and smoke does not exist for the Red materialist. Yet he dies the confessor of a cause, and his superiority can be likened only to that of the early Christians or of the Baptist.[14]

Pushing ahead, we now find ourselves faced with this

[14]Ernest Bloch, *Das Prinzip Hoffnung*, quoted by F. Heer in *L'athéisme, tentation du monde, réveil des chrétiens*, Paris 1963, 187–188.

antinomy: if disinterestedness is essential to the moral act, is it possible for a man who believes in an eternal reward to perform genuine moral acts? Is 'religious morality' not essentially egoistic? From this point of view must we not again speak of the incompatibility of morality and religion?

The conflict between heaven and earth is another aspect, therefore, of the conflict between religion and morality.

Marxism is an Economic Humanism

Even if it is understood in terrestrial terms, there is a risk that the liberation of man will remain an abstraction if it fails to take account of the real situation. Now an analysis of history shows the decisive function of material conditions, or, more precisely, of conditions of production that result from productive forces and productive relations. The various historical eras (the primitive community, the slave system, the feudal system, the capitalist system) must be interpreted in the light of their respective productive systems. As regards the present age, it is particularly easy to establish that technical progress is at the root of all other developments, that it regulates history and accounts for the common definition of our civilization as industrial, technical, atomic and space-age. Ideologies, artistic expression, political events and even psychological attitudes are decisively influenced by it. Conditions of production make up the 'infrastructure' of history; the other manifestations of man are its 'superstructure'. Basically, historical materialism consists in the view that the superstructure is controlled by the infrastructure. The conditions of production are not held to be the sole factor in history, but only the fundamental one. It is not denied, therefore, that the superstructure (particularly ideologies, as we shall see) retains a certain autonomy and effectiveness of its own. But at the level of great masses of people and extended periods of history there is a necessary correlation between infrastructure and superstructure, showing that historical development as a whole is not only based on, but is determined by, economic development. The possibility of tackling history, like nature, scientifically, is based on this deterministic outlook. Also based on it is the possibility of discovering the necessary laws of history, of foreseeing its future developments and of organizing revolutionary action with the aid of these data.

This possibility of studying social facts and of organizing *praxis* in a scientific way is considered by Marxism to be one of its most decisive conquests: it constitutes a brilliant counter-proof of the historical materialism on which it is based.

This interpretation derives from the idea that human psychology is essentially based on economic values. It does not necessarily prejudice the originality and genetic autonomy of other spheres of value, especially where individuals are concerned, but gives economics the primary role. Marxist man is fundamentally, if not exclusively, economic man.

Man's alienations are not to be reduced to economic alienation, therefore, but they certainly derive from it. From the conflict between capital and labour in the economic sphere is derived the assertion of one class at the expense of the other. Finally, the state is based on the interests of the wealthy class, and so it legalizes the established disorder. The fundamental alienation is situated at the level of productive relations. Here the infrastructure that determines the superstructure must be sought.

Ideologies, in particular, are determined by the infrastructure. Every economic system has a corresponding ideology which theorizes about it, justifies it and guarantees its stability. Ideologies are 'rationalizations' of an objective situation: any history of philosophy that intends to be realistic must be based on economic history.

Here, too, we are dealing with an historical law, however, one that is valid for long periods and for great masses of people. It does not prejudice the autonomy of an ideology in particular groups or individuals or for a limited period of time. This conditioning of thought by economics is the typical form in which the historicity of thought appears in the Marxist system.

The concept of alienation in the economic sphere is specified by the concept of 'value', which is defined as 'quantity of work'. Under capitalism, productive relations are such that new wealth, the fruit of the labour of the proletariat, actually goes to the employer, swells his capital, and consequently increases his very great powers. The produce of labour, which belongs to the worker by right, is taken from him and turned against him. This is economic alienation. In substance it is economic injustice, deepened in meaning and range.

If alienation is the evil in the Marxist universe, then, economic alienation is the radical evil, the 'original sin'. Whereas, in the Christian universe, psychic and moral imbalance, social disorder and intellectual deviations find their explanation in original sin, in the Marxist universe they are rooted in economic alienation. The state of 'fallen nature' is the reflection, not of a subjective act, but of an objective historical system. Capitalism, or the *bourgeois* spirit, is the original sin. It is an offence against man, not against God. It does not consist in man refusing to serve, but in the fact that he is enslaved.

This conception of economic value clashes with the current one based on the concept of utility, and it is perhaps difficult to sustain on the strictly economic plane. But precisely because of this, it overcomes the classical liberal mentality by bringing a new human and personalistic factor into economics. Labour, in fact, does not derive its value from the utility of the product, but from its human quality: the product gets its value from labour.

If, on the one hand, Marxism 'economicizes' man, man,

on the other hand, humanizes economics. It should also be noted that this concept of value cannot be justified in the light of experience or of *praxis*. Like the concept of liberty, it forms part of that axiology which is somehow anterior to *praxis*, and of which I spoke at the beginning.

Consequently, as with the concept of man, new and more specifically Marxist dimensions of the concept of liberty emerge. It cannot be reduced to economic liberty, but is founded on it. The liberating efficacy of *praxis* should be expressed, therefore, primarily in the economic field: by transforming the economic situation it ensures the transformation of the entire human situation and the suppression of all imbalance and alienation. When man is free from economic servitude he is certainly free. Once the 'original sin' has been destroyed, the others will disappear as a result. More precisely, *praxis* is defined in relation to nature on the one hand, and society on the other. These two are intimately joined, however, in the unity of the phenomenon of production. In other words, the process of overcoming the present situation should be a transformation of nature (resulting in an ever more complete dominion over it) and of society (with the aim of setting up a new social order). Technical progress is pursued by capitalism and Communism alike, but whereas capitalism reduces human progress to technical progress, Communism sees technical progress as human progress only insofar as it involves a transformation of human relations.

As an essential and fundamental component of man's liberty, economic liberty shares in the absolute quality of that liberty. The assertion of economic liberty as an absolute and fundamental value is one of the most characteristic features of Marxism; it constitutes its axiological materialism, which is no less important within the whole system than historical materialism itself.

In this light, labour is no longer simply a means of sustenance, much less a punishment for man's original failure, but the natural activity through which man carves out a place for himself, creates himself and frees himself, by dominating and humanizing nature. Man's nature, or position in the universe, is specified in dynamic terms as that of the producer, the worker, *homo faber*. The static definition of man as a rational animal is replaced by that of man as a worker. If he is essentially related to nature and society, this complex of relationships is based on the productive relationship. Thus Marxism asserts the dignity of work with exceptional eagerness; it even proposes a mystique of work and of technology—a technological humanism. In Marxism the assertion of man's dignity means the assertion of the dignity of work. Man's dignity is founded, not on blood or on money, but on his real capacities, primarily those concerned with production. The idealistic theme of man as the demiurge of the universe, creating himself through his own activity, undergoes new developments here. If the only work that Hegel knew was of a spiritual and abstract kind, in Marx we are dealing with the concrete, material, daily work that conquers and dominates nature.

This summons to life in the concrete rather than to abstract theories of liberty or perfection means that Marxism is an answer to the genuine problems felt by every man. Its analysis of economic alienation courageously denounces the inhuman and very real situation in which very many workers lived and still live. It is the situation of a great part of humanity, tormented by hunger and want, in unjust and unstable working conditions, deprived of the material infrastructure which would allow them to live a really human life. Marxism takes up these dramatic problems, proposes a solution that may appear in many cases to be the only concrete one, and pledges itself to work effectively towards it.

These aspects, though on the one hand they give a quality

of concreteness to the ideal of the liberation of man, on the other hand, in accord with the typical Marxist dialectic, they project the light of the ideal onto the concrete world. This also emerges from the connection between economic and ethical theories: while the economic incarnations of the ideal concretize the ethical obligation, the ethical viewpoint imprints a new, ideal significance on economics.

Economic alienation, the radical evil of humanity, is at the same time moral evil; it is the fundamental injustice, an immorality incorporated into the objective structures of the economic and political system. All the moral imbalance, the many objective injustices and the subjective attitudes of egoism and individualism, which mark the capitalist era, are derived from it. *Praxis*, aimed at overcoming economic alienation, is, therefore, the rebellion of moral conscience against an immoral condition; the struggle beween the two moral systems is the historical struggle between good and evil. The system of liberty and economic prosperity which is intended to issue from this struggle will be, at the same time, the reign of a morality that will consecrate the final victory of goodness. Man will then be 'confirmed in grace', or, more exactly, 'confirmed in nature'.

As with the concepts of man, of liberty, of *praxis* and of alienation, so, too, that of religion receives its most specifically Marxist interpretation in the economic field. The antinomies between humanism and religion which we have encountered up to now are actually present in other forms of atheism, even if in quite different contexts.

What characterizes Marxism is not its view that religion is a form of alienation, but its thesis that religion is essentially connected with economic alienation.

The conflict mentioned earlier between secular and religious values is thus clarified. The alienating, narcotic effect of religion on this secular sphere damages the economy in a

fundamental way by inducing the proletariat to resign itself
to the unjust situation in which it finds itself. Therefore
religion is the natural ally of capitalism or reaction. The
alliance between altar and throne derives from the alliance
between altar and capitalism.

Given the ethical nature of economic involvement, we are
faced with a new aspect of the conflict between morality and
religion. Being anti-progressive, religion is immoral. Religion,
not irreligion, is the sin. The religious man is psychically and
morally abnormal.

Marx writes:

> The social principles of Christianity have justified slavery
> in ancient times, have glorified medieval servitude, and
> are capable of approving the oppression of the pro-
> letariat if need be, even if with a slightly contrite air.
> The social principles of Christianity transfer to heaven
> the compensation for all infamy, and thereby justify the
> perpetuation of this infamy on earth. The social principles
> of Christianity declare that all infamies committed by
> oppressors against the oppressed are the just punishment
> for original sin or other sins, i.e., that they are trials
> imposed by the Lord, in his infinite wisdom, on souls that
> are saved. The social principles of Christianity preach
> cowardice, contempt of self, lowliness, submission,
> humility—in a word, all the qualities of the rabble.
> The proletariat that refuses to be treated like rabble
> needs its courage, its self-respect and its taste for in-
> dependence much more than its bread. The social
> principles of Christianity are crafty; the proletariat is
> revolutionary.[15]

---

[15]'Der Kommunismus des "*Rheinischer Beobachter*" ', in *Deutscher Brüsseler
Zeitung*, 12 September 1847, *Marx-Engels Gesamtausgabe*, IV, 200.

Religion (and with it the existence of God) is excluded, therefore, for axiological reasons specified in the economic sphere. It is an alienation, both in regard to man's natural aspirations, which are essentially terrestrial and basically economic, and in regard to his ethical and economic ideal.

Here, as in the rest of the system, the theme of alienation has an essentially axiological significance: religion alienates, not so much because it launches man into an illusory reality (as such it is a form of ignorance), as because it creates an illusory system of values, which, by distracting man from the genuine system of values, constitutes an obstacle to *praxis*.

Once again we are dealing, not simply with an historical or factual conflict, but with an essential incompatibility.

This view of religion also enables us to grasp the precise meaning of the problem of evil in Marxism. In a theistic framework the problem of evil arises after the existence of God has been proved and one is led to analyze his action in the world. Theodicy, a 'justification' of God, becomes necessary on account of the accusations brought against his wisdom and goodness owing to the existence of evil. In Marxism, as in some other forms of humanistic atheism, the framework is reversed: if God existed man would be condemned to evil, would have to give up trying to overcome it. God is denied, not because evil exists, but in order that it should not exist. God is denied, not because he would have to be good if he existed, but because if he existed he would have to be evil. God is denied, finally, not because he would be incompatible with evil, but because he would be incompatible with good.

Marxism approaches the problem of the origin of religion on the same level. It is said not only that religion is in conflict with secular values, but that religious alienation derives from secular alienations. Now the fundamental secular alienation is economic. From it, therefore, religion is derived.

Why, then, is man found to be religious, given that religion is an illusion? Marxism, like illuministic atheism, holds that religion is a form of ignorance destined to disappear with the progress of the scientific world-view. It also maintains, however, along with Nietzsche, Freud and many others, that the intellectualist explanation of the phenomenon is inadequate. The psychological roots of this ignorance must be sought in the depths of man, in his atheoretical life, be it conscious or unconscious. The problem of truth is resolved by means of the problem of values. And so there follows the description of the defence-mechanisms referred to earlier.

But, for Marx, even this explanation is inadequate and requires to be deepened in a way consonant with the general vision of man and of history. The roots of the superstructure end in the infrastructure.

According to Marxism, therefore, religion originates as a compensation for the economic frustrations of the proletariat, and is favoured by the ruling class who see it as a means of consolidating their position; from another angle, it reassures the conscience of the exploiter, offering an easy entrance ticket to heaven in return for some alms.

Here is Lenin's view of religion:

> Faith in a beyond arises from the helplessness of the exploited in his struggle against the exploiter, just as belief in divinities and demons arises from the helplessness of the savage in his struggle against nature.
>
> Religion, calming with the hope of heavenly recompense the man who suffers deprivation all his life, teaches him patience and resignation. To those who live off the labour of others it teaches the practice of benevolence here below, thus offering them an easy justification for their existence as exploiters and selling them cheap tickets to participation in heavenly felicity. Religion is the opium of the people. It is an unrefined

species of spiritual brandy, in which the slaves of capital
drown their humanity and their claim to an existence
worthy, at least in a small way, of man.[16]

If this is the origin of religion, then its destiny is easily
foreseen. Provoked by an imbalance that is historical, and
ultimately economic, it is destined to be swallowed up again
when the imbalance disappears. Socio-economic progress is
necessarily correlative, therefore, to the decline of religion.
Consequently, combating religion involves, not just the
dissipation of ignorance, but, above all, the suppression of the
historical conditions that gave rise to it.

In the future Communist society the process of restoring
history and human psychology to normal will be completed,
and all alienation will end. On the question of religion, therefore, all men will assume the normal attitude, that of atheism.
More exactly, atheism will consist, not in the denial of God,
but in the total absence of the problem. Not only religion,
but the religious problem itself, is provoked by a system
producing economic alienation. Consequently, it is destined
to disappear when the latter does. Ideal Marxist man is satisfied, as we have seen, with the earth and the indefinite progress
of terrestrial existence.

However, this analysis of religion in a Marxist key must
not be ended without mention of the profound new basis for
the problem in contemporary Italian and French revisionism.

We may cite, e.g., the thesis supported by the Italian Communist Party in its Tenth Congress: 'It is a question of understanding how the aspiration towards a socialist society not only
can make progress in men with religious faith, but can find
in the religious conscience a stimulus with regard to the
dramatic problems of the contemporary world.'

[16]Lenin, *Socialismo e Religione, Opere complete*, Rome 1955, X, 73-74.

Commenting on this text, Lucio Lombardo-Radice, a member of the Federal Communist Committee of Rome, writes: 'It would be difficult to overrate the novelty and importance of this thesis, approved by the last Congress of the Italian Communist Party (not without opposition—it was one of the most controversial theses, and discussion is still in progress). It was the first time, if I am not mistaken, that a Communist party, directed by a group of convinced Marxists, affirmed that "even in the present stage of history, there can be a capacity for revolution in religion".'[17]

Faced with the disconcerting phenomenon of Christian progressivism, which the orthodox Marxist, if he notices it at all, interprets in terms of tactics, quite a number of present-day Marxists are led to distinguish the historical forms of religion, which have been, and often are, reactionary, from its essence, which they consider capable of revolutionary involvement.

Declarations of this kind are difficult to reconcile with orthodox Marxism, for which the anti-progressive nature of religion provides the most typical justification of atheism. Is it possible to defend this thesis coherently without favouring revisionism? Can the following two affirmations be reconciled: 'religion is an alienation' and 'religion has a revolutionary capacity'?

Undoubtedly, the Marxist critique of religion which has just been presented is not based exclusively on its anti-progressive character. The first topics that we analyzed (humanism, ethical humanism and demiurgic humanism) are really independent of socio-economic progressivism. But the topics concerned with terrestrial and, above all, economic humanism, which are the most typically Marxist, are centred

---

[17]Mario Gazzini (ed.), *Un marxista di fronte a fatti nuovi nel pensiero e nella coscienza religiosa*, in *Il dialogo allo prova*, Florence 1964, 90.

on this problem. In this area, consequently, I can see no possibility of outlining a distinction (from the Marxist point of view) between alienation and anti-progressivism. In what sense would a religion that was no longer in conflict with revolutionary *praxis* be still an alienation? It should not be forgotten that, for the Marxist, alienation is an axiological category, and the criterion of value is *praxis*.

Marxist Humanism is Communal

As we have already seen, Marxism lays great emphasis on the social or communal character of human existence. Marxist man is not an isolated individual, but is essentially inserted into a network of relationships with nature and with society. He must not be reduced to a closed interiority, to a *cogito*, but is open to the world (being-in-the-world) and to other men (being-with).

The fundamental bond of this communion, which unites man to nature and to other men, lies in productive relations. This communion is not restricted to the economic sphere, however, but permeates all human activity. Any solution to the problem of man that considers only the isolated individual is purely rhetorical. Man's destiny is one with that of the human community, indeed with that of the whole of reality. Man cannot be transformed unless history is transformed.

This organic view of man is included in an organic, and, in this sense, dialectical view of the whole universe. The universe is not just a mass of phenomena, but a single, coherent whole, in which objects and phenomena are essentially interrelated, and condition each other reciprocally. The Hegelian dialectic is translated here into natural terms. According to this conception, each being and phenomenon can be understood only in the light of the totality. The communal dimension is essential to man, both in his being and in what he ought to be, on the level of reality and on the level of value. The essence of man is social. The isolated individual is an abstraction. The real man is, as Marx puts it, a 'being of a species' (*Gattungswesen*), or a social organism. But the individual may be integrated into society either as means or as end, as slave or as free man. The ideal man, towards whom history is necessarily orientated, is a member of a community of free and equal men. Indeed, the individual can realize himself as end only in a community (without classes, without the state, without coercion) in which each member is an end. This means that each man must overcome the egoism and individualism that cause him to try to dominate others and to reduce them to means. In short, liberty can be achieved only in love. The eschatological society will be a community of love. The organic view of reality outlined by Marx has some affinities with the Christian concept of mystical body (by which, moreover, it was probably influenced), but what is a supernatural unity for the Christian, now becomes a natural unity. The unity that was formerly founded on the Man-God is now based solely on man, or, if you will, on divinized man.

The human ideal is not a purely personal liberty, therefore, but liberty lived out in a fraternal community, in the classless society of the future. Faith in man means faith in the future of humanity. The basis of the new society will be a productive system full of respect for every man's dignity, in which each will give according to his capacity and receive according to his needs. In this society egoism, the fruit of economic alienation, will be finally overcome, and inter-personal relationships will be regulated spontaneously and without constraint, by justice and love. Each will be for all and all for each.

As we have seen, the existing situation of alienation is itself of a fundamentally social nature: it is the exploitation of man by man, with all the individualistic, egoistic atmosphere that goes with it. In a *bourgeois* society based on the master-slave relationship, man is still the same as in Feuerbach: an isolated, individualistic being in an egoistic, atomized world that is the theatre for the war of every man against every other man. He is degraded to the level of means, and, in turn, considers others as means. He is alienated in two senses, therefore: first, he is deprived of his liberty, which is taken from him by other men and particularly by the state, and second, he is deprived of his essence as a communal being—deprived of human solidarity. Effective liberty and solidarity are replaced by a juridical, state-centred liberty and solidarity that are illusory and serve only to consolidate the real servitude. Alienation is a social fact for the further reason that it strikes individuals by striking the whole class to which they belong. Every man's destiny is one with that of his class. Therefore, release from alienation cannot be secured simply through an increase in productive activity, but also necessarily implies the trans-formation of human relationships towards justice and love, and the emancipation of all the proletariat.

In order to be effective, the transforming action must unify, in its turn, all those who are bound by the same chains, and bind them into a single movement of rebellion: 'Workers of the world, unite.' And now the real subject of Marxist *praxis*, the protagonist of history, the creator of liberation— the messiah—enters the scene. He is not Hegel's abstract idea, or Feuerbach's isolated man, or Nietzsche's superman, but the human community in its best expression, the proletariat. The messiah is actually alienated, annihilated and crucified (here we meet the Christological origin of the Hegelian concept of alienation). But one day he will be glorified.

Proletarian solidarity is a condition of the effectiveness of *praxis*: it will be so much the greater the more numerous are the adherents of the movement. Its vocation is to overstep the confines of nationalism and to spread on a world-wide scale: internationalism—catholicity, if you will—is one of its essential marks. In fact, all the workers of the world live in the same alienating conditions, and must overcome them through a communal fight for liberty. Thus the mark of unity is linked with the mark of catholicity. It can mean unity of organization or unity of action. Every gap in the unity of the workers, whether on the national plane (the splintering of the workers' movement), or on the international plane (the conflict between Russia and China springs to mind), is detrimental to the effectiveness of their action: consequently, it is evil. This unity does not suppress legitimate diversity and autonomy as expressed in terms of the variety of national approaches to socialism. This theme has undergone much development in the post-Stalin era in response to the new needs of a pluralistic civilization.

There are two categories or social classes of men: the capitalists, who, by oppressing the workers, trample on human dignity and so are enemies of man; and the workers, who, being committed to the construction of a just system, are the defenders of man. These two classes represent good and evil in the world. The workers, the genuine chosen people on the way to the promised land and to the messianic era, bear the salvation of the world on their shoulders.

Like Israel and like the Church, they are certain that the fulness of time will come, and that the meaning of history lies in the journey towards it. Like ancient Israel, they believe that the fulness of time must come to pass on earth, not in heaven. But they differ from Israel in that they await liberation, not from God or his envoy, but from their own action; man is saved by man, the people by the people. This is not the people of God, however, but the people of history. The civilization which this people will build is not the kingdom of God, but the kingdom of man.

Although, like Israel and like the Church, it forms only a part, and in an organized form only a small part, of mankind, the proletariat knows that it has a universal missionary vocation, that it is called to carry out a task on which will depend the destiny of all mankind. The proletariat prepares tomorrow's mankind and in a certain sense prefigures it: it is the image of the city of the future.

It follows that for the individual worker success in life coincides with the success of his class. But the success of the working class is the success of mankind: the proletariat walks with the flow of history. Marxist humanism is proletarian, therefore, and expressed in a class, but this is only a provisional arrangement; its aim is to enable the proletariat more effectively to carry out the universal task to which it is called.

In order that the redemption of the proletariat, and so of mankind, should be possible, every member must regard the cause as the supreme value, and must subordinate his personal interests to it. In concrete, then, the community becomes the supreme value to which everything must be sacrificed. The Marxist has no purely private life; he always acts with reference to the community. His life is essentially a service to society; his first commandment is that of love—of world-wide dimensions—and it can demand even heroism, even the giving of one's life for those one loves, for one's fellow-workers. He is called to fight and to sacrifice himself for ideals that will certainly be attained, but perhaps only by tomorrow's mankind. He will not see the triumph, but the certainty of fighting for a just and noble cause, of walking with the flow of history, makes him aware that he has not lived in vain.

The theme of man's communal vocation is rich in consequences. Among them are the concept of the party, the collectivistic conception of property and of the family, and the idea of the dictatorship of the proletariat.

The proletarian struggle for liberation will be effective only if organized. The party is the expression of this need:

it unites the most active elements of the proletariat, and through them incorporates the whole class. *Praxis* in all its aspects must be directed by the party: it is (to coin a term) essentially 'partitic'. Marxism is a partitic humanism.

The partitic aspect extends to all areas of the worker's life and specifies for him the meaning of his communal obligations. Fidelity to party directives is the concrete synthesis of all moral imperatives. This obedience is not blind or unjustified, however, since, in fact, the party derives its authority from its being the interpreter of the sentiments and interests of the working masses. It is the conscience of the proletariat and, for the same reason, the voice of history. Whereas religion requires obedience to men who represent God, Marxism requires obedience to men who represent man—men who express the conscience of history.

This implies a concept of authority that tends to exclude every arbitrary action. The exercise of authority is, in fact, legitimate only insofar as it faithfully reflects the interests of the proletariat, and thereby faithfully reflects the flow of history. Such fidelity requires that authority be in continuous contact with the masses, in whose collective conscience the voice of history is expressed. Just as religious authority seeks the word of God in the sources of revelation, in the same way Marxist authority seeks the word of history in the popular conscience. As in the Church, so in Marxism, the conscience of the individual is fallible, but that of the mass is infallible. To ensure this fidelity to the people, the party must be notably democratic in its structure. If rigid discipline is essential to the effective implementation of decisions once taken, it is no less essential that decisions should be the fruit of extensive democratic consultation and frank debate at all levels. If the masses must follow their leaders docilely, it is only because they have elected them and because, in consequence, they then embody the general will. Besides being preceded by consultation with the masses, decisions should be made collegially. Collegial direction is another powerful aid to the suppression of individualism, since a college will reflect the popular conscience more easily than would an individual. The authoritarian forms of government and the cult of personality must be considered deviations from Marxist doctrine. Party leaders, therefore, have unlimited jurisdiction and power to teach, and this is derived, not from the authority of God, but from that of the people.

By virtue of its harmony with, or 'connaturality' to history, the proletariat is in a state of rectitude that enables it to gain objective knowledge. From this point of view, too, Marxism is a philosophy of *praxis*. Whereas the capitalist is bound by his economic interests to produce false and anti-historical ideologies, the proletariat is bound by its interests to produce the true ideology, namely, Marxism. This is not just one among the many ideologies generated by history; it is the one that reflects the objective order; it is the absolute and definitive world-view. Fidelity to reality presupposes that philosophical research be, not the work of isolated thinkers, as such exposed to error, but a collective work, directed and planned by the living teaching authority of the party; whence the collectivistic and partitic notion of truth and of philosophy.

Where the Communist party comes to power it must gradually lead the entire population to live the community ideal, in other words, to make its own interests coincide with those of the state. It is easy to see that the actualization of such a programme should begin in the economic sphere. The fruits of the labour of all must be put at the disposal of all, since wealth has an essentially social function. But this can be done only through the decisive intervention of state planning and the nationalization of the means of production. In a system allowing private property and free initiative, private interest is the stimulus to production, and profits go to private sources, to the capitalists. This is institutionalized egoism. In a community-based outlook on life, an economic system must be attained in which production is organized in the light of the real needs of the collectivity. Therefore, Communism does not deny the right to private property, but rather aims at the exercise of this right by every citizen. However, whereas in a liberal system this right is considered unlimited, Communism limits it in the light of the requirements of the common good, which demand that production be planned and private property collectivized.

The same principles hold with regard to the family. Here, too, Marxism opposes the *bourgeois* conception of matrimony, regarding this as conjugal or group egoism. Marxism does not sanction free love, notwithstanding accusations to the contrary; rather it argues against the licence and sexual exhibitionism that are rife in the Western world (Soviet films are known to be generally among the more restrained in sexual matters).

Matrimony has primarily a communal significance in Marxism: it is a service rendered to the revolutionary cause, and it generates and forms tomorrow's militants. The choosing of a partner should be undertaken with this in mind. The problems of divorce and birth-control are resolved on the basis of what benefits the state.

The socialist state is the true guarantee of the sound education of children. Education cannot be left to the subjective views of parents; it must be conducted according to the needs of the objective order, of which the party—the conscience of the proletariat—is interpreter. And it must serve the supreme value, the construction of a Communist society.

The right of the child to an objectively valid education prevails over that of the parents to educate him according to their own subjective views. Private, uncontrolled education,

imparted by the family or private school, runs the risk of producing a 'private' *bourgeois* man, not moulded according to
the objective requirements of his communal, socialist vocation.

This community life demands generosity. If, on the one
hand, it promotes a rapid rise in the standard of living of the
masses, on the other hand it asks of them, particularly those
privileged under the old system, renunciations sometimes quite
serious in nature. The common good calls for transformations
in existing structures and habits of life that cannot be effected
without personal sacrifice. Asceticism has no value in itself
and will disappear in future Communist society; but during
this stage of transition, the cause requires a system of high
tension and austerity. It is not just voluntary groups that are
called to live in an atmosphere of emergency, but the great
masses; and not for short periods, but for entire generations.
On the other hand, the transforming action meets with
lively resistance from the remnants of the *bourgeois* mentality
that is firmly rooted in the populace.

In these circumstances, continuity and efficacy of action
require that the socialist political system be strong and stable.
Where the proletariat has gained power, parties other than the
proletarian have no *raison d'être*. They would, in fact, be the
expression of particular interests in conflict with those of the
collectivity. They would polarize those remnants of the past
that conflict with the needs of the future. They could only
have the effect of impeding the progress of humanity, of
retarding the rhythm of history. A system is required, therefore, in which only the sane forces in the nation can express
themselves, and in which defeatist and reactionary organizations are proscribed. Goodness and truth have all the rights,
while evil and error have none. The sane forces in a nation
are embodied in the workers' party: consequently, this must
be the only party. Such a system would be called 'popular
democracy' or 'dictatorship of the proletariat'.

The meaning of Communist dictatorship should emerge from its doctrinal context, therefore. It is not considered to be the ideal or ultimate system, but a transitory one imposed by the state of emergency in which a nation that wishes profoundly and rapidly to transform its structure, must live. It is, like the state, a necessary evil—a lesser evil. In principle it is a question of dictatorship tempered by the internal democracy of the party and by dialogue between the party and the masses. Liberal economic systems uphold their un-limited respect for liberty against the authoritarianism of the Communist state. In reality, however, the democracy and liberty of these systems are purely formal: all rights are recog-nized, but their effective exercise is impossible. The reins of command lie in the hands of the capitalists, as a result of which a minority rules society in the light of its own interests and not those of the majority. In existing society all systems legalize the control of one class by another—the dictatorship of a class. It only remains to choose between the dictatorship of capitalism (a small minority) and that of the proletariat (the vast majority).

Like all dictatorial regimes, Communism defends the common good with ideological intolerance. Any counter-revolutionary *bourgeois* ideology whatever is a threat to the proletariat's conquests and must be opposed on that account. Since error has no rights it can, at best, be only tolerated in order to avoid greater evils.

Hence the need for radical limitation of religious liberty and for decisive atheistic propaganda. Religion, in fact, as we have seen, is the natural ally of capitalism, and con-consequently threatens the very foundations of the new socialist society.

State religion has given way to state atheism. Each has led to intolerance for analogous reasons: according to Marxism, liberty of conscience means liberty from the incubus of religion.   Reasons of expediency may recommend that the survival of religion be tolerated, but it cannot be considered of positive value in the life of the state.

One might be tempted to try for a compromise solution to the conflict between the Marxist and religious ideals: namely, the absolute laicizing of the state and a clean-cut separation of Church and state, resulting in the admission of religion as a 'private affair', though proscribing it from public life. The following facts might be thought to support the historical legitimacy of such a view: the existence of socialist states guaranteeing religious liberty constitutionally; the effective persistence of religious practice in them; the opening of the Communist Party to militants with religious convictions.

In reality, however, the conflict between Marxism and religion is so profound that any formula like that towards which some Western Marxists are turning must logically lead to a more general re-thinking of the entire system. Religion is antithetical to Marxism precisely as religion and not just as a public phenomenon. Consequently, even if religious liberty is sanctioned juridically and a certain amount of religious practice tolerated, this does not prevent Marxist organizations from fighting it tooth and nail and aiming at its complete extirpation.   The least one can say is that the believer under a Marxist regime will be in a position of *de facto*, if not juridical, inferiority.

In the Western world some Communist groups are tending to dilute the theory of the dictatorship of the proletariat and to arrive at a frank acceptance of pluralism, not only as a means of access to power, but even as a form of government in the future socialist society. Again it is a question of an evolution of the utmost importance, necessitated by the pluralistic world in which we live. On this point, too, there seems to be a parallel evolution in progress in both the Marxist and Christian worlds, influenced, in each case, by the same social environment. Contemporary Catholicism holds that intolerance, which she herself exercised, and up to a point theorized, in other days, is not one of her essential attitudes, but is linked with determinate historical situations now irreversibly past. Western Marxists make analogous declarations. Could Marxism effectively reconcile the acceptance of pluralist democracy with the premises of its own system?

The Catholic Church, sincerely accepting confrontation with other ideologies in a pluralist society, is aware that it thereby deprives itself of many possibilities of exterior efficacy and of expressing the faith of many of its members. It does not attempt to hide the fact that the results of this method come more slowly and less evidently. Notwithstanding its faith in the truth which it bears, it knows that by relying solely on free membership it risks remaining a minority in many nations and in the whole world; it also knows that its lofty programme will be carried out to a very limited extent by the masses. It holds, nevertheless, that its method of liberal confrontation, with all the limitations and risks involved, conforms better to the nature of its mission, and is more likely to obtain for it the living adhesion that it asks for.

Can Marxism realistically assume an analogous attitude?

Its evolution in this direction will be followed with the greatest interest. It must come up against serious difficulties from within the system, as the experience of socialist countries has proved. I cannot examine them here. In my judgement, however, the nucleus of these difficulties lies in the criterion of *praxis*. If *praxis* is the criterion of value, and if it coincides, in concrete, with the success of the proletariat movement as embodied in the Communist party, one is led to the conclusion that the party will recognize a system in the measure in which it shows itself favourable to this success, but will logically be forced to drop it as soon as it becomes an obstacle thereto. If it is to avoid this difficulty, Marxism must deepen the very concept of *praxis* itself by bringing out its personalistic roots, and on this basis must recognize the existence of values that are autonomous in relation to the success of the party.

Before concluding this analysis of the communal character of Marxist humanism, let us ask ourselves what evaluation of religion is demanded by it. From Marx's point of view, we are faced here with a new and fundamental aspect of the incompatibility of humanism and Christianity. For him, Christianity is essentially individualistic and egoistic: it expresses the separation of man from his communal essence. This consecration of egoism is one of the most important aspects of religious alienation. The tension between morality and religion is specified here as the tension between love and religion. Placed once again in the position of having to choose, Marxism chooses love. This interpretation of Christianity condemns a religious outlook which, with its political and economic conservatism, canonizes individualism and especially the unlimited right to private property; with its eschatologism and depreciation of 'works', it justifies a terrestrial life of egoism and resignation; with its prospect of the 'eternal reward', not even love can be disinterested.

Christianity speaks of love, but at bottom there is only an ineffective and hence illusory sentiment. Or else it speaks of charity, in the sense of a humiliating almsgiving that takes the place of justice.

Love, to be genuine, must be effective; it must be translated into practice. Marx was particularly polemical with regard to literature on social matters—largely inspired as it was by the liberal mentality of the times—and with regard to the individualism of the Protestant religious outlook.

Marxism is a Revolutionary Humanism

When the proletariat acts in order to affirm its rights and liberate itself, it clashes inevitably with capitalistic interests.

The capitalists take up their stand and defend legality and constitutional order to the bitter end, for it is really *their* interests, and not those of the whole community, that are expressed in the *status quo*. Real legality, as represented by the proletariat, comes into conflict with the formal legality expressed in the laws of a capitalistic state. Consequently, the social action of the proletariat necessarily turns into a struggle organized and directed by the party.

Marxism is a militant form of humanism; every Communist is a combatant. Man's life on earth is a struggle (as Christianity wishes it to be), not, however, a purely interior, abstract struggle, but a concrete, exterior, social struggle between the exploited and the exploiter. The proletariat, like the Church, must go through a militant phase while awaiting its triumphant phase.

This struggle is fought out basically in the economic field, but it acquires moral significance, as does economics in general. The conflict which animates history—the conflict between good and evil, the 'two cities'—becomes incarnate in the class struggle. *Praxis* is the active solution to the problem of evil. The socio-economic struggle is the motive force of history; it permeates and provides a key to every aspect of human life. Nothing is extraneous to it: there are no neutral men, events or attitudes, and in practice there are no indifferent acts. He who is not with the proletariat is against it. In particular, there is no culture, philosophy, art, literature, cinema, or science that can call itself neutral; all forms of culture are militant, and if they do not militate for progress then they favour reaction.

Antinomy and contradiction are the soul of history and of all becoming. This is a law of the dialectic that also rules the natural world. Internal contradiction provokes the disintegration of a reality, an historical epoch, and generates another. Once again it is the study of man and of history that points the way to the discovery of the laws of nature. All this is the more comprehensible insofar as nature, as we have seen, is subservient to man.

The affirmation that contradiction is the soul of becoming is Hegelian in origin. But for Hegel this contradiction developed, and must be resolved, in the intellectual sphere, whereas for Marx the contradictions are real and must be overcome by a real struggle. The Marxist critique of alienation does not consist merely in the revelation of its existence and theoretical composition, but involves its practical suppression. The real contradiction is between alienation, the evil, on the one hand, and the struggle to overcome it, on the other. For the proletariat there is a passive, undergone contradiction and an active, provoked contradiction.

But the liberation struggle carried on by the proletariat cannot rest content with obtaining concessions within the framework of existing structures; the very structures, unjust and oppressive, legalize servitude. Therefore evolution is not enough; there must be revolution. The success of *praxis* coincides, in concrete, with the success of the revolution. Marxism is a revolutionary humanism. Even here, the attitude involved is no more than an emergent awareness of the laws of the historical dialectic, or rather of the dialectic of all reality, whose progressive becoming does not consist solely of quantitative mutations, but necessarily entails 'dialectical' or 'qualitative leaps'. Real contradictions become progressively more acute, and at a given point cannot simply be resolved evolutively: the leap, the sudden passage from one historical epoch to another, from one system to another, the 'substantial change', must intervene. These leaps do not break the continuity of history, however, insofar as the past lives on in the present, in which it is 'falsified' (the law of the 'negation of the negation'). Revolutions are the motive forces of history.

Revolution means qualitative, but not necessarily violent, change. Contemporary Marxism has certainly attenuated Marx's quite categorical position on violence, which he described as 'the midwife of every old society pregnant with the new'. Historical conditions have changed, in fact, and nowadays Western democracies sometimes offer the proletariat the means of a peaceful conquest of power. However, the ruling classes often put up such a strong and violent resistance that they cannot be overcome except by violence; when non-violent methods are seen to be ineffective, violence becomes legitimate and obligatory. There is no question of exalting violence for its own sake, but merely of having it as a last resort in case of necessity. As such it may be used to vindicate one's alienated rights, to reclaim the wealth whose purpose is the service of all; in a word, to regain one's liberty. Violent revolution is a revolt of slaves against masters, a legitimate act of defence.

Therefore, revolutionary *praxis* is the criterion of truth and value. What contributes to the success of the revolution is true and good, what thwarts it is false and evil. Marxist morality is concretely summarized in this principle. It consists in free and conscious adhesion to the laws of history. The dialectic is not just a metaphysical and historical law, but also a moral law. What follows the flow of history is good.

Once again, because of its counter-revolutionary character, religion seems to be incompatible with the Marxist system of values. It defends legality or constitutional order; it attributes divine backing to authority. Thus it condemns rebellion against 'legitimate' authority and the recourse of the masses to violence in order to gain respect for their rights. The use of violence by the *bourgeois* state to defend its legality, i.e., to defend the privileges of the ruling class and to drown in blood the revolt of the oppressed, is, on the contrary, quite legitimate.

Marxism is a Scientific Humanism

Marxism sees itself as a scientific humanism—as a certain and organic view of the world worked out according to a critical, experimental method. As we have already mentioned, however, it is science pursued for the sake of *praxis*, not for its own sake.

First and foremost, Marxism is a 'world-view', a system of truth and values affirmed with the unshakable certainty of a faith.

Attempts to interpret the whole of Marxism in a purely methodological way are not wanting. But they are insufficiently based on the historical point of view, and in any case they are vigorously disowned by Leninism. The latter is certainly conceived as an ideology and attaches great importance to the ideological struggle.

With the clarity of its solutions it is opposed to the intellectualism of contemporary thought and the crises of truth that afflict it. With the vigour of its ideology it is opposed to ideologically neutral Western states, which are incapable, as such, of justifying theoretically the values they promote. The Marxist state, in actual fact at any rate, is not neutral (in this sense it is not 'lay'), but has a definite ideological character.

By now it is clear that the absoluteness of the Marxist system is incompatible neither with its pragmatic orientation nor with the historicity of truth.

One of the most suggestive aspects of the Marxist world-view is its organic character, which enables it to make sense of every side of reality, history and life by projecting the light of the whole onto every part. The whole is always present in the part, and the part in the whole. So there is a Marxist interpretation of everything that is and that happens. The unity of the system is reflected in the unity of the personality committed to it. The Marxist militant strikes us as a man

full of certainty and conviction, with a personality fully
formed and unified by his faith: in higher and lower activities;
in intelligence, affectivity and action; in personal and social,
private and public, interior and exterior life.

Marxism claims that its world-view is rigorously critical.
In other words, it wants to be fully justified and respectful of
rational requirements. It is not accepted through sentiment
or because of some superhuman authority, but is acquired by
reason and justified by it at every step. The intervention of
human authorities such as the party, or even the classics
themselves, is legitimate only insofar as they reflect the
objective order and help the individual to conform to it.
Here, as elsewhere, abuses of authority are certainly possible,
and present-day Marxists deplore those committed in the
Stalinist era.

Philosophers who wanted to work out a critical world-
view with the aid of modern thought have been inspired either
by a strictly philosophical ideal (as in the various forms of
rationalism) or by an ideal of experimental science (as in the
various forms of positivism). Both requirements are fulfilled
in Marxism and it is not always easy to see how they can
harmonize. On the one hand, *praxis* requires an objective
and absolute vision of reality, one that is, therefore, autonomous with regard to the sciences: on the other hand,
praxis involves knowledge that adheres to the results of the
sciences. Defence is a primary requirement—defence, e.g.,
against internal deviationist currents as represented by Soviet
mechanistic positivism, which tended to make Marxist
theory coincide with the latest results of the experimental
sciences, or against rationalistic philosophies of a Hegelian
kind and, indeed, the classical conception of philosophy in
general.

It is not easy to see how the sciences can be made tests of
philosophical theories without reducing the latter to scientific

theories with all their hypothetical character. Up to a point, the problem is analogous to that posed by the relationship between theory and *praxis*, and must be solved along the same lines. Indeed, *praxis* is one of the fundamental forms of experimentation. It is related to the human sciences, such as sociology and history, as laboratory experimentation is related to the natural sciences. History is the great laboratory of socialist science.

More precisely, two kinds of relationship between science and philosophy can, I think, be distinguished in Marxism. In the first place, the philosophical world-view must be such that science is possible.

Marxist philosophy is justified in its entirety because it alone makes science possible, it alone creates the ontological conditions for the possibility of science. Such are the foundations of Marxist materialism, whether on the natural or historical plane. Only a philosophy that excludes mystery makes science possible. On the other hand, anyone who believes in mysteries or holds that reality is unknowable has no faith in man's capacity to penetrate its laws and thus to rule it. So he is obliged to await light from on high in order to know reality, and the intervention of divine providence in order to rule it. Everything is referred back to 'hidden causes'. In order for science to be possible, the full intelligibility both of natural and of human reality must be affirmed, and mystery rejected. Now only a materialistic philosophy excludes mystery; spiritualistic philosophies admit one section of reality, namely, spirit, which escapes full human knowledge.

The same conclusion is also reached in another way. Only a philosophy that recognizes the reality of matter, its causality and its determinism, makes science (natural as well as human) possible. It is material causes that furnish the scientific or verifiable explanations of phenomena. Now in a spiritualistic philosophy matter is belittled, reduced to an occasion for the action of spirit, as happens typically in Platonism. Thus it is compromised in its reality, its causality and its determinism.

Materialism is necessary, then, as a condition of the possibility of history.

In the second place, philosophy studies at the highest level of generality what experimental science studies at a sectional level. In this way are founded the philosophical laws of the dialectic, which regulate both nature and history. They derive from reflection on the results of the experimental sciences, which take the place occupied by common experience in traditional philosophy. As is the case with historical laws, philosophical laws are revealed in a concrete intuition and are not based on induction. Thus philosophy synthesizes the universal and definitive conclusions of science (e.g., that reality is in motion, in ascending evolution, etc.). These are then confirmed by particular results, but do not depend on any of them individually. Conversely, the various sciences depend on philosophy in a certain sense: they depend on it to establish their method, the conditions of their possibility and their most universal laws, for which they must then seek further applications.

There is mutual involvement, then, between science and philosophy, a dialectical relationship that does not compromise the originality of its terms.

One of the most commonly recurring themes in atheistic propaganda turned out by Marxists is the opposition between the scientific and religious world-views. Religion is opposed to the spirit of science in its method, which is authoritarian and emotional, whereas science proceeds by way of rationality. It is also opposed to science in its content: apart from tension in particular matters, there is the fundamental opposition between religion and materialism. The denial of God, like the entire materialistic outlook that involves it, is a condition of the possibility of science. Here, the denial of God is a rejection of the *Deus ex machina*, of the magical explanation in place of the scientific. Thus every scientific advance or technical break-through becomes a new proof of the non-existence of God. Advances in astronautics in particular have an 'outstanding atheistic importance'.[18] 'The history of scientific and religious development is the history of the constant decline of religious faith in the face of scientific truth.'[19] A choice must be made, therefore, between the religious and scientific views of reality and of life. Marxism chooses science.

Before concluding the exposition, I wish to reply to a final question. It is often said that after Marxism has destroyed every religion it becomes a religion itself—a religion without God. What are we to make of this statement?

At first sight it may seem to be simply a question of terminology, the answer depending on the meaning of the term 'religion'. In fact, the problem is deeper and more radical. In order to solve it, a distinction seems to be called for between religious metaphysics and religious experience. Marxism, denying all transcendence, certainly is not a religious metaphysics. But can the experience of the militant Marxist be called religious?

Many statements by militant Marxists seem to indicate an affirmative answer. In order to understand their position from the inside, we shall begin with the following psychological reflection: every man tends to unify his personality around a system of values. In the preceding pages I have attempted to describe the system of values by which the Marxist's personality is unified. Is it licit, then, to affirm a certain affinity between Marxist experience and religious experience? I think it is.

[18]The *IL' ICEV* report, *La propaganda ateistica nell' U.R S.S. e misure per intensificarla*, Milan 1964, 9.
[19]*Ibid.*, 8.

There is a living certitude, a 'faith', involved in both experiences, and it penetrates every aspect of reality, polarizing all forces and putting them at the service of one cause. In both experiences there is an ideal to be pursued in a vast community of brothers in faith, with the consciousness of working on a world-wide scale; it is an ideal that requires active discipline and a spirit of fidelity. In both experiences man must generously overcome his egoistic interests in order to dedicate himself to the cause of humanity, to the construction of a new world—a world which he, perhaps, will not see. In both experiences, man is animated in his commitment by an eschatological hope, i.e., by the certainty of marching with the flow of history. On this account his work is not wasted and will contribute to the inevitable victory of the ideal for which he lives and is ready to die.

Because of these qualities—this synthesis of the ideal and the concrete, the absolute and the historical—in a word, because of what it affirms and not because of what it denies, Marxism appears as an alluring movement, an historical alternative to Christianity.

Without wishing to anticipate the evaluative section yet to come, it seems possible at this stage to state that, in its main lines, Marxism emerges as a coherent development of the theme of liberty on the various levels of human existence, among which the economic is considered fundamental. Even the critique of Christianity seems to be substantially pertinent to the image of it fashioned by Marxism—an image which is not without its concrete counterpart in history. But in what measure does this image correspond to the genuine face of Christianity?

We shall have to confront this problem in the second part of the present study. For the moment let us note that the Christian response to Marxism, if it is to be logically valid and psychologically effective, cannot be limited to a discussion of atheistic denial, but must face up to the affirmations that call it forth. The ground on which the two visions are called to face each other is the problem of humanism.

CHRISTIAN HUMANISM FACE TO FACE WITH MARXISM

A Christian evaluation of Marxist humanism might be based either on the problem of God and religion or on the problem of man.

The former kind of treatment might seem at first sight more consonant with the character of Christianity, which, being a religion, must take up this point of view with regard to the various currents of thought and action. A discourse on this basis would be polarized predominantly, if not exclusively, by the profound divergences which set the two systems of thought in opposition—religion and atheism, spiritualism and materialism, eternity and temporality, etc.—and would necessitate a decisive choice of either man or God, earth or heaven.

It is difficult to contest the legitimacy of this approach, which is rather common in the Christian context and in religious contexts generally. It has the merits of clarity and simplicity that are often necessary for theoretical, and above all for practical reasons, in facing our problem, and it finds support in the Marxist classics, which assert the incurable conflict between Communism and religion in categorical terms.

Prescinding, nevertheless, for the moment from the scientific consistency of such absolute confrontations (whether produced by the Marxist or the Catholic side), one thing seems clear: this method runs the risk of not providing a solution to the undeniably serious problems which Marxism raises and to which it provides a solution. No answer can be given to

Marxism that does not begin with Marxist problems. Besides, these problems reflect an anxiety that is widespread in our times and that is in no way alien to genuine Christian sensibility.

To welcome Marxist problems certainly does not mean to welcome its solutions to them. Quite often today we hear talk, especially from Marxists, about a 'division of labour' between Christianity and Communism: the former should concern itself with God, leaving man to the latter. This idea takes it for granted that Christianity is a pure 'religion', i.e., that once freed from its historical contaminations and reduced to its evangelical essence, it becomes a purely transcendent, theological and eschatological message, and leaves the anthropological and terrestrial field of human experience wide open. A new type of man is postulated, Christian in religion, Communist in politics.

Before all else, Christianity is undoubtedly a religion, a relationship between God and man in which man acknowledges unreservedly the primacy of God. The meaning of Christianity would be distorted by reducing it to a humanizing movement, just as it would be distorted by reducing it to a message of salvation.

On the other hand, however, Christianity cannot be resolved into an affirmation of the primacy of God, but sees itself as an answer to the problem of man and of terrestrial existence in the light of God. A division of labour between Marxism and Christianity is unthinkable, therefore, because both put themselves forward as integral visions of reality and life. For this reason each tends to be present in every sector and finds that it must confront the other. Confrontation will reveal profound divergence even in the manner of conceiving earthly existence.

Consequently, acceptance of the problems raised by Marxists does not mean acceptance of their solutions to them. But neither does it mean their indiscriminate rejection. It may be true that Christianity differs from Marxism even in its conception of earthly existence. We must avoid generality, however, and define the divergence precisely, inspired by the higher requirements of truth—which must be acknowledged wherever it is found—and not by any apologetic concern.

In a religious setting, the quickest way to repulse a Marxist position is to show that it is essentially connected with atheism. But it is one thing to say that Marxism as a whole is atheistic, another to say that this or that thesis implies atheism: in exposing such links, one must proceed with scientific rigour. There may be Marxist positions which Christianity rejects precisely because it judges them to be anti-human rather than formally anti-religious. The aim of Christianity is not simply to defend God's rights, but to defend man's rights, too. In that case it will naturally oppose all violations of the rights of man with equal energy, whether committed by other systems or in the very name of religion itself.

Consequently, it is necessary to proceed very carefully in this matter also. It is sometimes said that Christianity rejects Communism on account of its conception of property. But is it not true that Chrisianity is affirming, ever more strongly, the social function of wealth, the legitimacy and the duty of state intervention, and, in certain circumstances, even the necessity of nationalizing the means of production? Christianity rejects Communism for its dictatorial character and its oppression of liberty. But has the Church not been frequently allied with dictatorial regimes in the course of history? Christianity rejects Communism for its revolutionary, violent, subversive character. But has not the resort to force in the defence of violated rights always been considered legitimate in Christian tradition? Christianity rejects Communism for its theory of class-warfare. But can organizations of a Christian inspiration work effectively in the defence of justice otherwise than through a certain class-warfare?

These examples are not intended to question the profound divergence between Marxism and Christianity, but only to highlight the need to abandon vague and approximate formulae and to single out with care the real significance and root causes of the phenomena under investigation.

Paul VI, in the passage already quoted from the encyclical *Ecclesiam Suam*, having mentioned some positive aspects of contemporary atheism, concluded: 'Shall we not be able to lead him (the atheist) back one day to the Christian source of such manifestations of moral worth?'[20]

To acknowledge the presence in atheistic thought of moral values Christian in origin is to assert a certain convergence, a certain community of solutions. However, these values are undoubtedly wedded to profoundly different contexts, which modify their meaning. Some take this as justifying a massive, global antithesis, notwithstanding the presence of a certain partial affinity. By virtue of this antithesis all possibility of dialogue is excluded by some Catholics and Marxists.

The difficulty is a very serious one and must not be underrated if we wish to avoid a superficial and precarious eclecticism. But precisely on account of its gravity, the assertion must be rigorously verified. As systems, Marxism and Christianity certainly differ at a deep level; but are they totally different? This is not a question of occasional convergences within the context of a general divergence. We are seeking the precise import of this divergence; we are asking whether all communion between the two systems is excluded by their central inspiration and deepest concern.

The answer to this query should emerge from the whole of the exposition which follows. It will meet Marxism on its own ground—that of humanism—and will take up its problems and evaluate its solutions. We should like at the same time to

[20]*Op. cit.*, 38.

point out the originality of the Christian contribution to the solution of these problems, and to question ourselves as to the possibility of a Christian humanism.

Christianity and Humanism

Divergence on the question of Christian humanism depends largely on the concept of humanism to which it refers. We shall see that the progressive clarification of this concept, in confrontation with Marxism, brings certain decisive aspects of the problem into focus. But the basis of humanism seems to be expressed in the following principle: man is invested with a certain axiological absoluteness, in the sense that he may never be reduced to a means, but must always be treated as an end.

Now this principle lies at the heart of Christianity: being the history of salvation, it is totally ordered towards enabling man—every man—to fulfil himself as an end. It is not a question of an artificial modernization of Christianity, but of a thesis that forms a part of its primitive nucleus, its historical originality. In fact, it is through its spirit of universality that Christianity has infused into human history this respect for man as such. If the modern world is characterized by its sense of humanity, its source is the Christian message. Thus the innate modernity of this message is revealed.

If by liberty we mean the full realization of man as end and the overcoming of all that stands between historical man and his ideal fulfilment, then Christianity becomes a vast liberating movement. Furthermore, if we mean by alienation all that is opposed to human liberty, then, in fact, man is in many ways in a state of alienation or servitude. Christianity looks towards the day when this state of affairs will be fully and finally rectified by means of the battle between good and evil, which is the soul of history.

Christianity rejects, therefore, as alienating, any kind of

relationship in which man is reduced, in principle, to the status of means—whether in relation to society or in relation to God himself. In the Christian universe there are many ends, and in this sense as many absolutes as there are persons.

But the absoluteness of the ends excludes neither co-ordination nor subordination; rather it requires these things. According to Marxism, as we have seen, the common good may demand even the sacrifice of the individual's life, in other words, the renunciation of his own fulfilment as end in order to contribute to the fulfilment of the community. We shall have to return to this rather delicate theme. For the moment we should note that, even from a Marxist viewpoint, not all subordination among ends is excluded, but only that which reduces man to a means: only this kind of subordination has the character of alienation.

There is certainly no point in hiding the difficulties inherent in the coexistence of a multiplicity of 'absolutes' in the axiological order, particularly that of reconciling their subordination with their autonomy. But are not these difficulties inherent, perhaps, in the heart of Marxism, as far as interpersonal relationships are concerned? It seeks a solution (this is the intention at any rate) by transforming the master-slave dialectic into a dialectic of friendship. Christianity, too, though conscious of profound differences, sees in this dialectic the key to the interpretation of total dependence on God. Just as the overcoming of alienation between men does not consist in destruction of one by the other, but in a transformation of the relationship, so it is between man and God.

We are now in a position to grasp the validity and limits of the Marxist theory of religious alienation at this fundamental level: the affirmation of God would, in fact, be alienating if our relationship with him were exhausted in the master-slave dialectic, e.g., in a voluntarism that would expose man and his destiny to the divine free will; but it ceases to be so if the relationship is understood in terms of a dialectic of love, as an encounter between two liberties. Finally, religious alienation, like every other form of alienation, must be fought in the name of religion.

It is quite licit, on the other hand, to reverse the question and ask whether man could fulfil himself completely and attain his freedom even on the hypothesis of the non-existence of God. Axiological absoluteness does not, in fact, exhaust the content of liberty. Liberty also implies the total fulfilment of those profound aspirations that constitute man: freedom certainly, but for what? These aspirations are terrestrial, according to Marxism. But are they exclusively so? Are earthly prospects really sufficient to satisfy man's expectations in full?

Let us assume the most attractive hypothesis, that of the realization of the ideal city promised by the Marxists. In the meantime, however, billions of men have died, and will die, without having seen it. What are we to think of a universe in which so many men can never fulfil themselves as ends, a universe in which so many are alienated in such a final way? It will be said that their sacrifice was not in vain, that their blood fertilizes the fields of the future. It remains true that the individual has been sacrificed to the cause, that in the final analysis he has been reduced to a means.

But even those who will see the new sun rise will one day be faced with death, will one day hang over the abyss of nothingness. Will the certainty of having lived for a noble cause be sufficient to stifle the anguish of being present at one's own dissolution? Will the certainty that humanity will continue to live and progress suffice to make the dying man accept his inexorable destiny without regret or rebellion?

Whatever reply one may wish to make to these questions, and even if one chooses to leave them dramatically unanswered, it is difficult to deny that they issue from the depths of man and that they are genuine human problems. The religious answer may be rejected, but the problems themselves can neither be rejected nor reduced to by-products of the class-struggle. Whatever forecast may be made for the future of religion, it is hard to imagine that all questioning about the ultimate meaning of life and death will one day be rooted out of the heart of man.

Furthermore, to resign himself to total destruction would mean, for man, to cease to desire life, to renounce happiness, to renounce liberty. Between life and death there is inevitable conflict. What could be more alienating than total annihilation? Death is the supreme alienation, and the militant Marxist, having fought (at times victoriously) against partial alienations, finds that he must capitulate before total alienation—he must lose the decisive battle. Nor can this alienation be escaped by projecting onto humanity that fulfilment of the ideal which is denied to the individual.

The community is certainly essential for individual fulfilment, but it cannot be substituted for it. In the measure in which the communal ideal, communal happiness and communal immortality must replace those of individuals, they would become an illusory consolation, a projecting of the self outside of itself, an alienation that would distract man from the solution of his personal problem. For Marxism, in a word, the absolute is not man, but humanity.

If this is true, then the liberation of man cannot be fully achieved in a mortal life. The aspiration to liberty postulates a type of existence that is different from the present and stronger than death. This type of existence must be 'totally other', must enable man to exist without further fear of being lost. From the depths of man, where he rediscovers himself, a call goes up towards a world of realities and values greater than man, greater than the earth. Complete fidelity to man demands his supersession.

But in order to satisfy man's expectations God must be God. In other words, God must be the totality of being and of value, and must, for this very reason, be infinitely superior to man, totally other than he and his complete master.

This sense of God's greatness, his incalculable superiority and total dominion, lies at the centre of religious experience. It is sometimes expressed, especially in the language of the mystics, in terms that suggest the annihilation of man. Religious sensibility can understand this intemperance, which is more often affective than doctrinal. In reality, God's greatness does not destroy that of man, but forms the basis of it. Man cannot be great unless there is someone infinitely greater. His destiny must be in the hands of infinite love.

In the last analysis, the identity of being and love in God is the foundation of humanism. This identity guarantees that the laws of being are ultimately those of love, and thus allows a positive answer to be given to the question of the meaning of being. The Christian universe is such that every person in it has the opportunity of fulfilling himself as end; salvation is offered to all. The master-slave dialectic is superseded by the dialectic of love.

It is not the existence of God that would alienate, then, but his absence. Indeed, if God did not exist, man could not fulfil himself: the death of God would mean, in the end, the death of man. Having killed God, man would not succeed in outliving him.

But the liberty which Christianity offers to man does more than satisfy his most secret aspirations. It overwhelms them. The Christian ideal extends, not merely to full humanization, but to divinization.

So far is God from wishing to enter into competition with man that all his action is directed towards divinizing man by uniting man to himself. Man can become God only if God exists. The foolhardy dream that man hoped would come true if he denied God will really come true only because of the love of God. From this moment onwards the ways of salvation, of liberation and of the divinization of man coincide with the ways of unity and love.

The history of salvation is the history of the march of humanity towards an ever more intimate union with God. At the centre of this vast plan of unification we find a man who is God—a man who is joined to God in personal unity. But this man was called to be God so that all mankind might be called along with him. He is at once an individual man and the model of man. He is the model of a new humanity whose history is destined to be founded with that of God.

Christianity and Ethical Humanism

It may, at first sight, appear unnecessary to state the ethical character of Christianity. In fact, no one doubts that it involves a complex of moral laws. But the question really is whether this ethic is purely 'religious' or also humanistic; whether, in other words, it has as its sole supreme principle the glorification of God, or also caters for the liberation of man; and whether, moreover, it is based exclusively on the free will of God, or also recognizes the necessities built into man's nature.

The solution to these problems is implied, to a large extent, in our earlier reflections. If, in the Christian universe, not only God, but man, too, is endowed with absolute value, then ethics will not be orientated to the glory of God alone, but also to the liberation of man. Respect for man's dignity, which inspired God's creative action, should inspire man's action, too. A metaphysic of love generates an ethic of love through which man prolongs God's action by pursuing the same ends as he.

Respect for man is imposed on God himself because his nature demands it. In order to be faithful to himself, God must be faithful to man. Ethical laws are not established arbitrarily by God, but express determinate ontological demands. First among these is respect for the person—divine or human—and for each person at his own ontological level. The Christian ethic is a defence, not just of God's rights, but also of man's rights. Voluntarism would be a religious alienation of morality and would have to be rejected precisely in the name of religion. In this sense religious ethics do not cease to be 'autonomous'.

But every form of voluntarism, including, as we shall see later, that exercised by the party, is alienating. If it wishes to be objectively valid, the partitic criterion of morality will prescind from the situational ethical judgement of the individual and its subjective bias.

Thus subjective intention is irrelevant to the moral evaluation of an act (and therefore of a person), which is based solely on the verifiable effects of the act. One can be morally guilty without willing or knowing it. But is it possible without depersonalization or alienation for a man to abdicate from making the final judgement as to the direction his life is to take? Moreover, does he not risk an obsessive fear of committing crimes against history without realizing it?

If morality is decided by the party, then besides the danger that the absoluteness or the subjectivity of morality may be compromised, a question-mark is placed over the value of man and hence over the humanistic character of Marxism. So whereas we began, in the exposition, with the thesis that *praxis* is not the exclusive criterion of morality within Marxism, we have gradually established that there is a fundamental ambiguity in the system on this point. To sum up, it appears that tension can be perceived between the principle of the absolute value of man and the principle of *praxis* as to which is the ultimate criterion of value. There is a risk of making man relative to the party, and the subject relative to the institution, and thus of alienating him.

But I think the root of this ambiguity is to be found in the Marxist ideal itself, in its concept of liberty. When we try to find an exact meaning for this concept, the economic liberty of the proletariat is seen to be an absolute and fundamental component of it. By its very nature this already makes morality relative to the interests of classes; and these interests do not appear to be subordinate to any other sphere of value. This relativity is consummated by party control, as a result of which the historical ideal takes on whatever shape the party gives to it. Party control of the ideal provides a basis for party control of *praxis*, morality and truth.

Thus the conflict between the absolute and the relative, the subjective and the objective, the person and the institution, is present in the very heart of the Marxist ideal.

On the other hand, the categorical imperative, 'act in such a way as to consider the person always as an end and never as a means', must be considered profoundly Christian. If it is specified that it must refer, as is only natural, to every person, divine or human, according to his value, it will be found to coincide with the commandment of love which summarizes Christian morality and its historical originality.

As the progressive realization of love, and thus of the fulness of humanity, the moral life is a vast liberating movement.

But love means disinterestedness. Is there not conflict, then, between an ethic of love and an ethic of recompense, even if the latter is eschatological? This conflict exists, up to a point. The Christian is obliged by the fundamental commandment to love God and his neighbour in themselves, and not merely for the reward which his love will earn. The desire for recompense cannot become the exclusive or primary motive of the moral life.

On the other hand, however, can it be licitly affirmed that an act ceases to be moral in the measure in which it pursues a reward? It seems difficult to justify such a conception. In any case, it is distinctly foreign to Marxism itself, which does not condemn as immoral the revolutionary action by means of which man pursues his own personal liberation and that of humanity. This self-seeking would be immoral if it interfered with the interests of the community, but not if it were in harmony with them, in which case it would become a powerful incentive to the moral life.

We shall return to this theme when dealing with the communal dimension of humanism. For the moment let us take note of the requirement, already observed by Kant, that in an organic system of values, morality and happiness, it should be possible for personal interest and generosity ultimately to converge. However noble a gratuitous sacrifice, with its pure generosity, may be, a universe in which the most noble among men cannot fulfil themselves as ends must be judged harsh indeed.

But once again such a synthesis cannot lead to a purely terrestrial view of human existence. In that view, in fact, sacrifice of life, the summit of moral generosity, coincides with the return to nothingness, the supreme alienation. The antinomy of morality and happiness does not seem to be resolved in Marxism. Giving of self for the happiness of others does not suffice to stifle the frustration of personal aspirations. Kant's intuition that morality postulates the existence of God and the immortality of the soul in order to ensure the final convergence of morality and happiness, seems to be valid.

Perhaps a realistic examination will reveal that this antinomy strongly echoes something in human psychology, insofar as an ideal of pure generosity, without any prospect of personal advancement, risks being ineffectual for the great majority of men. Why should this surprise us when we ponder the difficulty of heroism, even for the man who is certain of an eternal reward for it! We must enquire, precisely from the viewpoint of efficacy, and in the light of the criterion of *praxis*, whether the ideal of pure generosity—of sanctity without God—is capable of attracting the masses.

The importance of this question in relation to the evaluation of Marxism may be easily gathered from the fact that the Marxist programmes for the construction of the ideal city of the future may demand immense sacrifices from entire generations. To the extent that the masses might be unable to face such sacrifices, to the extent that they might reveal themselves incapable of living for a long time in an atmosphere of heroism, they would have to be placed under a dictatorial regime, where the appeal of ethical values might risk being replaced by terrorism.

On the other hand, for the believer, the certainty of another life, where the synthesis of morality and happiness would be achieved, becomes a source of generosity and effective action, and can drive him on, without regrets, to total sacrifice: for he who saves his life shall lose it, and he who loses his life shall save it.

Christianity and Demiurgic Humanism

The Christian takes the same pride as the Marxist in man's liberty and creative power to which he attributes a decisive influence on history and on man's destiny, whether as individual or as community. He admires man's evident capacity to dominate nature, to transform socio-economic structures and to bring an ever greater unity into the universe—all this through technology and social action. For the Christian, as for the Marxist, man is a true craftsman of history; he is not simply an object, he is a subject. And nothing authorizes him to take up a passive attitude.

The Christian, like the Marxist, notes, nevertheless, that it would be naive to attribute pure liberty or unlimited creativity to man, making him the absolute master of history and of the universe. Human liberty, analyzed realistically, appears as incarnate. Up to a point, it dominates nature and history, but they condition it in their turn. The Christian universe, like the Marxist universe, is conditioned by insertion into its real context, but initiative is not thereby destroyed. If it is true that man liberates himself, it is equally true that he is inadequate to the task.

There is no incompatibility, therefore, but rather a dialectical relationship, between efficacy and dependence, activity and passivity, initiative and conditioning. Which is another way of saying that not every kind of dependence alienates, but only that which becomes an obstacle to man's liberation. Dependence is not the same as servitude. On the contrary, there are kinds of dependence that favour and strengthen human action and thereby promote its liberation.

For the same reasons, not every acknowledgement of insufficiency or sense of limitation is harmful to human dignity; on the contrary, it would be harmful to develop a myth of self-sufficiency that is not borne out by the realities of the situation.

Even in the moral sphere it is not contrary to human dignity to admit the existence of imbalance in historical man, as a result of which he is not spontaneously generous but must be helped to be so, even by factors extrinsic to him. While Marxism and Christianity disagree at a deep level on how to interpret this *status deviationis*, and on how to overcome it, they are agreed that it exists.

Therefore, even the Christian rejects as alienating a kind of dependence on God that would demand the abdication of his own initiative, and would reduce man to a simple occasion or instrument, depriving him of any decisive impact on his own destiny or on world history. On the other hand, he sees no reason to consider as alienating the kind of dependence that makes God a condition of the possibility of initiative and ethical commitment in man. If man's dignity does not prevent him from admitting that he is conditioned by his fears or by realities inferior to him, why should it prevent him from acknowledging his dependence on a reality superior to him? If it does not prevent him from recognizing that he has been inserted into an historical plan with its inescapable necessity, will it conform better to his dignity to see in this plan the blind law of matter or the limpid design of one who is love?

Christianity has always been aware, of course, of the doctrinal difficulty of reconciling the demands of human initiative with those of divine dominion, and it is quite prepared to admit that this relationship is a mysterious one. We shall have to enquire later on about the legitimacy of this recourse to mystery in a crucial world-view. Suffice it for the present to highlight the necessity of questioning the fundamental presupposition of rivalry between man and God, in the light of the dialectic of love.

But perhaps we ought to appeal to a decisive judgement, that of Christian experience, rather than to speculative discourse. This will reveal that genuine prayer has never dispensed us from making an effort to do moral acts. How often have we not prayed precisely in order to overcome the temptation to despair, to find again the strength to act? If there is a spark of real generosity in our lives, its source is the energy drawn from prayer: the energy of an Ignatius of Loyola, a Vincent de Paul, a Don Bosco, or a Charles de Foucauld. Such men are certainly rare, but they are rare in the sense that they have achieved an exceptional degree of fidelity to the demands of Christianity. It is in these cases, therefore, rather than in the multitude of the mediocre, that the true face of religion must be found.

As we shall see, man's historical initiative will be all the more effective insofar as its ever widening bonds of solidarity are made more intimate by his worldwide vocation. But in order to be truly human, this initiative must also be expressed in an atmosphere of civil liberty; otherwise there is a risk of seeing religious alienation replaced by a no less serious political alienation.

But, above all, the Marxist must finally acknowledge his helplessness in the face of death, and, consequently, the fragility of the cosmic construction to which he is dedicated. Once again, action becomes invocation—the invocation of a love that is stronger than death, and whose intervention in history assures man of an immortal destiny and guarantees a lasting significance to history. On this condition alone can we be justified in believing that the laws of being are precisely those of love; thus alone can we give a more solid foundation to humanism than is given it by the initial act of faith in man. Once again it is not God's action, but his absence, that would alienate, since it would leave man's condemnation to death without appeal of any kind. In the last analysis, it is impossible to believe in history without believing in love.

As a result of this active presence of love, not only does human action find a basis, but it has horizons of efficacy opened to it that it would never have been able to reach otherwise. Because of this presence, man is enabled to work for his eternal destiny, or rather, for the destiny of the whole human community. Called to live the divine life and to live within Christ, man sees the possibility of effective action that greatly exceeds his natural capacities and shares in the divine demiurgic efficacy.

Christianity and Terrestrial Humanism

Its attitude towards secular values will be decisive in establishing the nature and limits of Christian humanism. For the Christian, as we have seen, man's destiny transcends earth and time: liberty is fully attained only if attained forever. The possibility cannot be excluded that the sense of eternity will make him dizzy, and, when he faces up to it, will accentuate the precariousness of temporal existence. Every man is liable to this fugacity and becomes more so as he gets older. Why should it surprise us, then, if one who has discovered that he is called to an immortal life capable of fulfilling his deepest expectations, is tempted at times to submit to the contrast between eternity and time, even to the point of thinking that the spiritual ideal lies in flight from the world; even to the point of declaring that 'what is not eternal is nothing'? This is the same reaction as the one we noticed in the conscience overcome by the revelation of God's greatness.

When it has overcome this momentary upset, however, Christian realism reflects that its eternal vocation must be realized in the temporal order, and that temporal life cannot be explained away in religious terms but implies a whole area of secular values whose development conditions religious values, sometimes decisively.

In its relationships with the world the Church is concerned with balancing two requirements: the first, that of affirming the primacy of spiritual values and hence the subordination of all other values to them; the second, that of affirming the consistency and autonomy of secular values in their own sphere.

Medieval Christianity had emphasized the first requirement, and had thus made possible a civilization in which all values appeared to be permeated, in a somewhat monolithic way, by religion. Politics, art, science, education, professional organizations, etc., were affected in this way. Ecclesiastical authority presided over these diverse sectors of human life. Political authority, in particular, was subordinated to it and considered its 'secular arm'. The defence of religion was viewed as one of its fundamental tasks. As soon as this stress was laid on the Church's rights, its dominion came to be expressed in the dignity, the wealth and the honours conceded to it by sovereigns, who thus made the pope and bishops into temporal powers.

If this type of Christianity assured the Church of a privileged position and the possibility of giving a religious inspiration to various human activities, it also had some very regrettable results. The temporal power of the Church, which ought to have been a sign and an instrument of spiritual action, often risked becoming an obstacle to this action. It distracted the clergy from its essential mission by absorbing it in secular problems. It rendered the Church's mission less evident by contaminating it with dubious temporal interests. The alliance between throne and altar made the Church co-responsible for abuses committed by sovereigns whose actions the Church seemed to support. The concrete link between the spiritual and the temporal continually exposed ecclesiastical authority to the temptation of turning spiritual values into instruments in the service of a temporal cause. Christian monarchs were all the more exposed to this temptation, since they saw religion as the consecration of their power and were thus able to seek to use it for their own ends. Serious meddling in the life of the Church resulted from this. Again, the clergy, as a privileged class, was situated socially on the side of the rich and powerful. Thus it could easily become estranged from the life and sensibility of the masses, and be steered towards conservative views in social and political matters. With the secular arm at its disposal for the promotion of religious values, the Church could be tempted to avail of it in order to limit and repress religious liberty: hence, persecutions, violence and religious wars. These methods violated objective personal rights; they encouraged a Christianity of conformity rather than of free choice.

This conception of Christianity is strongly marked by an integralistic or 'clerical' mentality, typified by the monolithic and institutional emphasis. The monolithic emphasis derives from a concern to unify personality and civilization around a sphere of values, in this case, religious, and is open to the risk of making instruments out of other spheres of value, compromising the consistency of its own sphere. Institutionalism is the tendency to embody values in a determinate institution, and risks making the 'success' of the institution in question the exclusive criterion of value.

This type of Christianity can give rise to various forms of religious alienation. It should be noted that religious alienation is not merely an alienation of the secular sphere by religion, but also of religion by the secular sphere. Indeed, it not only impedes the fulfilment of the secular sphere according to its own requirements, but also 'secularizes' religion itself.

The benefits that the Church brought, not only to religion, but also to civilization, seemed, for many centuries, to be adequate compensation for these risks and misfortunes. Adolescent peoples found in the Church a maternal tutelage that enabled them to grow and to attain adulthood. The Church also played a vicarious role in secular life: in other words, it took on many tasks which, of their nature, related to other organisms. As it happened, these organisms were not concretely prepared for the tasks in question. Finally, the powerful position of the Church could be viewed as a service rendered to society at the time. This situation marked the period known as 'Constantinian', which began when the Church ceased to be clandestine and became the state religion.

The assertion of the primacy of the spiritual order also implies the decision to sacrifice the temporal order where this would contribute to the furtherance of spiritual values. Here, too, a profound diversity of emphasis is possible. A monastically inspired spirituality laid great stress on the dangers of the world and on the necessity of distrusting them, of fleeing from the world and of scorning its vanities. Its basic attitude to creatures is one of detachment: *conversio ad Deum* presupposes *aversio a creaturis*. Creatures are to be used only to the extent that is indispensable to enable one to consecrate oneself to the service of God. In this context, the very expressions 'world', 'worldly' and 'spirit of the world' often have a negative sense. This spirituality tends to extend its sphere of influence from the purely monastic setting to other forms of Christian life, which are considered perfect insofar as they approach the monastic ideal.

This kind of ascetical foundation, while it clearly highlights the primacy of the spiritual order and the renunciations which it requires, may lead the Christian to neglect his duties in the temporal order. It may render him less sensitive to the urgency of constructing a more just human society, of working towards a solution of economic and social conflict, and of fighting for the recognition of the rights of man. The impression is created that the consistent Christian is an exile on this earth, that he is lost to the tasks of the earthly city, in a word, that religion alienates.

The Church of today remains faithful to the basic concerns of medieval Christianity. At the same time, the evolution of historical conditions and of human psychology demands new emphases and new doctrinal developments. The factors in this evolution all derive, basically, from a new awareness of man's rights, especially his autonomy, at every level of secular life. On the one hand, secular institutions are tending to emancipate themselves from the Church's tutelage. On the other hand, they are gaining an increasingly vivid awareness of their duties to the community. As a result, many tasks which the Church performed in a vicarious manner are being absorbed by secular institutions, above all by the state, and one can foresee the growth of this tendency.

As we have seen, this awareness of autonomy has matured in modern times in opposition to the Church, which was accused of wishing to conserve for itself powers which lay outside its competence. And the Church often reacted to this accusation in terms similarly polemical. Hence the state of divorce between the religious and civil spheres which is expressed in the 'Syllabus'.

The new attitude of the contemporary Church is the outcome of two apparently contrasting movements: one, a movement of detachment, of purification from matters temporal; the other, a movement towards involvement in the temporal order. Thus the Church continues to desire both detachment from, and involvement in, the world, but in forms and with motives that are appreciably different.

The Church maintains today that it must free itself, as far as possible, from compromise with the temporal order, if it is to be a sign of the mystery of Christ. The Council laid great stress on the poverty of the Church and its detachment from secular values. This attitude is connected with the new accent placed on service as constituting the Church's mission, just as the wealth of the Church and its temporal power were connected in the past with the defence of its rights and primacy. The Church, which in the past judged it opportune to manifest its primacy by assuming the trappings of temporal power, now maintains that this primacy is more clearly expressed through poverty. The theme of poverty, in its most general acceptation, transcends the economic order to a large extent, and penetrates the whole complex of secular values.

This loss of power is not simply tolerated by the Church as an historical necessity, therefore, or as a concession to laicism. It is seen as a purification, a 'dis-alienation' that enables the Church to appear in the world in the originality of its spiritual mission, without the mediation of forms which today would serve to hide rather than reveal it. On the other hand, the autonomy of the temporal and lay order is not a concession granted by the Church, but simply the just recognition of the rights of a humanity that has come of age. From now on, adhesion to the Church should be the fruit of a free and personal choice, not the result of the temporal prestige enjoyed by the Church. The Church believes that it can be more effective in today's world with poverty than with wealth.

But the attitude of the Christian and of the Church towards the world is not expressed adequately by the concept of detachment or poverty. Today more than ever, the Church is concerned to be present in the world, no longer with a tutelary or vicarious function, but in new forms more suited to its specific mission.

And the Church knows that the development of an authentic religiosity presupposes a normal secular, economic, social and political life. For this reason, the Church sees how urgently necessary it is that her sons should be sincerely committed to the construction of the earthly city—a just and fraternal world within which the flowering of a more mature religiosity will become possible.

This intercommunication of sacred and secular orders in the actuality of Christian life is vigorously stressed by the contemporary Church, which aims at proposing a message capable of giving a sense of direction to all that exists, of penetrating all sectors of action, and of being a ferment in civil life. Hence the necessity of a presence which, while it respects the autonomy of the secular order, will not be purely extrinsic and negative, but rather an effective inspiration.

It would be inaccurate, however, to think that the Church is aware of secular values only insofar as they can be instruments of the apostolate and dispositions for a more mature religious life. This would still be a 'clerical' conception of the relationship between religion and civil life. It would mean that the Church would be concerned with progress only in its 'religious' implications. It would have no interest in the human advancement of those masses where the prospects of Christianity asserting itself are not sufficiently proximate;

or, at any rate, it would have to attune its interest to the possibility of giving progress a religious orientation.

In reality, there is a more profound and general reason for this commitment, and today the Church is more explicitly aware of it. It is the defence of man's natural rights. First among these is the right to live in a world in which he can fulfil himself as end. Every man, independently of his religious dispositions, has a complex of natural rights to human perfection, to which rights there correspond, on the part of others, determinate duties. The Church of today vigorously proclaims these rights and duties. It gives full value to, and encourages, secular progress, because it enables humanity to respect the rights of man ever more effectively.

The commandment of love involves, not only the eternal salvation of men, but also their temporal advancement. Therefore, the Christian is a builder of the earthly city. Although his vocation relates primarily to eternal liberation—to evangelization—it also extends, in a subordinate way, to terrestrial liberation or humanization. The meaning of this vocation has been maturing in Christian consciousness with the passage of history. Even if the Christian has religious motives for promoting human values, for respecting man's rights and for working towards an increasingly realistic affirmation of them, it remains true that he is working in the construction of an earthly city considered also in its intrinsic value.

And so, overcoming the integralistic, monolithic emphasis, he accepts the internal dynamism of the various spheres of value—the laws of art, technology, science, politics, economics, etc., and becomes involved, through informed, qualified, organized action, in an effective intervention from within these sectors.

The fact that, as far as he is concerned, the definitive solution to human problems cannot be reached on earth, does not dispense him from searching for the partial solutions accessible to him. The fact that, for him, historical progress is on the way to eternal horizons, does not prevent him from believing in earthly progress and in a new humanity, or from becoming involved in a great historical project. This attitude enables the Christian to collaborate sincerely with men of other ideologies in the actualization of secular values; it enables the Church to extend the area of its interests and influence far beyond the Catholic world and far beyond the formally 'religious' sphere.

For this complex of reasons, we are witnessing an attitude to the world, which, viewed as a whole, has altered its emphasis from distrust to trust, from polemics to dialogue. Divorce between the Church and the world, between the religious and civil spheres, gives way to composition. Religious alienation on this earth is conquered in the name of religion.

It is not merely a question of telling the Christian that he has a terrestrial mission. His involvement must spring from original motives; it must be undertaken in the name of religion. The Christian presented with a purely eschatological version of his faith will rarely be prepared to do this, but will be inclined to judge the whole project abstract and utopian, even if only implicitly. Drawn by the immediate needs of daily life, he will 'let himself go' in the secular order and will thus create a profound dualism of the temporal and spiritual aspects of his life. He will live in the world as though he had not encountered God; he will encounter God as though he were not obliged to live in the world. By a para-doxical dialectic, an eschatological Christianity generates a purely terrestrial involvement in the secular world.

Apart from the impression of sterility (is it merely an impression?) which undoubtedly marks this kind of religiosity and love as disembodied, there is a risk of producing Christians who reveal an inferior idealism to that of the Marxist, in secular matters.

If it is natural for Marxists, not having a transcendent

horizon, to express all their idealism in the secular world, a religiosity, on the other hand, which, without distracting from the construction of the earthly city, did not project onto it the strong light of idealism, would produce alienation. Christianity can alienate either because it is too idealistic or because it is not idealistic enough. Thus the space left vacant by the Christian is not so much the field of worldly involvement pure and simple, as the field of worldly involvement impregnated with idealism.

The incorporation of secular values into the total viewpoint involves blending the originality and autonomy of these values with the need to form them into a hierarchy. Conflicts between the various spheres of value, unavoidable as they are in the complexity of human experience, will have to be resolved in this light, and the sacrifices which the total development of personality or civilization can demand from this or that area must be confronted.

It is extremely revealing that the contemporary Church, though it approaches secular values with a new sensitivity, feels, nevertheless, the necessity of reaffirming the necessity and urgency of asceticism, of detachment, of renunciation. While its attitude towards human nature, its conquests and its sensibilities, is substantially optimistic, nevertheless, the Church realistically draws attention to the state of alienation in which man finds himself, and the original sin that provoked it. While it acknowledges the value of secular civil life, it declares the latter's insufficiency in relation to the solution of human problems and points out the risk that the said life brings with it, that of narcotizing man, of alienating him by rendering him insensible to ideal values. The trusting optimism with which the Christian immerses himself in the secular movement is tempered by a summons to vigilance, by a sense of risk—the risk that human progress may turn against man.

Again, although he sincerely believes in progress, the Christian does not look forward to an era of complete interior and communal equilibrium, of unclouded joy and unreserved generosity. The myth of a 'terrestrial paradise', which would feed marching humanity with hopes that no datum of experience confirms, is being gradually played down by the more perceptive Marxists. They are abandoning primitive historical triumphalism. The Christian, on the contrary, knows that the roots of his alienation are not simply external to man, but also internal. He knows that his imbalance is born with him and is destined to disappear only at the close of his earthly adventure. Will not this striving towards a non-attainable ideal be a form of alienation? But perhaps the Christian is announcing a more profound truth—a truth to be grasped beyond the myth—namely, that 'attainable' ideals are not sufficient for man: his expectations transcend them all.

The new Christian ideal of life and of civilization sets going a process of 'dis-alienation' of religion. It reveals the possibility of a theoretical and operative equilibrium which would allow respect for the originality of values within the framework of an organic vision and experience of the world. Such a prospect is not just a theoretical solution. It is a historical task and duty.

Christianity and Economic Humanism

Through its involvement in the promotion of values, Christianity is becoming increasingly aware of the fundamental status of economic values and their decisive influence on the individual and on humanity. But it does not thereby exclude the possibility of distinguishing historical laws from economic laws, and particularly, from the dynamism of the class-struggle. Although human liberty cannot be reduced to economic liberty, the latter certainly plays a highly important part in man's development.

On the other hand, Christianity concurs with Marxism in denouncing the state of alienation in which the majority of men still suffer, and criticizes the liberal capitalist system insofar as it is responsible for this state of affairs. Christianity also recognizes that other alienations derive from this: in fact, economically alienated man lacks the conditions or infrastructures necessary for a harmonious development of his personality.

Thus the Christian is called to fight economic alienation, to become involved in liberating the proletariat through work and social action. His love for man would be illusory if it did not take the form of a protest, if it did not become an operative transforming force.

Work and social action are expressions of the initiative that impels man to build his new reality, to make himself a demiurge of the universe and of history. In dominating nature through work, especially technology, he humanizes it and furthers the unification of the universe around man.

If there have been, and still are, alliances between capitalism and the altar, this is not because religion is reactionary in nature, but because it has been unfaithful to its own central inspiration, or, at the least, because it has been insufficiently aware of its mission in the secular sphere. Once again, in such a case it is not just the secular order, but religion itself, that is alienated.

The Christian conscience is in process of maturing on this point. The Church's preoccupation with human advancement leads it to take a special interest in the less developed individuals and communities—the poor. It becomes the 'Church of the poor', not only because it is poor itself, nor simply because it is sensitive to the human and Christian dignity of the poor, but because it is concerned to enable the poor to overcome their poverty. This is not a case of the mere paternalistic exercise of charity, but a practical recognition of

every man's right to economic liberty. It is this new and more
authentic face of religion that today invites many Marxists
to revise their interpretation and evaluation of the religious
phenomenon.

There is a certain 'historical materialism' which contrasts,
not with Christian spiritualism, but with a Platonic version of
it. This is a materialism that affirms the economic conditioning
of all human activity and the correlation between economic
and general historical laws, but recognizes, nevertheless, the
autonomy of the other areas of human activity, the superstructures.

Our quarrel with Marxism on this point is not based on its
assertion of the historicity of man, but on the fact that it has
not asserted this historicity in all its implications and that it
has not grasped the originality and autonomy of the various
areas of human knowledge and unconscious life. As I
mentioned earlier, it is not a question of denying that conscious
life is conditioned, but of grasping its complexity, of fully
acknowledging the decisive contribution of depth psychology,
and of allowing the subjective dimension of historicity to
emerge.

To affirm the autonomy of the various spheres means to
abandon any attempt to formulate laws adequate to the
historical process; it means recognizing that history slips
through the schematism of our categories to a large extent.
It is impossible, without forcing the matter, to fit the science
of history into the pattern of the physical sciences, not to
speak of conferring on historical laws the absolute quality of
metaphysics. Marxist materialism, while it acknowledges the
autonomy of the various spheres of value in principle, runs the
risk of compromising it in practice, however, insofar as it is
not content to see economic laws as capable of illuminating
and orientating *praxis*, but tends to construe them as absolute,
adequate explanations of human dynamism.

Nevertheless, contemporary Marxists are becoming more cautious on this point, too, which is as much as to say, more realistic. The threat of thermonuclear war—of cosmic suicide —puts a question-mark over the inevitability of progress and dramatically reveals its contingent aspect.

But some details of historical materialism seem to merit an especially attentive examination. According to Marxist materialism, the integral liberty of man, while not being reducible to economic liberty, is based on it. Economic alienation is at the root of all alienation. Spontaneously good and balanced, man has been deranged by economic disorder. So while it has recognized the autonomy of the various spheres of human activity in principle, Marxism notably limits their importance in practice by contesting the autonomous quality of the problems, conflicts and alienations encountered within these areas.

Does a historical and psychological analysis confirm this diagnosis? It seems doubtful. If man were indeed spontaneously generous in the beginning, why is it that his economic relationships were defined from the outset in terms of rivalry and conflict? Why did he establish economic systems that canonize the exploitation of man by his fellow man? The economic explanation of human relations, then, is not the ultimate one. It requires to be explained in turn. It would be difficult to explain, for instance, the markedly egocentric tendency of the child, in socio-economic terms. It is a characteristic that appears to be written into the human reality prior to its insertion into the economic context.

Although history is animated by a dialectic of interests, the economic aspect constitutes but a single stage, albeit a most important one, in a wider conflict—a conflict which hides its roots in man's egoism and limitations and brings individuals, groups, classes, nations, etc., into opposition for the most diverse reasons. How, for instance, can the conflict between Russia and China, or the present struggle for power in socialist states, be interpreted in terms of class-warfare? Moreover, it is difficult, within the economic sphere itself, to reduce conflicting interests to elements in the war of classes, particularly if the entire proletariat is treated as one class. Conflicts between workers and peasants, competition within an industry—these spring to mind as examples.

These reflections prescind from the Christian interpretation, which traces all imbalance in man and society back to a single source, namely, original sin. The said reflections are sufficient however, in my opinion, to give the lie to any interpretation of human psychology conceived in purely socio-economic terms. And if the interior imbalance referred to is antecedent to socio-economic structures, then it seems destined to outlive all exterior reforms and to constitute a problem which every man is called to confront in his own historical context. It is a personal matter.

The socio-economic interpretation seems to be inadequate, not only in the face of man's moral attitudes, but also in relation to his happiness. It is difficult to admit that man's unhappiness is rooted exclusively in his economic oppression, and that economic liberation will enable him to overcome it. Egoism, rivalry and the ethical imbalance already mentioned, are certainly responsible for much suffering and will outlast all economic systems. Furthermore, how can economic security be thought capable of suppressing physical pain and handicap, as well as psychic anomalies, limitations and inferiority complexes? How could it placate the tumultuous swarm of aspirations and anxieties that populate the secret life of man? The experience of economically more advanced and more socialized countries definitely discredits these forecasts.

And so, although a correlation can be established between socio-economic progress and the total development of mankind, there is no reason to affirm that the former is necessarily accompanied by the latter. Important as it may be that the new structures should come, this will not suffice in order to generate new men. Socio-economic progress creates conditions in which a greater human and Christian maturity becomes possible, but it also multiplies the pressures and risks. Man can be liberated by technology, but he can also be dominated by it. It can enable him to become open to the whole range of personal values, but it can also enclose him in a cold 'objectivity'. Economic alienation does not consist merely in separating man from the product of his work—the exploitation of man by man—but also, on a deeper level, in the reduction of man to an object, and of human relations to 'objective' relations. Even without being dominated by others, technological man can be alienated by being dominated by the objective laws of nature and technology, by being unable to escape from the meshes of this dialectic with a free project of his own.

Today, man must see beyond any ingenuous messianism and become aware of the ambiguous character of the civilization which he is building. It holds great promise and a terrible threat. The promise will be fulfilled and the threat removed only if personal values and subjectivity are given a new lease of life.

Consequently, we can understand why socio-economic *praxis* is an excessively partial criterion for judging the validity of a system.

Another important instance of the Marxist tendency to interpret the whole of reality in terms of economics is its explanation of the religious phenomenon. I have already had occasion to point out how profoundly human are the situations that give rise to religious anxiety, and I have said that, for this reason, no matter what judgment one might wish to make about the religious world-view, it seems difficult not to acknowledge that it responds to a problem that is irreducible to other spheres of knowledge.

Furthermore, insofar as contemporary Marxism recognizes a revolutionary message in religion, it implicitly abandons the attempt to explain the genesis of religion in terms of class-warfare. Would it not be logical for Marxism to pursue the matter to the point of affirming the autonomy of the religious dimension and formulating with greater caution its prognostications about the disappearance of religion?

The Christian may actively pursue economic liberty, but he does not see it as the essential constituent of the liberty to which he is called. This attitude may look like renunciation, but it derives precisely from a desire not to renounce a global experience of values. It enables that great majority of men who have not achieved economic liberty, and will not achieve it in the near future, to escape having to look upon themselves as failures in life. The humanist ideal will be truly universal and 'democratic' when it is concretely accessible to all, even the poorest and least fortunate, the sick and the dying.

Christianity and Communal Humanism

It is true that one often comes across a form of Christianity that is lived, perhaps even theorized, in individualistic terms. But it would be difficult to think of a more radical deformation of Christianity than this. In essence, Christianity is a vocation to love, a vocation to community. It should be embodied as such in the secular and religious spheres, in the temporal phase and in eternity.

Christianity, like Marxism, maintains that man considered in isolation from society is an abstraction and does not exist. Man cannot reach complete fulfilment or liberate himself except in a free and fraternal community. Christianity, like Marxism, considers it a fundamental duty of man to work on this earth towards the creation of such a community.

Nevertheless, according to Christianity, the secular community on this earth does not exhaust man's communal vocation, which aspires to eternal existence. This prospect does not dispense man from temporal involvement. On the contrary, it provides him with new motives for it.

Thus the Christian is called to put his love for his brothers into practice here and now, and, in union with them, especially with the poorest and most oppressed, to become an historical force capable of effective action in the world. It is not simply a question of love of the individual but of commitment to the construction of humanity on the community level. Spiritual, eschatological love would be illusory if it did not issue in concrete action and concrete secular liberation. Though neither being, nor wishing to be, a movement of secular liberation, the Church requests its lay members to become involved in such movements and to create them if necessary.

The individualistic attitude and the systems which it generates are states of alienation for the Christian, too. Indeed, they are such in a much stronger sense for him than for the Marxist, since they are opposed, not only to man's temporal vocation, but also to his eternal vocation.

Thus, at its various levels, the secular movement of liberation is the organization of love with a view to effective action. One can even speak of a 'partitic' aspect in the action of the Christian. But political values are realized within the framework of the complete picture. For this reason, the partitic criterion must be governed, in turn, by absolute ethical requirements, principally respect for the person.

Naturally, though remaining faithful to absolute requirements, political directives must be embodied in changing historical situations. In the formulation of situational judgements, the subjective element will inevitably appear. But what subjectivity has the right to direct community life in the secular sphere? The question of forms of government arises here. On this point both Christianity and Marxism, being absolute and total world-views, are very much attracted to strong dictatorial systems, in which a minority or an individual exercises authority over the majority by virtue of the right pertaining to him of representing the objective order, the common good. The rights of the institution prevail over the rights of the individual. For a long time, Christians showed sympathy, perhaps even preference, for these absolute monarchs, who guaranteed the prestige of religion with the protection of the law. In popular republics, on the other hand, the system has been maintained up to now by the overbearing power of a personality (Stalinism) or a party oligarchy.

But in both the Christian and Marxist worlds, people are becoming conscious of subjective rights. In a society that has reached adulthood, this consciousness is accompanied by the need for frank acceptance of the democratic system, with all its component parts and all its risks—in particular, the acceptance of pluralism of ideologies and parties, of majority rule, of respect for the opposition, etc. Undoubtedly, as the Marxists have shown, a formal or juridical democracy is not enough. It remains necessary, however, in order to make possible the exercise of real democracy. While there could be formal democracy without real democracy, there could be no real democracy without formal democracy.

If the evolution of the Marxist world on this point is still hesitant and localized, that of the Catholic world is clearer and more decisive. It implies recognition of the rights of the person even where this could injure the position of the ecclesial institution.

Religious liberty is a theme on which the opposition between the two viewpoints emerges very clearly. An integralistic conception of the defence of God's rights and those of the Church had led to the neglect, even the denial, of this liberty, in the past. Today, in proclaiming it, the Church not only wishes to vindicate the right of Catholics to profess themselves as such, but recognizes the right of every man to act according to his conscience, even where this directs him to oppose Catholic doctrine. The vigorous resistance encountered by this thesis in the Council is easily explained when we think of the profound evolution—we are tempted to say revolution—which it manifests.

In relation to Marxism, then, a Christian can no longer question its right to free organization and diffusion on account of its atheism, but only because Marxism itself fails to guarantee respect for liberty either doctrinally or in practice. The same principle applies, naturally, to any movement that makes an attack on civil liberty, even if it does so in the name of religion.

From these principles it follows that a party can boast its right to determine what direction the state will take only insofar as it can count on popular backing freely expressed. No party may unilaterally declare itself the conscience of the proletariat unless it is freely acknowledged as such by the proletariat. It is not enough to be certain of the objective validity of one's own political programme in order to obtain the right to put it into effect: it is necessary to pass by way of subjective consent, expressed from conviction. The principle of respect for the person and for subjectivity naturally opens out into pluralism. On the political plane, communal humanism demands that the entire community should be the effective subject of power and should be able to determine its own destiny.

As we have seen, there is ferment at the very heart of Marxism on this point, and this ferment is inspired, basically, by a personalism and a desire for fidelity to the masses that are certainly present in the system. But if this evolution is to be consistent it must rediscover the very concepts of *praxis* and historical efficacy. If this efficacy is understood in purely 'objective' or 'institutional' terms, then that method will be considered efficacious, and therefore valid, which succeeds in establishing a determinate socio-economic order. All this coincides with the success of the Communist party. All the values that will be made relative to the party are defined in relation to it. But if the 'objective' pole of the socio-economic order is integrated with the subjective pole, that method will be considered efficacious which actuates its plan without offending against respect for the person and his legitimate autonomy; which, in other words, by placing socio-economic *praxis* within a wider context, ceases to treat it as the sole criterion of value.

Moreover, even according to the spirit of Marxism, economic progress is pursued, not for its own sake, but as a component of human maturation. The method that would achieve economic progress at the cost of higher personal values would, therefore, be inefficacious. If historical proof is the final test of the validity of Marxism, it is licit to ask in what measure has this proof been given. I would answer in the measure in which the Marxist system is the object of free adhesion. The Marxists will demonstrate that they really believe in their historical success when they accept the risk of liberty.

Such a method presupposes the capacity to repudiate any 'efficacy' deriving from power-structures maintainable only if liberty is suppressed. It also presupposes the capacity to accept a minority status indefinitely, while recognizing that one has a universal vocation. It seems to me that Marxism has not given this proof as yet. We can ask whether it could possibly be given until such time as a profound revision of the concept of *praxis* is carried out in the way already indicated, thus enabling Marxism to affirm the absolute character of the fundamental rights of the person and of the moral imperatives deriving from them.

This point also seems to be of decisive importance in evaluating the fidelity of Marxism to its original personalistic inspiration. A society that does not guarantee the exercise of fundamental personal rights—that makes men relative to institutions—certainly does not enable every person to fulfil himself as an end.

It is also important to determine the relationship between person and institution if we are to evaluate the humanist character aspired to by the Marxist ethic, particularly in its message of solidarity. If the person were actually made relative to the party, then love would cease to have the person as its ultimate object. In other words, man would cease to be capable of friendship. Genuine love participates in the absoluteness of the person and would be destroyed if constantly exposed to interference from the party. Even familial love could be distorted by this threat.

If the party as an institution becomes an absolute substitute for the person, then the universality of love is also compromised. By treating the party rather than the person as such as the criterion of value, one is led, logically, to the position of loving whoever serves the party's cause and hating whoever opposes it. But the universal vocation of Marxism imposes on it a universal criterion of value.

Moreover, human coexistence, whether of persons or of institutions, can be fraternal only if it is based on mutual trust. Everyone must be able to count on the loyalty of everyone else. This trust is a particularly essential component in the context of dialogue.

But on what can such trust be based except on a common willingness to respect certain values as absolute? How can one dispel the fear of being deceived or made an instrument by a companion whose ultimate criterion of value is the success of his own institution?

In no way am I questioning the personal loyalty of Marxists. It is a question of trying to find out whether this loyalty is sufficiently justified by the system. It is my view that a fraternal coexistence which aims to ascertain its theoretical rationale must acknowledge the existence of absolute values.

The system we are examining is humanistic in central motivation, but comes to be embodied in an anti-humanistic regime. This is not the result of pure chance. It cannot be attributed to human weakness or adverse circumstances. The fact that, up to the present, this situation has come about wherever Communism has come to power, is explained by the fact that the principle of *praxis* is the sole criterion of value.

The gravest threat to Marxist personalism is not the community spirit, therefore, but the party spirit; not that the individual is sacrificed to the community but that the majority is sacrificed to a minority. The dictatorship of the proletariat is exposed to the danger of becoming the dictatorship of the party over the proletariat, and, by the same token, of some personalities or power-groups over the party. It is a case of tension between the community itself and the institution which ought to be its expression but in reality kills it, and not of tension between the person and the community. The risk for Marxism is not that of being too communal, but that of not being communal enough. The life of the true community is based on free personalities and strengthens them.

In accepting pluralism, the Marxist also finds himself faced with other difficulties. In view of the close link which he sets up between *praxis* and ideology, he must, in order to be consistent, affirm that, since *his* ideology is the only one that is fruitful in practice, the state should adopt it and keep the others in a state of inferiority. There is a tendency in Marxism towards confessionalism on the part of the state (as distinct from that of the party). This is typical of the integralistic mentality.

In the Christian environment, attracted for a long time by the idea of a confessional state, the lay formula is now widely recognized as legitimate and is often preferred. Thus is it implicitly admitted that fidelity to civic duties and respect for authority can in fact be inspired in different citizens by quite diverse, and not necessarily religious, world-views.

Some Western Marxists are trying to overcome the integralistic mentality and to see the possibility of effective 'lay' status for the state. They are now proposing the hypothesis of a plurality of ideologies, religious ideology among them, all capable of nourishing *praxis*. We have already noted how this development implies the re-thinking both of *praxis* as the criterion of value, and of the alienating character of religion.

If the community is the end and the subject of power in general, then the following must be said about wealth in particular: agreeing with Marxism, Christianity proclaims (against liberalism) the social function of wealth, and denounces the insufficiency of an increase in production that is not matched by a more equal distribution. It acknowledges, moreover, that, today more than ever, this can be achieved only by definite state intervention, giving direction to the spontaneous dialectic of egoism and community. This intervention can—indeed must—impose on the use of private property whatever restrictions are demanded by the common good, including, where necessary, nationalization of the means of production. According to Marxism, this is the only formula that will enable wealth to perform its social function. But perhaps the awareness (so strong in Marxism) of the historicity of the relationship between man and the product of his work ought to lead to a modification of the universality of this claim, and to a greater conditioning of it by the changing circumstances of time and place. Thus the distance between the Christian thesis that man has a right to private property with the limitations imposed by the social function of wealth, and the Marxist thesis that the means of production are essentially the property of the community, tends, if not to disappear, at least to diminish. Both concepts, in fact, are inspired by the same concern to enable man to enjoy his own liberty without alienating that of others. The divergences here have regard more to the basic criteria on which the doctrine of property is worked out than to the doctrine itself.

The problem of the relationship between the community, on the one hand, and the state or party institution, on the other, comes very sharply into focus in connection with the family. Even from a Christian point of view, it would be an impoverishment of the person to make a fully autonomous system out of familial values and to restrict his horizon to them, thus creating a *bourgeois* and egoistic type of relationship. The family takes its place in the wider context of national, ecclesial and human communities, and should view its own values in this light.

But it will be possible for the family to execute this wider mission only if it embodies those values which are proper to it, only if it enables conjugal love to be expressed according to its own laws and with respect for personal values. Genuine family love would be alienated, therefore, if it were made instrumental to state or party. The Marxist tendency to question the autonomy of familial values is connected with a monolithic concept of axiology. Once again, this must be replaced by a concept of the unity of the person that will allow full play to every sphere of values according to its needs.

The common good may also demand state intervention to control the education of the young. But how far can this intervention be pushed? Can the state consider itself the supreme authority in the educational sector? This question is correlative, naturally, to the question of pluralism. When a single institution authoritatively claims the right to determine the objective good, then it alone can educate men to conform to that good. Once again, recognition of the autonomy of the person guarantees the autonomy and originality of a particular sphere of values.

From the Christian point of view there is a dimension of man's vocation that commits him to act in a communal manner in order to form a more just and fraternal earthly community, where every man can fulfil himself as an end. But this is only a part of the Christian response to the problem of solidarity. However important it may be, it is still deeply inadequate. In fact, if the interpersonal relationship is favoured by a just and liberating political system, it will largely transcend the level of solidarity and will penetrate the secret of the individual.

I have pointed out the danger of a technological alienation of man. Among its more alarming features is the decline of love which would take place if love were reduced to 'objective' solidarity, in the sense of action aimed at determinate 'objectives'. The relationship of love is not just between 'producers', 'citizens' or 'militants' but between persons, with all the inimitable drama of their subjectivity.

When communion between men is grasped at this profound and authentic level, its limitations in our present condition are immediately grasped. First, there are qualitative limitations. However deep the friendship between us may be, it must halt before the impenetrable fortress of the subjectivity of consciousness. However intimate our social ties may be, we are quite alone when it comes to the fundamental choices that decide our destiny. In the last analysis, man is always alone. Furthermore, the antinomy between personal advancement and generosity to others, which forces man to choose between two orders of values, neither of which may be ignored, seems to admit of no solution in the secular sphere. There is the further limitation of time: the tendency of love to prolong its encounter endlessly is irrevocably smashed against the wall of death at the moment of supreme solitude.

Finally there is the limitation of extension: although universal in aspiration, human love normally reaches only a restricted circle of people. It is impossible for man to give himself totally to all, to achieve the unity to which he aspires.

Many fundamental expectations of love consequently remain unsatisfied and alienated. Thus it is love itself that calls for an area of essentially different relationships, so that it can reach fulfilment and overcome its alienations. This will be an area in which a more profound intimacy can be established —endless in duration and universal in range.

Christianity discloses unsuspected horizons for these expectations, revealing to man the ultimate meaning of his communal vocation. God has decided to communicate his life to men, taken, not one by one or in isolation, but communally, as a people.

Divine life is communal in nature, therefore; it consists of insertion into a community. Life, for the Christian, is life with someone. Besides being a juridical and hierarchical community—and at a deeper level—the Church is a community of life and love. It tends to gather in the whole of mankind, and its formation constitutes the centre and the end of history.

It is a question of a new area of relationships between men, an area immensely more intimate, more lasting and more universal. These are relationships so close as to make one reality, one single organism, of the persons who love each other, and this, not just in a moral or psychological sense, but ontologically. These are relationships destined never to be destroyed, but to be intensified and to explode into joyous eternal communion. These are relationships which do not compass merely a small part of mankind, but are destined to create bonds between all men, between past and present, present and future: the whole of history seems to be penetrated by this vast movement of unification. The people of God are simultaneously the people of history.

In their terrestrial phase, nevertheless, these relationships, however intimate and real, do not fully emerge into the light of day, and, consequently, do not yet achieve that fusion of spirits which is the dream of love. This will be the task of 'eternal life', which is not an encounter of the solitary soul with God, but an immense community of consciousness, the fulfilment of full and eternal communion with one's brothers; it is the joy of a family, in which each will partake of the joy of all, and all of the joy of each. This is the promised land towards which we are travelling; this is the new humanity that we are painfully constructing, the ideal of history.

Man's end is specified by this dimension. The reply of the Roman Catechism, according to which man's end is to 'know, love and serve God in this life in order to enjoy him in the next life in Paradise' remains valid, certainly. It is still true that man must glorify God and pursue his own happiness. But we feel today that these descriptions lack something, namely, the communal dimension. Doubtless it is implicit. But we find it necessary to make it explicit. Man is on this earth to build a human community of temporal and eternal love. Other men, separately and in community, are not just occasions for loving God and saving oneself, but are likewise ends themselves.

Love also has its place in man's end; rather, raised to divine life, men can love with that depth and fruitfulness with which only God can love. They will be able to reach among themselves that intimacy and joy which can be achieved only in the communion between the divine persons.

This theme is not simply a sector of Christian truth. It is

a dimension that traverses the whole, a central focus that gives new meaning to the entire message and provides an ultimate answer to the problems raised for contemporary thought by the movement towards socialization. As we shall see, the unification of humanity then becomes part of the wider movement towards the unification of the world.

The touchstone of any ideal could be its capacity to respond to love's expectations, and the ideal in which love is stronger than death will have responded in full. No matter how great and noble it may be, an ideal that yields to death will always be a frustrated one.

For this reason, Christianity believes that the new community must be based on the vitality of a man who has died and risen from death—a man who is God. The community must pass through resurrection.

The future community will be the expression of this victory of Christ, and in him of the whole of humanity, over death. It will be the joyous, definitive proof that love is stronger than death.

Christianity and Revolutionary Humanism

The effective exercise of love to which the Christian aspires strikes out against an alienating situation and against human egoism with its interest in defending constitutional disorder. Effective action takes place through a struggle, in which those whose concern is to defend certain values associate and confront those who fight for contrary values. This confrontation will be primarily on economic matters, where the conflict of interests determines the class-struggle. It is difficult to deny that these tensions have the role of motive forces in history, and that history proceeds according to a dialectical rhythm.

It is often asserted that the method of class warfare is incompatible with the Christian commandment of love, which is directed towards collaboration. Thus if incisive social action demands war, the Christian message would seem to be inefficacious and reducible to a romantic appeal for mutual comprehension.

The Christian principle of love is undoubtedly universal, and therefore extends even to political or economic enemies. Class hatred is incompatible with Christianity. But the universality of love does not interfere with the effective defence of one's rights and one's class through political, party, or syndical combat, etc. This defence is legitimate as long as it aims, not to destroy the adversary or to contravene his rights, but solely to uphold one's own rights against his unjust demands.

As we have noted, class warfare does not mean class hatred. If the universality of love admits even violent warfare, in certain circumstances, in the defence of injured rights, why should it exclude non-violent combat? Who would deny, for instance, the legitimacy—even the necessity—of the negro struggle for equal rights with the white man? On the other hand, if we cease to generalize, and attempt to specify the meaning of collaboration between classes, it will easily be seen that this takes on a dialectical character, in that each of the 'collaborators' will render his contribution from his own angle, which is necessarily conditioned by his situation and interests.

The struggle takes place within existing structures, but where these structures legalize injustice and defend privilege, it can (and must) tend to reform them. It must pass from evolution to revolution. It will tend to be a peaceful revolution, so that it will be consonant with the respect due to the human person, and also because the efficacy of violence is generally more superficial and precarious, appearances to the contrary notwithstanding. Violence can be upheld, if at all, only as the last resort of legitimate defence.

It would be inexact, therefore, to contrast Marxism and Christianity, without further ado, as the method of revolution and the method of evolution, as though Christianity were constitutionally committed to the defence of established order or formal legality. When this type of presentation is not duly clarified, it helps to spread the image of a reactionary Christianity.

Should we take it, then, that the Marxist and Christian views on revolution coincide? Such a conclusion would be all the more serious insofar as it is in revolution that the fundamental concept of *praxis* takes concrete form.

Now it is still at this decisive level that the divergence occurs. The Marxist conception of revolution as an absolute value and a criterion of value does not really appear to be reconcilable with the *Marxist* principle of the absolute value of the person, nor with the connected principle of the universality of love. For this reason, from a Communist point of view, class-warfare tends to be associated with class-hatred.

For the Christian, on the other hand, the class struggle—the proletarian revolution—must be seen in an integral personal context. It must be accomplished with respect for the ethical imperatives that flow from that context. Revolutionary *praxis* may, perhaps, be taken as a criterion of value, but it is subordinate to these imperatives—subordinate, in a word, to the imperatives that derive from the absolute value of the person and, consequently, of humanism.

The originality of Christianity with respect to Marxist humanism does not consist solely in its placing the socio-economic revolution within an integral system of values, however, but in its declaring the inadequacy of any structural reform for the realization of the new humanity. Christianity seeks the source of the objective social dialectic that moves history in a personal, subjective, interior dialectic. Man is in conflict with other men because he is in conflict with himself; mankind is divided because man is divided. The dramatic conflict between the spirit and the flesh, or between egoism and generosity, is congenital to man. He is spontaneously carried, as we have seen, in the direction of egoism.

This interior tension places a fundamental choice before every man—a choice which defines his value, his impact on history and his eternal destiny. This choice, however much it may be conditioned by the infrastructures, is, in the last analysis, an incommunicable act of the individual. He is all the more a man to the extent that he takes an active and free hand in his self-determination; he is all the more alienated to the extent that his choice is determined by exterior conditions. The socio-economic revolution must create conditions in which the individual's choice will have maximum liberty, but it cannot be substituted for that choice without giving rise to new forms of alienation. Thus a genuinely human choice—that interior revolution by virtue of which generosity prevails over egoism—will become possible. Christian 'conversion' is not merely a question of man turning to God, but also of man turning to his fellow man and overcoming egoism. It is a revolution accomplished under the banner of love.

The Church, which is the saving community, is, therefore, an organism fighting the forces of evil in this world. But the forces of evil must not be identified with any historical institution, nor the struggle between good and evil with any political, economic or military conflict—or with any 'holy war' (the integralistic mind tends to make this identification). The struggle in question is considerably more profound, and the demarcation line between good and evil passes through the interior life of every man rather than between institutions.

It would be inaccurate, on the other hand, having once distinguished between the social and interior revolutions, to set them in opposition as though there were a gap between them or as though the former dispensed with, or was alienated from, the latter. The man who has sincerely decided to love will tend to put his decision into practice. Thus the interior revolution could become a new ferment of social revolution.

Christianity and Scientific Humanism

Religion, for many Christians, is much more a complex of rites, a system of moral prescriptions, the satisfaction of a psychological need for security or the fact of belonging to a definite social group, than a view of the world and of life. They belong to it just as they belong to any other element in their cultural *milieu*. They simply accept it as part of the environment, never making it the object of a personal critique and choice.

Such a concept of religion, if it is confronted with a doctrine presented as being objective and critical, can easily appear to be in an inferior position. This may be so either because it is less suited to respond to the demands of reason, or because it is objectively sterile and inefficacious.

Christianity certainly cannot be reduced to doctrine. It permeates the whole of human existence. For this very reason, if its influence is to be exercised in a human and efficacious way, it must be, first and foremost, a profoundly unifying vision of the world, a vision capable of satisfying all the requirements of a rigorous critique.

The organicity of the Christian world-view is of interest here, not so much from the point of view of scientific methodology, as in relation to the kind of personality it will generate, compared to that of the Marxist. It is not a purely logical, but an axiological organicity. It has already entered our discussion of terrestrial humanism.

In this matter we shall come across one of the most profound convergences between Marxism and Christianity, and also the root of the most important divergences. Both Marxism and Christianity tend to reconstruct the unity of the human personality from a baseline of alienation or interior fracture, and both see a correlation between unity of the person, the unity of mankind and the unity of the universe. Now this common impulse towards unity, especially if understood monolithically, renders some apparent convergences rather doubtful: many of the difficulties that have emerged at various levels of our discussion point back to the concepts of the organicity of the system and of its dialectical structure. Ultimately we are led back to the idea of the organicity of personality. On the other hand, we have watched the emergence of a manner of articulating the system that is organic without being monolithic, and of a personality that is integrated without being integralistic.

But such a system could aspire to shape the adult personality only if it were rigorously critical. The Christian must believe the truth of what he cannot see, but he can, and must, also know why he believes. If it is true that faith is an act of the whole person, and not simply of reason, it is also true that it is an intellectual act. Consequently it must respect the natural dynamism of thought. Man cannot be asked for an assent that he is incapable of giving—that would be an alienation.

The critical spirit with which the Christian is asked to justify his world-view implies trust in human reason, both philosophical and scientific. While he acknowledges the extreme complexity of the problems which he is asked to solve, the Christian believes in man and in the power of his thought. Reason engaged perpetually in problems would be sterile; it could not recognize the value either of God or of man; it could never give direction to an existence.

We can ask whether, in the last analysis, Christian belief in the value of thought is not more firm than that of the Marxist. It finds limitations in the Marxist system that could seriously compromise it. Unless it is further specified, the pragmatic criterion of truth can lead to truth being made an entirely historical concept, and can thus deprive the Marxist of that operative force which derives from an absolutely certain world-view. If truth is defined in relation to the party, there is a risk that divine voluntarism will be replaced by a no less alienating human voluntarism. It is the very requirements of *praxis*, therefore, as we have seen in the course of the exposition, that should stimulate Marxism to pass beyond *praxis* as the sole criterion of value and re-evaluate the criterion of objective evidence. And the requirements of action should stimulate it to a discovery of contemplation and the autonomous value of truth. Strange as it may seem, however, this re-evaluation of objective evidence must take account of the danger involved in the exclusive cult of 'objectivity'—the danger that Marxism will be exposed to the temptation of relativism. It is through a re-evaluation of subjectivity, of the individual's capacity to make absolute judgements, that the basis for a realistic view can be found.

The autonomy of human thought does not exclude all forms of dependence, but only those that alienate by preventing either reason in general, or specific acts of knowledge, from proceeding according to their own laws. Marxism does not consider the subordination of thought to party directives alienating; Christianity does not consider the subordination of human to divine thought alienating. In reality there is no alienation involved in submission to a mind whose infallibility has been critically ascertained. On the contrary, the rejection of this new horizon of truth would be an impoverishment. The Christian adheres to revelation from the moment that he ascertains its origin in an infallible mind, not before.

On the other hand, insofar as the party line reflects thought that is susceptible to error, it cannot be imposed without violating a fundamental personal right, the right of critical thought. It is striking to note how a system that arose in the name of liberty has found it possible to suppress liberty so openly. The sterility of socialist countries in the field of

philosophy is a consequence of this, and is responsible for the
fact that any deepening of Marxist doctrine itself is achieved
today, with rare exceptions, by Western Communists alone.
Truth lives on liberty. In order to make itself felt as a genuine
philosophical message, Marxism has need of that very social
liberty, that very dialectic of ideas, that is threatened by its own
methods. The withholding of liberty seems to imply lack of
faith in the possibility of gaining confirmation of the official
theses through free research. Liberty can be granted only by
the system that believes in the power of its own truth.

The pragmatic criterion of truth is also placed in doubt
on account of the serious split in world Communism that has
been provoked by the conflict between Russia and China.
Which of these is the proletarian community whose *praxis*
is to be the criterion of truth and value? Which is the genuine
Marxism? Which is the community of workers in whose
consciousness the real meaning of history is to emerge?
Which Communist party can regard itself as the conscience of
the proletariat? After the schism, which authority has the
right to pronounce excommunication? Whatever may be
the answer to these questions, it will be difficult to base it on a
criterion of *praxis* which is itself being questioned. Once again
we are referred back, from within Marxism, to the need for
a more developed criterion of truth.

Faith in thought can also be compromised at the heart of
Marxism by laying too much stress on the dependence of
philosophy on the conclusions of science. If, at first sight,
this dependence seems to project the prestige of science
onto philosophy, it ends up by drawing philosophy into the
relativity of science.

However, the Christian shares the Marxist's admiration for
the success of science in penetrating the world. He also shares
a desire to work out a world-view that fully respects the
conclusions reached by science. These conclusions have

certainly raised problems in the past, and will continue to do so, when faced with the conclusions reached by religion. Furthermore, theologians and philosophers alike have been tempted (perhaps the temptation has not been entirely overcome) to pronounce on strictly scientific questions. Similarly, scientists may be tempted to pronounce on strictly philosophical or religious questions. 'Scientific' proofs of the existence or otherwise of God spring to mind as examples. But these border violations in one direction or the other, whether they are committed by believers or by atheists, are the result of immaturity in men and in the times, and seem destined to disappear of their own accord with the maturation of epistemological and axiological awareness.

They reflect an integralistic, monolithic mentality, a mentality in which the desire to unify all values is not tempered by respect for their autonomy. Thus science becomes instrumental to the demands of class warfare, to a concern with apologetics or to an ecclesiastical or partitic voluntarism.

The epistemological and axiological maturation which we have mentioned implies, on the contrary, the recognition of a plurality of methodologies that will enable every science to proceed autonomously according to its needs. Christianity is fully disposed to accept this maturation. In this case, as in others, integralism does not form part of its structures but merely constitutes an historical form that is in process of being discarded.

It may be asked whether the same disposition is to be found in Marxism. Again the difficulty arises from the pragmatic criterion of truth (in particular from its partitic quality), and the solution lies in the development of that criterion in a pluralistic direction. No one would wish to question the greatness of the conquests achieved by Soviet science under Communism. But science clearly transcends its competence when it purports to prove the validity of a world-view.

By aspiring to be scientific this view ceases to be critical. For this reason the more liberal Marxists are abandoning such forms of argument, recognizing their scientific inconsistency. This awareness should give rise to greater caution when attempts are made to give a 'scientific' basis to dialectical materialism and to reduce it eventually to a scientifically fruitful theory.

Soviet historiography seems to be a typical manifestation of how science becomes an instrument. De-Stalinization has placed a radical question-mark over forty years of production in this field, and de-Khruschevization has done the same for the years following. The balance is discouraging, therefore, and there is nothing to support a more optimistic outlook for the near future. When one thinks of the prime importance given to history by Marxism (history is called upon to provide documentation for its success and hence for its truth), and, on the other hand, when one considers the practical impossibility of carrying out free, and therefore objective, historical research under the Marxist system, one becomes aware of the serious tensions that afflict the system and threaten its very foundations.

The Christian appreciates the value of scientific achievements, but believes that they cannot furnish the solution to all human problems, particularly those involving the general meaning of existence and of the universe. Science raises many problems which it is constitutionally incapable of solving. When the astronaut returns to earth after his marvellous voyage, filled with new experiences, according to the Christian these do not hold the solution to his problem, however inspiring they may be, and cannot suffice to bring him happiness. He needs immensely wider horizons—horizons greater than the world and greater than man. Man is greater than the space that he explores.

Here, then, is the real alternative for man: either he encloses himself in a world where all things are clear to him but too small in relation to himself, his problems and his aspirations, or he lays himself open to a world that is greater than he but clouded in mystery. Is it right that he should reject realities solely because they are greater than he is? In the name of what kind of progress does one wish to extinguish man's ultimate and greatest expectation, his final and greatest hope?

For, in the last analysis, he who denies mystery denies hope. How bleak and stifling would be this world of clarity without hope—a world which, one day, man would have explored to its very depths and in which he would have found everything but what he was seeking.

Here again Marxism has posed in terms of a radical alternative a problem which is solved, on the contrary, in terms of dialectical complementarity. There is no question of human knowledge being forced to choose between intelligibility and mystery. There is, however, a need to recognize the compenetration of these two planes in the actuality of a total experience.

To acknowledge mystery is not to deny that reality is knowable, but rather to perceive the limits of knowability. It does not mean renouncing the spirit of criticism, but rather pushing one's critique to the point of grasping the inadequacy of those of our solutions that claim to remain within the area of clarity.

On the other hand, this euphoric faith in the power of reason seems to correspond less and less with modern sensibility, since modern man is tempted, precisely by his critical sense, to renounce every rational system rather than wait for reason to penetrate reality adequately and provide a fully satisfactory solution to his problem.

But without waiting for science to give us answers which it cannot give, it remains legitimate, as well as entirely suited to the sensibility of our times, to reflect on the fact of science and on its most universal conclusions in order to work out a world-view in harmony with them, a world-view that provides the conditions of their possibility.

As Marxism has realized, a philosophy that aims to guarantee the conditions of the possibility of science must affirm the authenticity of matter and its causality. An 'acosmistic' or occasionalist view of matter would deprive science of any foundation whatever. Therefore it is accurate to say that science necessitates the denial of a God understood as a surrogate of natural causality, a God who would prevent nature from being itself, science from grasping the real and technology from dominating it.

Does the assertion of the exclusiveness of matter lead without further ado to the negation of God and of the spirit? We are again faced with the difficulty of reconciling the authenticity of partial causes with that of the total cause, and it is not my intention to conceal the gravity of this problem, which is illustrated, moreover, by the many centuries of effort (as yet unconcluded) devoted to it by Christian thought. The difficulty is overcome insofar as divine presence and action are found to be situated at another level and do not compete with the being and action of nature. Science can exercise a demythologizing and purifying influence on this aspect of our knowledge of God.

Then we are faced with another difficulty, that of reconciling spirit and matter in the same natural universe—in human reality, to be precise. This tension is certainly not unknown to speculative Christian tradition or to speculative religious tradition in general. Indeed it is not easy simultaneously to affirm the material nature of man and attribute a certain autonomy to his spirit; it is not easy to escape the temptation of posing the problem in terms of ontological or axiological rivalry and being thus left with a choice between a materialistic conception of man, on the one hand, and a dualistic spiritualism in which the body is seen more as a prison than as an essential constituent, on the other.

Despite the uncertainties that characterize the wearisome search for equilibrium down through the history of thought, contemporary Christianity is increasingly more decisive in affirming the reality of matter and questioning the necessity of a choice between soul and body in order to describe man.

The body is not some sort of packaging or prison for the spirit, therefore, but an essential constituent of man. It is not an obstacle to man's spiritual life but an essential condition of it. The importance attributed to material, especially economic, infrastructures for the spiritual life itself is ultimately based on this vision.

Matter acquires a new dignity from the fact that man is open to the religious dimension. Thus man's bodily activity (which is carried on within the framework of his total vocation), as well as the world of nature itself, contribute to the construction of the eternal personality and the eternal community.

But the Christian theory of matter discloses horizons more unexpected still. By virtue of the incarnation, not only is there a man who is God, but a body that is divine and the object of adoration. This body is to be offered for the salvation of humanity. It exists both as priest and victim, therefore, in the work of redemption. In the resurrection this body becomes the expression of the final victory of Christ over evil and death, and, acquiring a glorious state, is inserted into the eternal life of God.

But it is not the physical body of Christ alone that is called to these heights: united with Christ's life, the bodies of all the redeemed will share in his destiny. Furthermore, the whole of nature, just as it has participated in the drama of salvation, is called to participate in its eternal epilogue. And so the whole of creation groans in the expectation of reaching the freedom of the glory of sons of God.

Thus is consummated the movement of liberation and unification that simultaneously traverses the interiority of every man, the history of mankind and the event we call the universe. New heavens and a new earth arise. And all things are recapitulated in Christ.

Conclusion

As we have been noting from the beginning, the problem of convergences and divergences between Marxism and Christianity cannot be broken down into a multitude of details. It bears primarily on central inspirations. At this level it would be difficult to exaggerate the profundity of the divergences separating the two systems, for they are present everywhere, and since we are dealing with basically unified systems, these divergences confer differences of meaning on every expression of life and thought. For the same reason, however, neither can the profundity of the convergences be denied. They, too, are present everywhere and ensure that differences in meaning are never total. This dual aspect of the relationship seems to explain the contrasting attitudes taken up in the Christian world towards Marxism, ranging from indiscriminate rejection to facile concordism. The divergences are concealed in formulae very Christian in appearance, while the convergences are expressed in formulae markedly anti-Christian in appearances. Hence the difficulty of drawing an objective demarcation line between convergences and divergences. They are co-present everywhere. Hence, too, the particular complexity of dialogue with Marxism.

Difficulty is not impossibility, however. If our interpretation is valid, the convergences, however delicate the task of pinpointing them may be, exist and are profound. They can form the basis of fruitful doctrinal dialogue (I do not intend to raise

here the question of dialogue in the sense of political collaboration. This raises quite different problems and in any case lies
outside my competence).

A central aspect of this dialogue might well be the question
of humanism, which separates convergences from divergences
fairly clearly. In the crisis of truth and of values that marks
our times, both Marxism and Christianity claim to be unified
and complete world-views, capable of giving meaning to a
host of details in the light of the totality, of transforming
everyday life with the sparkle of idealism, and of bringing a
message of hope to man. It is a question, not just of doctrinal
systems, but of types of personality and civilization. These
visions aim to enable man to fulfil himself as an end. They
direct his action and the movement of history and of nature
to this end. They support an ethic in which the absolute value
of man is a fundamental principle and the commandment
of love occupies a central position. In the pursuit of this
ideal, man is not just an instrument; he is the principal architect
through personal and communal action. His action is aimed
at the construction of an earthly city in which men will be
able to live together and in which man will really be an end.
In particular, this implies the humanization of the economic
relationship. This relationship conditions man's total development and is responsible for the fact that his influence on history
is exercised largely through his influence on the economic
infrastructures. The humanist ideal and its realization are
essentially social matters. Man will fulfil himself only in a
community, and his action towards this end will be effective
only when communal. The horizons of this community are
not circumscribed by any particular region or category, but
stretch to the ends of the earth. The communal character of
the human vocation is especially evident in the social function
of wealth and in the legalization of state intervention to limit
private property when it appears to conflict with its social

function. Social action to realize these objectives sets off
from a situation of alienation that can be overcome only by
doing battle with those who attempt to canonize it. This war
is waged within existing structures but tends to reform them;
in this sense it can become revolutionary. The world-view
that inspires action cannot control it effectively unless it has
been critically justified itself, and is capable of accepting the
contributions of science. Therefore, it must recognize the
fundamental reality of matter, particularly matter as constitutive of man, his causality and the laws of his being. The
whole of history is constituted by a vast movement to liberate
and unify man, the human community and the whole universe.

It is difficult to contest the fact that convergence is real
and profound on these points, not to mention others. Along
with this we should place the critique of the many alienations
defined in contrast with these values. With regard to religious
alienation in particular, the Christian is in agreement with
the Marxist precisely insofar as religion actually alienates.

If this is true, then we must admit that some of Christianity's
most characteristic intuitions recoil against it. How is this fact
to be explained? History has undoubtedly occasional versions
of Christianity in which these intuitions were lost sight of on
the practical, and even on the theoretical, plane. Thus
Christianity has been criticized in the name of Christian values
and compromised in syntheses that are not Christian. But
perhaps it is an over-simplification of the problem to say that
Christianity has merely 'lost sight of' some of its truths,
that these have been rediscovered by other systems, and all
that Christianity has to do is recover what it once possessed
by returning to the spirit of its origins.

In reality, many of these 'Christian' truths are present only
virtually in primitive Christianity and in the inspired books
themselves. In other words, we find the principles from which
these truths may be inferred, but not the truths themselves.

It would be difficult to show, for example, that the social encyclicals of recent popes are derived purely from revelation. More generally, it would be inexact to affirm that all the spiritual problems of our time are resolved in the Gospels, even if the Gospels supply the inspiration and the broad directives which make their solution possible, as well as the germs from which these solutions mature. One must acknowledge a certain incompleteness in revelation with regard to new situations and new problems. The Christian community, under the direction of the *magisterium*, has a duty, in this area too, to supply 'what is wanting' in divine intervention, or more precisely, to lay itself open to divine action, which continues to animate history. The fidelity of Christianity to its origins cannot be simply conservative but must also be creative. Christians have been guilty, not only of losing sight of ancient truths, but also of failing to discover new ones when they were needed in new situations; not only of failing to put doctrine into practice, but also of neglecting to develop doctrine itself in keeping with the rhythm of history.

It follows that in affirming the evangelical inspiration of certain truths present in other systems, e.g., in Marxism, Christianity does not intend to question the originality of what these systems contribute to the evolution of human knowledge or to claim all the historical credit for itself.

In fact it cannot be denied that this evolution of mankind stimulates the evolution of Christianity itself and that, consequently, movements like Marxism, which arose in opposition to religion, may subsequently contribute to its maturation and enrichment. By focusing attention anew on the basis of the problem, this process can help, in turn, to reveal the need, e.g., in Marxism, for re-thinking and maturation.

Awareness of the convergences and of the basis which they provide for dialogue obviously cannot lead to any camouflaging of the divergences, even to serve the needs of dialogue itself. They spring up just as soon as any of the points enumerated above are dealt with in greater detail. The most macroscopic of them derives, as I mentioned earlier, from atheism. In order to measure its profundity we shall have to attempt a more direct reply to the question of whether Marxism is essentially atheistic.

First, let it be noted that the term 'essential', as applied to a doctrinal system, is not always very clear. We need to distinguish at least three meanings of the term:

(a) In the strict sense, doctrines that regulate all the others, or at least the most original tenets, are essential to a system— for these we shall reserve the qualification 'fundamental'.

(b) Essential in a broader sense are doctrines whose role is to give global significance to the world-view. They may be fundamental or derivative.

(c) Other doctrines necessarily connected with those already mentioned may be termed essential in an even broader sense.

The importance of these distinctions, which may appear rather academic, will emerge more clearly when we apply them to Marxism.

First of all, if our interpretation is correct, it seems reasonably clear that in sense 'c', atheism is essential to Marxism. In other words, it is not a purely personal tenet of Marx, but a thesis connected with the foundations of his system.

Again in sense 'b', atheism seems to be essential to Marxism. It does not merely affect certain sectors of the system; it traverses all its solutions and characterizes Marxist humanism as a whole. We have seen at every stage of the exposition how the various tenets of Marxism invoke atheism.

Finally, with regard to sense 'a', we must be much more cautious. As a denial, atheism (in Marxism as in other systems) is a derived, not a primitive, position. Therefore, the assertions that demand it are independent of it. In other words, atheism is not one of the 'fundamental' theses of Marxism.

So it is that the affirmation of the absolute value of man, along with many of its implications in the fields of ontology, morals, economics, theory of knowledge, etc., does not demand atheism. I have attempted to prove, on the contrary, that these theories can be actuated in many cases only on the hypothesis that God exists. If they lead to atheism, this is because they are joined to another decisive principle, that of the existence of axiological rivalry between man and God, human action and divine action, human reality and divine reality, and, consequently, between morality and religion, secular (especially economic) values and sacred values, the community spirit and the religious spirit, etc. This principle is not itself atheistic and is often developed, as we have seen, in deeply religious contexts. This means that Marxist atheism derives from two ranges of premises, neither of which, taken separately, demands it. Each is in fact susceptible to development in a religious direction.

Insofar as the political, economic, social theories, etc., of Marxism are dissociated from the principle of axiological rivalry, they no longer imply atheism either as a presupposition or as a consequence. By acknowledging the existence of a revolutionary side to religion, the Marxists already seem to have done some re-thinking on this principle.

It remains true, nevertheless, that to dissociate the political, economic and social theories of Marxism from the principle of axiological rivalry is not the same as to affirm their compatibility with Christianity. Christianity, as we saw earlier, is not just an answer to the problem of God. It is also an answer to the problem of man. Its resources in the face of Marxism are deployed from these two points of view. They call Marxist humanism itself into question. In other words, serious antinomies subsist within the Marxist system and within the concept of *praxis*, so that the humanistic inspiration is constantly grappling with anti-humanistic elements.

Any doctrinal or practical thesis that contradicts the absolute value of man may be termed anti-humanistic. Opposition to humanism could come either from the prospect of a world in which not every man would have the opportunity of fulfilling himself as an end, or from the prospect of a system of values that would not guarantee the respect of men for each other. Now, as we have seen, a life in which death had the last word could not be considered fulfilled, could not be considered to have realized its fundamental aspirations. A love that ended in death, a community destined to disintegrate, a history in which, in order to build up mankind, one had to lose oneself—these things do not constitute victory over alienation. A system of values made radically dependent on history and on the party does not guarantee respect for man, nor, in consequence, the possibility of life in fraternal community. Such dependence would mean that, structurally, alienation could never be overcome. And if the criterion of value coincides with the success of a particular institution, e.g., the party, then the movement is exposed to the constant temptation to impose itself on the masses and re-establish the enslavement of the majority by a minority.

The basic problem posed by the re-thinking of Marxism seems to be reducible to the question of whether *praxis* is the sole criterion of value. This leads back, in turn, to the fundamentally socio-economic and partitic vision of the ideal. Hence the historicization of values (particularly moral values) and truth; the monolithic inclination in axiology and the denial of autonomy to the various areas of secular and religious values; the idea that the party dictates what is valuable and what is true (leading to the pre-eminence of the institution over the person and the community, and of the 'objective' over the 'subjective').

What the Christian will reproach the Marxist for, in the last analysis, is not the fact that he is a humanist, but that he is not humanist enough; nor the fact that he does battle with alienation, but that he does not do so radically enough; nor again the fact that he denounces the master-slave dialectic, but that he remains a victim in his turn.

What he must do is not to import values in an eclectic way, but to get back to the roots of his original personalistic and communal inspiration, to insert socio-economic *praxis* more decisively into the whole scheme of things, and thus to arrive, by way of maturation from within, at a pluralistic expression of the criterion of value and of truth. In a word, Marxism must become decidedly more faithful to man.

Appendix: Two 'Models' of Marxism[21]

I must thank Professor Garaudy for the attention he has given to the articles which I wrote on Marxism. His frank and lucid attitude marks him off as one of those who encourage dialogue and give one grounds for hope.

In his lecture, Professor Garaudy examines some confusions which, he claims, lie at the root of the objections raised against Marxism by Fr Gollwitzer and myself. I must say that I agree with him to a large extent in denouncing these confusions, and the next lecture which I will present shows how close is my interpretation of Marxism to his.

How can I be in agreement with Professor Garaudy's critique of my interpretation of Marxism? I think the answer to this question is of some importance in determining the precise significance of our dialogue.

Besides, the answer is indicated by Garaudy himself. Having said that only a deformation or mechanistic interpretation of Marxism would fall within range of our critique,

[21]An intervention in the discussion following Roger Garaudy's paper at the Herrenchiemsee (28 April—2 May 1966) convention of Christians and Marxists. In that paper, Garaudy, referring to the present essay, had amply discussed some difficulties which I had urged against Marxism.

he adds frankly: 'I realize that only too often there have been, and still are, deformations and anti-humanistic interpretations of this kind in texts that relate to Marxism'.

Anticipating my next thesis, I believe that a distinction must be made between two 'models' of Marxism, a 'personalistic' model of the Garaudy or Schaff type, and an 'integralistic' model as developed, for instance, by Stalin or Ilichev. The demarcation line between the two models is their attitude to the absolute value of the person, which allows us to measure the profundity of this divergence. It seems to me that the first type of Marxism is more faithful to the original inspiration of Marx, while the second is still in force in socialist countries and seems to orientate their action. If integralism is a deformation of Marx's thought, it seems to be due to his disciples rather than to his adversaries. It might be asked whether Lenin and Engels are not partly responsible for this. At any rate, 'personalistic' Marxists must not be surprised if the most widespread image of Marxism in the West is that which reflects more generally its historical incarnations.

Professor Garaudy recalled the distinction between three levels of dialogue: ideas, their actualizations and their deformations. This distinction is undoubtedly very illuminating. On the other hand, if one is to judge a doctrine which proposes, not to contemplate the world, but to transform it, one must take account of what it has accomplished where it has been applied. In order to judge a doctrine that is presented as being based on *praxis*, one cannot avoid having recourse to this criterion. Of course Marxists are entitled to do the same in relation to Christianity and in fact they do so. We might note in passing, however, that the transformation of the secular world is not the prime object of Christianity, and that, consequently, the parallel between the two doctrines cannot be pushed to extremes. However, this problem merits special treatment.

The pluralism in Marxism is not surprising. On the contrary, it is a sign of life. Is it not true that Christianity itself displays internal pluralism, in particular a rather sharp opposition between the personalitic and integralistic types of thinking? Dialogue with others becomes possible only in virtue of this pluralism. In fact there is no external dialogue without internal dialogue.

We must become aware, nevertheless, of the difficulties which this situation can give rise to in our dialogue. Our discussions are normally with the most liberal Marxists and we bring up objections that do not apply to them personally, but to some of their companions and, above all, to Marxist institutions. On the other hand, however, Marxists are in the same position regarding their Christian partners in discussion.

My reason for pointing out this difficulty is certainly not in order to place obstacles in the way of dialogue, but to contribute towards making it ever more realistic and effective. It is normal that dialogue should take place between *avant-garde* elements in the Marxist and Christian worlds, but it must aspire to extend to an increasingly wide circle and to draw communities and institutions into its range.

We are only taking the first steps on a long and laborious road. But these first steps are very important, for they could well mark the beginning of a new epoch.

CHAPTER II

Marxist Solidarity and Christian Solidarity

The orientation of this discussion of Marxism would be somewhat distorted if the wrong construction were put upon Marxist unbelief. The Marxist certainly does not believe in Christianity, but he does believe in something else. Or rather, he does not believe in Christianity because he believes in something else.

Moreover, there is a general principle at stake here. In order to understand a non-believer, we must discover what he *believes*, not in the specifically religious sense of the term, but in its wider sense, connoting the affirmation of certain values. Negation is never a primary phenomenon either logically or psychologically; it is always consequent on affirmation. Now it is certainly important to know whether a person believes in God; but it is equally important to know why he believes or does not believe. It is important to ascertain the fact of faith or the lack of it, but it is equally important to grasp the significance of this fact.

Now the significance of a fact, in this sense, brings us into the sphere of values: we must ask what are the values involved in an affirmation or a denial. It is impossible to understand what a man says unless one understands, in a certain sense, what he is. To understand atheism is to search out the values incorporated in the denial of God by a person or by a given movement.

Malraux, referring to the spiritual crisis of Tchen, one of his characters, writes: 'When his new master raised against Christianity, not arguments, but other forms of grandeur, faith trickled through Tchen's fingers little by little, without a crisis, like sand'.[1] Not arguments, but other forms of grandeur —or better, an argument that consists of opposing one form of grandeur to another.

The difficulty of our attempt at penetration lies in the fact that the denial of God generally has not the same significance for the non-believer as it has for the believer. For this reason, comprehension implies a notable effort on the part of the believer to transpose himself. This effort is difficult but necessary, since without it all dialogue risks being partially frustrated or carried off into abstract argumentation.

Consequently, it seemed to me that if we wished to confront Marxism and Christianity, we would be led to the kernel of the problem by confronting the ideals which they lay before us and which distinguish them as the great alternatives of our time for many individuals and for civilization itself. We shall bring our attention to bear on the ethical message of Marxism, therefore, and, more specifically, on its appeal for human solidarity.

The relevance of this alternative is thrown into strong relief by a phenomenon of our times which, according to believers and non-believers alike, must be numbered among the signs of the times, namely, socialization.[2]

Having acknowledged the existence and importance of this phenomenon, both Marxism and Christianity offer themselves today as interpretations of it. In other words,

---

[1] *La condition humaine*, Paris 1947, 226.

[2] Regarding the Catholic Church, cf., e.g., paragraphs 4, 5, 6, 23, 24, 25, 26, 30, 63 of the *Pastoral Constitution on the Church in the Modern World* and paragraphs 1, 9 of the *Dogmatic Constitution on the Church*.

each claims the ability to discover its value and to fit it into a world-view which would reveal all of its significance.

What is socialization? Briefly, it is the actuation of man's social dimension; it is the making of society. It is based on the natural social dimension of man. But this dimension is historical and subject to becoming; it is actuated progressively. Man evolves towards increasingly socialized forms of life. He lives new sectors of his life socially (we may call this intensive socialization) and social ties reach even wider communities (extensive socialization).

This is a typical example of an historical law, of an inclination necessarily written into the process of man's becoming. Nevertheless, the phenomenon may justifiably be numbered among the signs of our time, since evolution has seen a dizzy acceleration in this direction in industrial civilization. Society tends to permeate all sectors of human existence (work, property, culture, entertainment, building construction, etc.) and has already reached planetary dimensions —indeed the hypothesis of a spatial society is now being framed. The stress laid on state intervention in the various spheres of human activity is among its most considerable consequences.

Being a dynamic phenomenon, an historical movement, this sign of our times is destined to make an increasingly deeper impression as time goes on. It has at once an actual effect and a prophetic content.

But socialization does not interest us here merely, nor perhaps even principally, in its exterior, 'objective' aspect, or in the progressive growth of relationships or social bonds that it implies. This evolution is accompanied by an evolution of the human conscience regarding the community and by the creation of a new sensibility characterized by the emergence of man's communal vocation, which bears with it new rights and duties whether in relation to others or to the various regional, sectional and worldwide communities. For the same reason, each human existence must be seen within the context of mankind as a whole. The present is related to the past and the future. Mankind is discovered to be a dynamic unity, one great people on the march. Awareness of the communal dimension brings awareness of the historical dimension.

In proposing themselves as interpreters of the movement of socialization, Marxism and Christianity must face each other on the question of the meaning of human existence and history. They must be concerned with the present and project themselves towards the future. Each must confront the other's message of hope.

Let us now examine, together, some aspects of these two messages.

MARXIST SOLIDARITY

Many believers are in the habit of thinking that the denial of God is equivalent to the denial of morality, and that the ultimate meaning of atheism is to be sought precisely in this desire to liberate oneself from all moral bonds. In other words, atheism would be the rationalization of a lived attitude. What are we to think of such an interpretation?

Certainly, it is partially true. There are forms of atheism whose psychological genesis answers to this description—in the case of the adolescent, for example, who rejects religion along with many other moral bonds that seem to him to belong to infancy, and sees in this liberation his accession to adulthood. More rarely, there are forms of atheism that pose expressly as justifications of complete moral anarchy: 'if there is no God, then everything is permitted'.

But this interpretation is only partly true, and perhaps it is necessary at this point to recall the extreme diversity of the forms of atheism, a fact that should lead to distrust of any univocal presentation. There are atheists whose lives, as far as we are given to judge, are integrated and generous. There are forms of atheism that promote high moral values, that seek, in the words of Camus, 'sanctity without God'. Finally, however paradoxical it may seem, there are theories that define their atheism in the name of moral values, and that reject religion because they hold it to be insufficiently sensitive to moral values, or to some of them at any rate. They reject religion, not in order to abandon morality, but to discover it. In the psychological development of these men, the passage to atheism is experienced as moral progress rather than as an impoverishment. On the doctrinal level, then, the foundations of atheism lie in the conflict between religion and morality, a theme that is among the most fundamental in modern atheism, particularly in Marxism.

In regard to Marxism, the immoralistic interpretation may seem, at first sight, to be confirmed by many of its assertions, which seem to be heavily critical of morality. But these are really directed against a particular type of morality—a morality that is *bourgeois*, individualistic, conservative, stagnant, defeatist, eschatological and heteronomous. This is replaced by a morality inspired by the idea of solidarity, and we must examine some of its aspects. The believer will often have to make profound reservations about its validity, but this does not entitle him to deny its existence.

The theme of solidarity is a dimension rather than a chapter —a dimension that spans the system from end to end. Its meaning would be distorted were it reduced to a collectivistic conception of property. Economic Communism itself must be understood in the context of a global vision of solidarity.

Thus an exhaustive discourse on Marxist solidarity would involve an exposition of the whole system. We must limit ourselves to some necessarily very incomplete indications.

Here we shall try to put ourselves in the position of our opposite numbers, to see the system as they see it, to see what values it presents in their eyes—those values that seem to postulate atheism.

The Communal Reality

The basis of moral solidarity in Marxism is an ontological solidarity, or organic (in this sense dialectical) view of the whole universe. This universe is not a conglomeration of phenomena, but a coherent, single unity, in which things and phenomena are essentially interconnected and condition each other reciprocally. The Hegelian dialectic is thus translated into natural terms. By virtue of this inter-communication, no being or phenomenon can be understood except in the light of the totality.

Specifically, Marxist man is not an isolated individual but an essential part of a web of relationships with nature and with other men. Man is essentially social; the isolated individual is an abstraction; as Marx put it, man is really a 'being of a species', a communal organism. Any solution to the problem of man that would treat him as an isolated individual would be purely rhetorical. The individual's destiny is one with that of the human community, or rather with that of reality as a whole. Man cannot be transformed unless history is.

Productive relations form the basic bond in this communion of man with nature and with other men. Man's social dimension is based on the social dimension of work. However, it is not restricted to the area of economics, but has a hand in all human activities. In this case, as always, the infrastructures form the foundation of the superstructures, though without absorbing them.

So man's social dimension is an historical reality. In other words, it grows in depth and extent as the relationships arising out of work become socialized.

The Communal Ideal

The individual can be integrated into society as means or as end, as slave or as free man. The ideal essence of man, towards which history is orientated, is that of a community of free and equal men. The individual can fulfil himself as an end only in a fraternal community where each member is an end and all forms of slavery and alienation have been abolished. This will be a classless, stateless society from which all coercion is banished. A purely personal ideal of man does not exist; the very concepts of liberty, happiness, perfection and human dignity are essentially communal.

Corresponding to these new exterior, 'objective' relationships between men there are new interior, subjective relationships. Historical evolution brings with it an evolution in human conscience, a new ethical attitude. Egoism and individualism will finally be overcome, and relationships between men will be regulated spontaneously, without coercion, by justice and love. All will be for each and each for all. In short, liberty can be achieved only through love, and the eschatological society will be a community of love.

The basis of the new society will be an economic system with full respect for man's dignity, a system in which every man will give according to his capacity and receive according to his needs. This will be a system that has left behind the economic conflicts responsible for the origin of evil. The fruit of the work of all will be placed at the service of all— wealth has an essentially social function. But this new society cannot be created without definite state planning and the nationalization of productive assets. We have already seen how Marxism as an economic system must be understood within the framework of a vision of the solidarity of all mankind. Seeing in the private ownership of productive assets nothing but institutionalized egoism, Marxism asserts that only by abolishing this system can we create conditions enabling men to live together fraternally. Thus the meaning of the historical movement of socialization is sought in this process of liberation and humanization, which is the meaning of history.

Faith in man means faith in a better future, faith in the possibility of creating a new humanity and building the ideal city. This faith explains Marxist optimism and forms the real basis of its message of hope.

Having demythologized heaven, however, contemporary Marxism is turning its attention to demythologizing earth. It acknowledges ever more expressly that not all problems will be resolved for tomorrow's mankind, nor all alienations overcome. The ideal city is being approached indefinitely, accompanied by the knowledge that it can never be reached. Even faith in the necessity of progress itself seems to be clouded at times by the prospect of an indefinitely enduring capitalism and, above all, by the threat of atomic suicide.

Marxist hopes still lie in a great historical project, but this is ceasing to be a great certainty. Thus Marxism is becoming much more realistic. But by virtue of that very fact the limits of the Marxist ideal are manifested.

A Critique of the Situation

The diagnosis of the situation and the critique of it in the light of the ideal are always accompanied, in Marxist method, by an outline of the ideal. Analysis of the human situation coincides with the analysis of the type of society into which man is inserted, the *bourgeois* society.

Diagnosis and evaluation are conflated in the pregnant concept of alienation. Alienation is the antithesis of liberty, happiness and human dignity. It characterizes a way of living together in which man is enslaved by his fellow man—a relationship that owes its inspiration to that between master and slave. Reduced to the level of a means, man tends to treat others as means, too. This is an atomized world, a theatre for the war, fought by all, against all.

Basic to this exterior and interior situation is the liberal economic system, characterized by the unlimited right to private property and free initiative. Personal gain is its stimulus to production, and profits go to private individuals called capitalists. Thus the exploitation of man by his fellow man grows, and with it, in consequence, grows the condition of slavery. This economic system—this institutionalized egoism—is humanity's original sin and the source of all evils.

The Historical Task of the Communist Movement

The historical task of the Communist movement is to overcome alienation, to transform the situation in order to bring it into conformity with the ideal, to liberate mankind by liberating the proletariat. Its love of mankind is not purely Platonic or interior. It aspires to be efficacious, to become a creative historical force, to become incarnate in new structures.

The transformation of the world begins with the transformation of the economic system, and the total liberation of mankind is based on its economic and social liberation. The first assault in the war against alienation must be made on the fundamental alienation and original sin, economic slavery. This liberation cannot be reduced to an increase in productive activity, but implies, even necessarily, the transformation of human relationships in the direction of justice and love.

To be effective, the transforming action must draw together into a single movement all who are bound by the same chains: 'workers of the world unite'. Here we see the real subject of Marxist *praxis*, the protagonist of history, the author of liberation, the messiah; in other words, the human community in its best expression, the proletariat.

The solidarity of the proletariat is a condition of the efficacy of *praxis*—an efficacy that will be all the greater the more numerous are the adherents of the movement. In any case, it must cross national boundaries and spread to the whole world. Internationalism, or catholicity if you will, is one of its essential characteristics. In fact the workers of the world all live in the same alienating conditions and must overcome them through a common revolutionary struggle. For the individual worker, therefore, success in life coincides with the success of his class. On the other hand, the success of the working class is the success of mankind, since the proletariat walks in the direction of history. Marxist humanism is proletarian, then, and is thus involved in a class distinction. But this is only provisional and its purpose is to enable a universal vocation to go into action more efficaciously.

This duty of liberation and struggle is a moral imperative, and through it the supreme imperative of love takes concrete form. In order that the redemption of the proletariat (and consequently of humanity) should be possible, each of its members must view this cause as the supreme value and subordinate his personal interests to it. Concretely, the community becomes the supreme value and everything must be sacrificed to it. Marxist man has no purely private life, but always acts with the community in mind. His life is essentially a service to society. His first commandment is to love, to love on a worldwide scale. This is a love that can lead to heroism, even to the giving of life for those he loves—his fellow workers. He is called to fight and sacrifice himself for ideals that will become realities only for tomorrow's mankind, perhaps, but the certainty that he is fighting for a just and noble cause, that he is marching with the flow of history, lets him know that he has not lived in vain.

The proletarian liberation-struggle will make headway only if it is organized. The party is the expression of this need. It brings together the most active elements in the proletariat and through them incorporates the whole class. *Praxis* in all its forms must be directed by the party—*praxis* is essentially partitic.

Thus the party affects every aspect of the worker's life and specifies for him the meaning of his obligation to the community. Fidelity to party directives concretely synthesizes all moral imperatives. However, this obedience is not blind or unjustified. Indeed, the party derives authority from its being the interpreter of the sentiments and interests of the working masses. It is the conscience of the proletariat and, consequently, the voice of history. Whereas religion requires obedience to men who represent God, Marxism requires obedience to men who represent man and express the conscience of history.

Thus there is a typically Marxist interiority, that of the man who lives solely for the party, for the working class and for mankind, who makes his ideal and his success coincide with the ideal and the success of the community.

We may synthesize the Marxist position in the words of Maxim Gorky: 'In socialism the true love of man has been organized into a creative force for the first time'.

Communal Humanism and the Critique of Christianity

Communal humanism is the basis of one of the most important sectors of the Marxist critique of Christianity.

The necessity of grasping the precise significance of the atheist's denial if we are to understand it at all has already been mentioned. Hence we must discover, not just why the atheist proceeded to his denial, but also what was its object—what exactly did he intend to deny.

Historically and psychologically atheism emerges as a post-religious phenomenon, a critical reflection on religion (on the Christian religion, in the Western world). In order to understand the atheist, therefore, one must reconstruct the image of God which he has formed for himself. Religion is called to the dock here, not just as a doctrinal system, but as a system of values and a living reality, as a phenomenon present in history. For this reason the critique of it takes the form of a protest.

The Marxist critique of Christianity denounces the individualistic character of its concept of reality and of the ideal, and hence of ethics and especially of love.

By turning man towards God, religion encloses him in an individualistic relationship and detaches him from involvement in the community. In the last analysis, it is an illusory replacement for the complex of real relationships. It deprives man of his communal essence and, from the moral point of view, canonizes egoism. This is a fundamental aspect of alienation. The rejection of religion means, for Marx, the rejection of this form of alienation in the name of man's communal vocation and in the name of love.

Let us examine more analytically this conflict between religion and solidarity. Marxism asserts that, according to Christianity, reality is an aggregate of beings, and society a conglomeration of individuals. They are unified only by an extrinsic relationship to God and by superficial relationships among themselves. These relationships are not constitutive of their being. And so, considered in itself, even the evolution of the universe, and particularly of mankind, is a succession of phenomena and facts which do not reveal a unifying significance. For this significance one is referred to a mysterious divine plan, which seems to dispense one from seeking the inner sense of the dynamism of history. Already, therefore, on ontological grounds, Marxism is opposed to Christianity, as a unified, communal vision, to an atomistic, individualistic vision.

But let us fix our attention primarily on the antithesis of the two ideals. According to Marxism, the Christian ideal is essentially individualistic. The highest aspiration of the Christian is to his own perfection, salvation and happiness. He is preoccupied with his 'soul', and the salvation of others interests him only insofar as it affects his own. Marxism proposes its communal ideal in opposition to this version of the human vocation.

The Christian ideal is essentially eschatological or other-worldly. Man is called to prepare for heaven rather than to build up this earth. Marxism, with its requirement of fidelity to earth, opposes this evasion.

Love is certainly implied in the Christian ideal, too, but it is love of God, not of man. Human perfection or happiness will consist of 'enjoying the vision of God'. The type of morality deriving from this ideal is naturally influenced by it. It is an ethic centred on a solitary relationship with God (alone with the One) and on flight from men. Thus the Christian is a man of God, but not a man of other men. He is the man who prays much and loves little. Consequently, other men are viewed as dangers to be avoided rather than as brothers to be loved. Preoccupied with God's rights, he has no interest in the rights of men. Or rather, for him, the defence of God's rights guarantees the violation of those of men (persecutions carried out in the name of religion, as well as religious wars, inquisitional methods, etc., spring to mind). He finds in the expectation of heaven good reasons to dispense himself from building up the earth. In short, the Christian is a man in whose interior life religion becomes, in the last analysis, a substitute for morality.

In the measure in which religion bears an ethical message, it is a question of commitment regulated by the prospect of recompense or 'eternal reward', and not by pure generosity. It is really only a superior form of egoism. A genuine morality, such as atheistic morality seeks to be, can only be disinterested.

In the eyes of the Marxist there is a tension between religion and morality that can be specified as the tension between egoism and generosity. Marxism chooses morality or generosity and rejects religion or egoism.

According to the Marxists, the most outstanding proof of the individualistic character of Christianity is its attitude to the liberal economic system, which, as we have seen, is merely institutionalized egoism. By defending this system, Christianity reveals the deep-seated motive of its moral attitude, which coincides with that of liberalism. The alliance between capitalism and the altar at the social level reveals an even more intimate alliance at the level of general attitudes to life.

So whereas Marxism, incorporating the values of socialism, moves in the direction of history, Christianity, entrenched in its individualism, runs against the grain of history.

Nevertheless, there is undoubtedly a lot of talk about love in Christianity. But if the two conceptions of love are compared, profound oppositions between the outlooks underlying them are seen to emerge (still according to the Marxists) even more clearly. Whereas Christian love is sterile, Platonic and hence ultimately illusory, Marxist love is efficacious and creative. Basically, Christian love is aimed at the welfare of the soul, not of the body, and at eternal rather than terrestrial salvation. It is more interested in pointing out man's duties than in defending his rights. Faced with injustice, it preaches resignation and defers justice to some future period; it does not fight for immediate justice. And when the Christian serves the body by doing 'works of mercy', he gives in the name of charity, or as alms, what he ought to give in the name of justice. His kind of charity ends up by dispensing him from justice. Always within the bounds of legality, it operates within existing structures, shunning revolution, and canonizes an unjust system with all the weight of divine authority behind it. Finally, it is love of the individual as such, and takes no account of the fact that the individual finds fulfilment only in the context of the community.

To this concept of love, Marxism opposes a love that is involved, concretely and decisively, in the secular world, especially in the economic sphere. Its object is to defend the rights of man, to achieve justice on earth, and to create a new community through unified, militant, revolutionary action.

Conclusion

We are now in a position to make a better attempt at formulating the meaning of Marxist atheism, at least in relation to the problem on hand. It is an atheism that involves the rejection of egoism and individualism and aspires positively towards a communal ideal. Now, perhaps, we can see more clearly why the denial of God does not 'mean' the same thing for the Marxist and the Christian; why, indeed, it can mean many things which, for the believer, are implied in his very act of belief.

Our discussion could be developed in two directions from here. The first would consist in examining Marxist solidarity in order to discover up to what point its methods, duly specified and, above all, confronted with historical experience, remain faithful to this inspiration. In other words, up to what point in Marxism does the communal ideal retain its respect for the value of the person? To what extent do community values not themselves end up by being subordinated and eventually sacrificed to the demands of the party?

But if it was necessary to point out the values present in Marxist solidarity, it is no less necessary to point out the fact that Marxism has, to a large extent, betrayed those very values for which it had fought, and in the name of which it had arisen in the first place. The outcome is the realization that, in the nations where it has been tried, it cannot count on a free consensus of the masses. This has been solemnly acknowledged by the Communist movement itself as regards the Stalinist period. The evolution that followed certainly represents progress of a kind, but it leaves the problems substantially intact.

As a result, quite a number of present-day Western Marxists express fundamental reservations about the Communist regimes, and feel that they must dissociate themselves from responsibility for these to a certain extent. The Soviet regime has ceased to be the ideal for many Marxists. The myth of the guiding-state has collapsed.

Insofar as the Communist experiment is judged to have been more or less unsatisfactory, we naturally wonder about the causes of its defects. To what extent are they due to the original system and to what extent due to a particular version of it or to the particular circumstances of its incarnation? For my part, I see these defects as partly due to each of the above causes, and consequently as largely due to the original system. Above all, however, they are due to the Soviet version of that system. This is also implicitly acknowledged by Western Marxists, whose effort to re-think the system is concerned with doctrine. For the present, however, it is a question of partial retouching or of declarations of intention. Now Marxism is an organic unit, and it would be difficult to justify sectional modifications without becoming involved in a total process of re-thinking. This does not take from the fact that the evolution in progress will be followed with the greatest interest.

But there is another range of problems which I think it is more urgent to face. Examining the Marxist critique of Christianity, we found ourselves in a paradoxical situation. Here was a spiritual movement, marked by its founder with the sign of love, finding in love its whole *raison d'être*, and it is being criticized and rejected precisely in the name of love.

Our problem is this. What has made such a massive criticism possible? What has been responsible for a reputation such as to provoke the apostasy of the working classes? What has made possible and plausible what seems to us to be such a radical misunderstanding of Christianity?

Our answer gets its bearings from the Council document on the Church in the modern world, which, having established the post-religious and post-Christian character of atheism, continues: 'Yet believers themselves frequently bear some responsibility for this situation . . . . . To the extent that they neglect their own training in the faith, or teach erroneous doctrine, or are deficient in their religious, moral, or social life, they must be said to conceal rather than reveal the authentic face of God and religion' (no. 19).

The document returns even more explicitly to this theme:

> Although by the power of the holy Spirit the Church has remained the faithful spouse of her Lord and has never ceased to be the sign of salvation on earth, still she is very well aware that among her members, both clerical and lay, some have been unfaithful to the spirit of God during the course of many centuries. In the present age, too, it does not escape the Church how great a distance lies between the message she offers and the human failings of those to whom the gospel is entrusted.
>
> Whatever be the judgement of history on these defects, we ought to be conscious of them, and struggle against them energetically, lest they inflict harm on the spread of the gospel. The Church also realizes that in working out her relationship with the world she always has great need of the ripening which comes with the experience of the centuries. Led by the holy Spirit, Mother Church unceasingly exhorts her sons 'to purify and renew themselves so that the sign of Christ can shine more brightly on the face of the Church' (no. 43).

And when speaking of modern atheists Pope Paul VI

had said: 'Sometimes, too, the atheist is spurred on by noble sentiments and by impatience with the mediocrity and self-seeking of so many contemporary settings. He knows well how to borrow from our Gospel modes and expressions of solidarity and human compassion. Shall we not be able to lead him back one day to the Christian source of such manifestations of moral worth?'[3]

Perhaps, then, the Marxist critique applies to us, not because we are Christians, but insofar as we are not Christian enough. Perhaps, in the end, the most telling arguments in a critique of Christians are supplied by Christianity itself.

If this is so, then the most radical response to the Marxist critique will be an honest admission of the personal and collective defects of our Christianity in this matter of solidarity, and an effort to rediscover at its source, 'which is in fact Christian', the meaning of our communal vocation.

CHRISTIAN SOLIDARITY

It is difficult to deny the existence of a markedly individualistic version of Christianity both in the past and in our own time. This version is lived, and sometimes even theorized, by such great masses of the faithful that it characterizes the collective religious conscience.

The liturgical movement has condemned it as regards prayer, and this revival of the communal dimension in worship is one of the most prominent aspects of reform. But individualism in devotion is just one aspect of a more extensive phenomenon, the eclipse of the communal dimension in the Christian conscience. So here, too, with regard to the whole life of the Church, the liturgical renewal should have the function of a sign.

[3] *Ecclesiam Suam* (E. tr.), 38.

Typical in this respect is the answer of the Roman Catechism: 'God created us to know, love and serve him in this life, and to enjoy him in the next in Paradise'. It may be irreproachable, but we feel today that something essential is missing—there is no reference to man's communal vocation. This reference is certainly implicit, but we feel the need to make it explicit.

The maturation in Christian conscience, of which the Council speaks in this as in other sectors, does not consist so much in the affirmation today, on the level of doctrine, of what was denied yesterday. It consists more in making explicit what was implicit in the past. This movement is of great importance. Although the implicit truths are not denied, they end up not being lived. In theory they are not denied, but in practice everything happens as though they were. Insofar as this is true, religion can actually become an alienation.

The causes of this development are quite complex, and man's innate egoism, which tends to make use even of religion, cannot be discounted.

Nevertheless, I shall also mention here some of the historical factors that have contributed to the phenomenon to a greater or lesser extent. They are usually legitimate in themselves, emphases rather than errors, but they finally result in a distortion of perspective when they eclipse other aspects of the problem. We are constantly exposed to this danger as individuals and as a community on account of the necessarily partial nature of all experience, including our religious experience.

If Christianity is the bearer of great human values, it is also true that it transcends them immensely in its religious and supernatural content. If it has a zone in which it encounters secular movements, institutions and ideologies, it is also deeply original in relation to the same. Different periods in history and different personalities develop now one, now the other aspect, never being sufficiently concerned to show how they are complementary. So it comes about that the stress laid on the transcendence and originality of Christianity serves to obliterate its human message; that the stress laid on the relationship with God develops into 'religionism', a purely cultural religious phenomenon; that the stress laid on the superiority of religious values, on 'God's jealousy', leads to contempt of the secular sphere, and to a conception of it, of the world, and of human relationships themselves, that views these things more as dangers or distractions than as the space left open for the incarnation of love ('Every time I entered the company of men, I returned less a man', says the *Imitation of Christ*, in other ways a most valuable book). We can understand how, in this context, the love of man can lose its central position, or at least can tend to be expressed at a 'religious' level and not to penetrate the secular sphere. Finally, it can remain at a moralistic level and not tend to become embodied in secular institutions and structures more worthy of man, or to become a transforming movement.

Christian doctrine is at once a vision of reality and a programme of action. Here again, different personalities can focus their attention more fully on either the dogmatic aspect or the moral task. The moral aspect can thus be developed independently of dogma, in a separate series of 'tracts' and categories, as, for example, doing one's duty, conforming to the will of God, obeying the commandments and gaining merit. Thus there is a risk of another deformation of Christianity, namely, moralism. It consists in reducing the Christian ethic to a codex, in losing sight of its profound originality.

The real Christian ethic is on a level with a world of realities, persons and events being actuated in us and in the whole of history: the indwelling of the Three Persons, incorporation into Christ, the communion of saints, the paschal mystery and its progressive actualization through the course of history, the existence of eschatological realities, etc. The divorce in question has made possible the elaboration of a morality and a spirituality from which the communion of life and destiny among men has remained absent.

In the reality which is the Church, then, as it is seen by Catholicism, the mystery and the institution, the communion of life and love and the hierarchical, juridical society, are co-essentials. Here, too, different emphases are possible, and the totality is distorted when one or other particular dimension is exalted. Post-Tridentine theology gave a predominantly apologetical twist to the study of the Church. It was a question of defending the Catholic Church, as the one true Church of Christ, against schismatic, and especially Protestant, deviations. Furthermore, it was a case of affirming the rights of the Church and the clergy against interference by monarchs, emperors, or politicians. The accent thus came to be placed on the juridical and hierarchical side of things, and the onto-logical and charismatic aspects were left in the shade. The emphasis was on the visible society rather than on the invisible communion.

Finally, in the modern age, Christian philosophical and theological thinking has been greatly influenced either by the empiricist philosophy (especially in the Protestant world) or by the rationalist philosophy (especially in the Catholic world). This has given rise to a philosophical tradition (often closer to Wolff than to St Thomas). Now while these philosophies diverge profoundly, they converge in their individualistic, static foundations. They consider realities singly and atomistically rather than globally. They view them statically, in their being, rather than dynamically, in their history. It is evident that reflection with a basis of this kind must show itself less amenable to the communal and historical dimensions of Christianity.

The Christian Vocation as a Vocation to Love

Let us now face the authentic content of the Christian message.

Jesus was God. He came on earth with infinite marvels to communicate to men, and these he communicated. But among them all one stood out. It was *his* idea, the one with which he connected the success of his mission in the world: the love of one's brothers. For him, this love is inseparable from the love of God and is the guarantee of its authenticity. How can you love God, whom you have not seen, if you do not love your brother, whom you can see? (1 *John* 4: 20-21; 1 *John* 3:17). The two great loves are the synthesis and summit of the law (*Mark* 12: 28-33; *Matt.* 22: 34-40; *Luke* 10: 25-37; *Col.* 3:14), and the condition on which God, who is love, will continue to live within us (*Eph.* 3: 17; 1 *Cor.* 13: 13; *John* 14: 15-23; 1 *John* 4: 12-16).

Often, indeed, Jesus limited himself to speaking of the love of one's neighbour, leaving the love of God implicit. This is his commandment (*John* 15: 12), the new commandment (*John* 13: 34; 15: 12; 15: 17; 1 *John* 2: 8), the manifesto of his revolution, the sign by which his disciples were to be recognized by the world (*John* 13: 35), the one commandment, which, when it is observed, means that the law is fully observed (*Rom.* 13: 8-10; *Gal.* 5: 14; 6: 2), the commandment on which we shall be judged (*Matt.* 25: 31-46), the commandment which, in the last analysis, will measure the value of our lives, will measure our success.

It would be difficult to be clearer than this.

But there is yet more. Specifying the meaning of the fraternal love that he requires of his disciples, Jesus says: Love one another as I have loved you (*John* 13: 34; 15: 12). St John, in a natural way, draws a very serious conclusion from this. Jesus, he observes, gave his life for us. Consequently, we ought to give our lives for our brothers (1 *John* 3: 16).

The Christian principle of love is extremely demanding, therefore: it binds unto death. It is not a counsel or a work of supererogation, but a command, Christ's first command. It is a command that we are free to follow or not to follow, just as we are free to be, or not to be, Christians, but no one can pretend to be a Christian and at the same time deny the first commandment of Christ.

So man's love for his fellow man is situated right at the heart of Christianity. It demands that, following the example of God, who is love, every man be recognized as an end. The harmony between man and God, between the salvation of man and the greatness of God, is affirmed at the heart of Christianity. It is impossible to be faithful to God without being faithful to man; it is impossible to defend God's rights without defending the rights of man. By vocation man is not merely a man of God. He is a man of men.

The love to which we are called is love unto death, heroic love. The Christian vocation is to heroism. It is offered, not to the initiated, not to some mystical souls, but to each and every person. The universal vocation to love is, in the first place, a vocation to heroic love. We can accept or reject this call, but we cannot deny that it has reached us. The day we reject it we may write in our diary: today I have refused to offer my life in heroic sacrifice.

Thus it would be difficult to conceive a more radical deformation of Christianity than that offered by individualism. And the appeal of the Council has a genuinely evangelical ring about it when it says: 'Profound and rapid changes make it particularly urgent that no one, ignoring the trend of events or drugged by laziness, content himself with a merely individualistic morality' (no. 30).

So the success of Christianity is connected with the creation of a great community, of a vast movement of love. Christianity is this or it is nothing. Perhaps many do not believe in the love of God because they have never encountered the love of man.

The 'practising' Catholic is not the man who 'goes to mass', but the man who loves. The great precept is not the festive one, but the daily one of love. The extent of 'religious practice' should not be calculated merely on the basis of the numbers 'going to mass', but also from the number of those who suffer hunger, who live in hovels, or who work in unjust and degrading conditions.

It certainly is not my intention here to devalue religious practice, in the current sense of the expression. Rightly understood, it remains the summit and foundation of life for the Christian, and his source of energy for every task. I have in mind a type of practice that is severed from love, that sometimes risks dispensing a man from love by tranquillizing his conscience. This is the practice of the priest and the levite in the parable told by Christ. While travelling from Jerusalem to Jericho, they saw a suffering brother and quickly passed on. We must not forget that Jesus, so understanding with publicans and sinners, with the prostitute and the woman taken in adultery, was hard and cutting when referring to certain 'church-goers' of his time. These men prayed and fasted, but did not love. Much will be forgiven to the sinner who has loved much.

Many Christians confess to not going to mass on Sunday, or to eating meat on Friday. Very few accuse themselves of not having loved, of having forgotten the suffering, the poor, the sick and the imprisoned, or of not having practised justice or fought to establish it. Is it because few sins are committed against the commandment of love, or is it because this first commandment has been forgotten? Has it become possible to feel oneself a Christian and not feel bound to love?

The Secular Dimension of Christian Love

Christian love is profoundly original with regard to all human love and every philosophical movement, on account of the religious, supernatural character of its motives and object. The Christian loves man for the love of God, as a son of God, as a member of Christ destined for eternal joyous intimacy with God.

But just as the love of God would be illusory if it were not embodied in the love of one's neighbour, so would religious love be illusory if it did not reach into the secular sphere. In either case there is religious alienation and a fictitious love that conceals (when it does not actually canonize) an effective atheism. We must not gloss over the risk that loving a man in Christ may turn out to be false love, and that many may prefer to be loved in themselves rather than in Christ. Jesus, for his part, in the preview he gives us of the universal judgement, cites examples of love that are taken from secular life in its most mundane aspects (*Matt.* 25: 31-46). And in the first epistle of John we read: 'But if anyone has the world's goods and sees his brother in need, yet closes his heart against him, how does God's love abide in him? Little children, let us not love in word or speech, but in deed and in truth. By this shall we know that we are of the truth' (1 *John* 3: 17-18; cf. *Jas.* 1: 27). The maturation of the Christian conscience in this area leads to a situation in which the demands of love in the secular sphere become progressively more explicit.

The commandment of love concerns, not only the eternal salvation of men, but also their temporal advancement. The Christian is engaged in building the earthly city, too. Although his vocation relates primarily to the eternal salvation of men, it also extends, though in a subordinate way, to their secular liberation. The fact that, for the Christian, the problems cannot be finally solved on earth, does not dispense him from seeking the partial solutions accessible to him. The fact that, for him, progress is directed towards eternal horizons, does not prevent him from believing in earthly progress and a new humanity, or from the actualization of a great historical project. Eschatological hope does not diminish the importance of terrestrial tasks; on the contrary, it provides them with new motives.

'The expectation of a new earth must not weaken, but rather stimulate, our concern for cultivating this one. For here grows the body of a new human family, a body which even now is able to give some kind of foreshadowing of the new age.

'Earthly progress must be carefully distinguished from the growth of Christ's kingdom. Nevertheless, to the extent that the former can contribute to the better ordering of human society, it is of vital concern to the kingdom of God' (no. 39).

The compenetration of the religious and secular aspects of love is part of that 'living synthesis' (Pastoral Constitution on the Church in the Modern World) which the Christian must urgently achieve in order to overcome his internal dualism and integrate his personality. This is a synthesis that the Christian community itself must accomplish, so that love may become truly visible and thereby become the sign, raised up among the gentiles, of the mysterious love of the Father.

Genuine Christian love aspires to create an earthly city in which all men may fulfil themselves as ends; a city in which everyone's rights will be acknowledged, without discrimination, in theory and in practice. Thus it is contrary to human dignity, and consequently to Christian love, that what belongs to man by right should be granted to him in a paternalistic manner, as alms. The Christian fulfils his duty of almsgiving, but he is aware that this is the solution of expediency, that it is a lesser evil, and feels that he must fight for a society in which everyone will possess by right what is due to him by right.

In this regard there are certain equivocations latent in talk about the Church of the poor, and these must be dispelled. The Church of the poor does not mean the Church of almsgiving and resignation, but the Church that fights in defence of the rights of the poor, so that, as far as possible, there may no longer be any poor. Human liberation cannot prescind from economic liberation.

If it is to be genuine, this sort of commitment must not consist solely of edifying theories or declarations of principle that reassure consciences and leave the reality intact. We must break, ever more decisively, the association that at times still seems to subsist between Christianity and socio-economic conservation, between Christianity and the last-ditch defence of constitutional order or disorder. Where this kind of alliance exists, religion becomes instrumental to egoistic interests. It becomes, in fact, an alienation. Religious alienation in all its forms must be denounced and fought in the name of religion. The believer must be found in the front line of those who courageously denounce, in the light and in the name of the gospel, the injustices and alienations of our society, particularly as regards the distribution of wealth and the regulation of labour relations. This lucid diagnosis will reveal the fact that effective action often cannot rest content to develop within existing structures, but demands reform of the structures themselves. It can also demand a more decisive intervention by the state, or a limitation of private property that will enable wealth to fulfil its natural social purpose.

'An improvement in attitudes, as well as widespread changes in society, will have to take place', says the Council, 'if the objectives are to be reached.

'God's Spirit, who with a marvellous providence directs the unfolding of time and renews the face of the earth, is not absent from this development. The ferment of the gospel, too, has aroused and continues to arouse in man's heart the irresistible requirements of his dignity' (no. 26, cf. no. 71). Thus love will become militant and capable of transforming the world through the consolidated action of those who, according to the anguished appeal of Vatican II, wish to be 'men who are truly new and artisans of a new humanity' (no. 30).

Notwithstanding its risks, the process of socialization has, therefore, a highly positive value as a movement towards that broader and more fraternal unity which constitutes the terrestrial meaning of history. If all this is true, then it seems possible for a renewed Christianity to accept what it finds legitimate in Marxism, harmonizing the personalistic and communal dimensions rather more fully.

This is a new face of Christianity, brought to light with special force by the personalities of John XXIII and Paul VI, and by the fruitful work of the Council. It has not failed to make an impression in some Marxist circles, which feel the need nowadays to re-think their evaluations of Christianity, even to the point of acknowledging its revolutionary character and of reaching out to the possibility of an encounter on the moral, political and economic planes. We have already seen how very partial this convergence is, but the fact that it is now being affirmed by a growing number of Marxists is significant. Insofar as it is seen possible for Christianity to accept the valid demands of Marxism and to become an historical force for renewal, what value would then attach to the Marxist critique of religion in the name of morality?

Christian Horizons of our Communal Vocation

But this is only part of the Christian answer to the problem of solidarity, and, although very important, it is still basically inadequate. However profound may be the human friend-ship that we achieve among ourselves, it must halt at the impenetrable wall of consciousness. However intimate our social ties may be, we are alone with the fundamental choices that determine our destiny. In the last analysis, man is always alone. The tendency of love towards a lasting encounter is irrevocably smashed against the wall of death at the moment of supreme solitude. Finally, love, universal in its aspirations, normally reaches only a restricted circle of persons: man cannot give himself to all. Thus in the secular sphere many basic expectations of love remain unsatisfied. Love itself, if it is to reach fulfilment, calls for an area of essentially different relationships, where it can reach a more profound intimacy and where it will be really universal as well as endless in duration. Christianity discloses unsuspected potentialities for these expectations by revealing to man the ultimate meaning of his communal vocation. God has decided to communicate his life to men taken, not as individuals, but as a community—a people (Dogmatic Constitution on the Church, no. 9; cf. Pastoral Constitution on the Church in the Modern World, no. 32). 'So from the beginning of salvation history he has chosen men not just as individuals but as members of a certain community . . . God called these chosen ones "his people", and, furthermore, made a covenant with them on Sinai' (no. 32).

The whole of salvation history is the story of this progressive unification of mankind. It is a question, not of a particular sector, however important, of the Christian message, but of a dimension traversing it as a whole. Man's perfection —his very life—is realized through unity. But the unity of the person is essentially an interpersonal matter: man achieves interior unity only by uniting himself to God, by accepting his offer of alliance, by entering into the intimacy of Trinitarian unity. But there is no union with God without union with one's brothers. The Trinitarian community reaches right into the human community, so that interior personal unity is achieved only in communion with men.

Original sin was not just the fall from grace, but also, for this very reason, the rupture of original interior and communal unity. Babel, with its confusion of tongues, symbolizes this dispersion of mankind. Communication between men became impossible because communion between them had ceased. From then on man's psychic equilibrium was also disturbed. There emerged within him a dualism of 'flesh' and 'spirit', and a conflict between two value-systems, egoism and generosity. Thus individualism was generated by sin. Every sin is an act of infidelity not only to God but also to the community. Every sin is a rupture of unity. The redemption, by virtue of the fact that it is the reconciliation of man to God, is thereby the interior reconciliation of every man and the reconciliation of men to each other. The Paschal mystery is the source of the unity sealed by the blood of the new and eternal alliance (no. 32). The parallel between Babel and Pentecost is enlightening. Pentecost makes men capable of communication once more because it re-establishes communion among them. The eucharist, a renewal of the Paschal and Pentecostal mystery, is thus the source of unity. It binds into one body those who are nourished by the same bread. Offered by the community, it generates the community. Moreover, all the sacraments, insofar as they are signs of divine life, generate unity.

Thus divine life is communal in nature: it consists in entering a community. To live, for the Christian, is to 'live with'. The Christian vocation is a 'con-vocation'. Besides being a juridical and hierarchical community, and at a more fundamental level, the Church is this community of life and love, the new people of God, the body of Christ. This is a new area of relationships among men, immensely more intimate, lasting and universal. These relationships are so close that they make of those who love each other one organism, one man almost, not, however, in the purely psychological or moral sense, but in the ontological sense. They become like branches of the same vine, members of the same body. Jesus compares the unity that binds Christians to that which binds the Three Divine Persons. These relationships will never be destroyed. They are destined to intensify and explode into joyous eternal communion. They do not just bind a small part of mankind, but are destined to create links between all men, between past and present, present and future. Mankind becomes a single great reality on the march. The whole of history seems to be penetrated by this vast unifying movement in which the process of socialization finds its deepest meaning (no. 24). 'The Church is a kind of sacrament or sign of intimate union with God, and of the unity of all mankind. She is also an instrument for the achievement of such union and unity' (Dogmatic Constitution on the Church, no. 1). And the opening declaration of the same document is symptomatic: 'The conditions of this age lend special urgency to the Church's task of bringing all men to unity with Christ, since mankind today is joined together more closely than ever before by social, technical and cultural bonds' (Dogmatic Constitution on the Church, no. 1; cf. Pastoral Constitution on the Church in the Modern World, no. 24). By becoming involved in this movement towards the unification of mankind in Christ, man will surely find his own interior unity. He will find generosity and the source of interior unity. He will find his life by losing it. He will unify himself in unifying mankind. The drama of each man flows into the drama of history.

In the terrestrial phase, however, relationships between men, however intimate and real they may be, do not emerge fully into consciousness and consequently do not actualize that fusion of spirits which remains the dream of love. This will be the function of 'eternal life', which is not a solitary encounter of the soul with God, but an immense community of consciousness, the accomplishment of full and eternal communion with one's brothers. It will be the joy of a family, where all will share the joy of each and each the joy of all (no. 32). This is the promised land to which we are making our way, the new humanity which we are laboriously building up, in other words, the ideal of history. We were created by God in order to build, with him and with our brothers, a community of temporal and eternal love.

The most serious risk for man is the eternal cleavage which is damnation. It not only involves 'loss of the vision of God', but also the loss of fraternal love. A destiny of eternal isolation emerges as the alternative to eternal communion, and the seclusion of absolute solitude as the alternative to perpetual union with the human community.

Consequently, a reliable criterion of the value of an ideal can be its capacity to respond to the expectations of love, to create an intimate, permanent, universal solidarity among men, and to give a profound meaning to the process of socialization and to the whole of history. In the last analysis, the ideal which is stronger than death will be the one that has responded to the expectations of love. However noble it may be, an ideal that yields to death is necessarily a frustrated one.

'The Marxist', writes Garaudy in a recent volume, 'asks himself the same questions as the Christian, is tormented by the same demands, lives with the same straining towards the future, but does not believe himself authorized to transform his question into an answer, his demand into presence . . . . The infinite, for the Marxist, is an absence and a demand; for the Christian, a promise and a presence'.[4] In the same book he admits frankly: 'Insofar as Marxism has left these problems

---

[4]*De l'anathème au dialogue. Un marxiste s'adresse au Concile*, Paris 1965, 86, (E. tr. *From Anathema to Dialogue*, London and New York, 1966).

without an adequate solution, young people have sought this solution elsewhere.'[5]

Certainly, the Christian knows that he is able to transform the expectations of love into a promise and a presence. In fact he knows that the authentic community will be based on the vigour of a man who has died and has risen—a man who is God. The community passes through resurrection. The community of the future will be the expression of this victory of Christ, and in him of the whole of humanity, over death. It will be the final joyous proof that love is stronger than death.

[5]*Ibid.*, 73–74.

CHAPTER III

Marxism and Integralism

The lively and contradictory reactions aroused in Marxist and Christian circles by the very idea of dialogue are extremely significant. They certainly show that the problem is a real one. Above all, however, they manifest a widespread presentiment that the attitude of dialogue will not be something superficial, but implies a concept of human existence, human thought and human community; that acceptance or rejection of dialogue constitutes an historic decision; that if it were to be accepted, along with all it implies, by both sides, we should be at a turning point in history. A disposition for dialogue is not just a simple decision involving the will alone, but a structural openness that affects one's system of thought and one's method of action.

Those who consider doctrinal dialogue between Marxists and Christians impossible often advance an argument not lacking in force. Both systems of thought, they maintain, are extremely organic. Each is a coherent whole. Any affirmation by either system can be understood only in the light of the whole system. Consequently, the Marxist and the Christian could never come to speak the same language. Even if they were to use the same expressions, they would mean different things by them.

What are we to make of this argument? For my part, I regard the difficulty as a very serious one. If a solution is possible, it certainly will not be a simple one. Since we are dealing with a radical difficulty, one which could compromise all further effort, it must be given priority and confronted candidly.

But first, what exactly is integralism? We might begin with an approximate description of it in relation to dialogue. It is a conception of values which views them as organic. It holds that no encounter is possible on the basis of determinate values unless there is an encounter on the basis of all values or at least the fundamental ones.

Integralism originates in the context of a 'faith', be it religious or lay. By 'faith' in this case I mean adhesion to a complex of ideal values, which generally involves membership of a community or institution. Clearly, integralism does not consist solely in total adhesion to these values (for instance, the glorification of God in the case of Christianity, or socio-economic liberation in the case of Marxism), nor solely in a willingness to subordinate all other values to them, but rather in the way in which this adhesion and subordination are conceived. They are conceived in terms of a monolithic axiology involving the primacy of the group over mankind or of the institution over the person.

Formally included in the description of integralism proposed here is the concept of a monolithic axiology. It involves a sharp sense of the primacy of a determinate sphere of values, and of the consequent need to define all other spheres in the light of this one, to relate them to it as means to end. Thus the autonomy and originality of the various spheres of value are seriously compromised. The organic conception of values easily comes to be reflected in a similar conception of truth and leads to a rigid interpretation of systematic unity.

This attitude is not defined solely in relation to doctrine, but also in relation to a community of 'faith', a group which is seen as the historical incarnation of the fundamental values and whose success is taken as the criterion of value. Thus the primacy of values is specified as the primacy of a group (political, ethnic, religious, etc.). This can easily lead to the view that history is a game played between two opposing camps, one representing goodness and truth, the other representing evil and error.

But the group can preserve its monolithic character only by being highly organized. In fine, then, values become incarnate in the institutions surrounding the group, and the primacy of values becomes the primacy of the institution over the person, of authority over initiative. A monolithic conception of axiology leads to a monolithic social structure. Thus integralism leans in the direction of totalitarian forms of government and all the political and ideological intolerance which such regimes bring with them. Finally, the success of the institution and the will of authority become the criterion of value and even of truth.

Among the more typical results of this attitude we might mention triumphalism, which consists in seeing the history of one's institution solely in terms of a series of 'triumphs', and in rejecting all self-criticism by the community. Triumphalism thus leads to the canonization of the accomplished facts of one's own institution.

There is evident opposition between this kind of attitude and that of dialogue, which is based on give-and-take at all levels. In fact the integralist is closed within his own system, group and institution, and he can acknowledge no autonomous values elsewhere.

He excludes the possibility of an area of values held in common by opposing ideologies. Thus he cannot allow an encounter, on a specific topic, with individuals who do not share his basic tenets. He cannot sincerely admire others on the moral or intellectual plane. He cannot grant them rights for example liberty, nor does he admit to having any duties towards them. Although he criticizes other institutions, he refuses to criticize his own in the name of the same principles: so he must criticize in others what he approves in his own camp. He finds it impossible to face others on equal terms and to open the way to genuine friendship. In such conditions dialogue is structurally impossible.

The temptation to integralism is as strong for Christianity as it is for Marxism. In the course of history both have yielded to it. Christianity takes as its central theme the affirmation of religion; Marxism takes socio-economic liberation. Both show a tendency to subordinate other areas quite rigidly to the fundamental values. Both maintain that the salvation of mankind is the work of a chosen people, the ecclesial community in one case, the proletariat in the other. As a result, these communities, and the institutions that grow within them (the ecclesial society on the one hand, the party and the socialist states on the other), become the centre of history. They represent goodness and truth and fight against evil and error. In the end, their success and the will of their leaders emerge as the criteria of value.

No dialogue is possible between a Christianity and a Marxism so conceived. Nor would it be possible if one side alone had overcome its integralism. Naturally, then, Marxism must ask to what extent integralism has been overcome, or is in process of being overcome (apart from good intentions), in the Christian world. And Christianity must ask the same question about the Marxist world.

The question to be asked by both sides does not concern a simple fact, but the very possibility of that fact. It is a question of finding out whether the two systems are structurally disposed for dialogue or whether, on the contrary, their integralism is essential to them.

For my part, I should like to ask the question in regard to Marxism. Here are the terms of our problem. Is Marxism integralistic, as the greater part of its adversaries and supporters think? Is it possible to criticize the Soviet type of Marxism, at the doctrinal and practical levels, in the name of Marx? Must the Marxist choose between Marx and dialogue, or can he set a dialogue going with Marx as a springboard?

I have declared the existence of an integralistic version or Marxism, still widely diffused and officially adhered to wherever Communism is in power. But it is rejected by many Marxists, who proclaim the necessity of being open to dialogue with those of other persuasions, especially with a section or the Christian world. They affirm theses that contrast with those of their companions in power, such as the affirmation of pluralism, the laicity of the state (in principle), the elaboration of a morality, recognition of the positive, re-volutionary value of religion, a questioning of the partitic character of truth and values, the affirmation of the autonomy of culture, the rediscovery of the problems concerning sub-jectivity, etc.

Moreover, Marxist intellectuals are aware that their new ideas imply quite a profound doctrinal evolution involving, in the first place, their conception of values. They often share our uneasiness in the presence of Soviet integralism. Most of the criticisms which the Christian finds it necessary to bring against this integralism and its doctrinal presuppositions are formulated, explicitly or implicitly, by these very Marxists.

Two series of documents testify to this evolution. There are those which express official tendencies, such as the motions at party congresses and committees and the speeches of leaders, and those produced in the field of philosophy, within which we can distinguish personal contributions and historical research (particularly into the young Marx).

Examples of official documents would be the theses of the tenth and eleventh Party Congresses, the speeches of Togliatti and Longo (in Italy), and the conclusions of the most recent session of the Central Party Committee (in France). Among the philosophers we might name the Frenchmen Garaudy, Mury and Goldmann; the Poles Schaff and Kolakovsky; the Germans Bloch and Havemann; the Hungarians Lukacs and Markus; the Italians Gramsci, Lombardo-Radice, Luporini, etc.

These two series of texts naturally differ in importance. From one angle, the first are the most important, since they express the views of the majority, at least within the party. But what they express is essentially political in orientation and is not concerned with doctrinal justifications for its statements. These justifications are to be sought in the personal contributions of the philosophers and in historical research into Marx. But a philospher's views, especially if he does not hold some official position in the movement, are binding on himself alone.

For the sake of objectivity, then, we must avoid attributing to the evolution in progress a breadth and depth that go beyond the data. If new tendencies are detected in certain Communist parties, even at official level, they must not be attributed forthwith to the international Communist movement. The fact that certain *avant-garde* thinkers have forged ahead with the revision of the system does not entitle one to view them as though they expressed the intentions of the party. If certain policies are adopted at the political level, this does not suffice as a proof of doctrinal evolution. In general, while taking account of new developments, we must never lose sight of the continued presence of the integralistic forces still in power in socialist countries—forces that are still quite influential in the West.

Nevertheless, these reservations do not prevent us from establishing one fact: something is changing in the Marxist world. Even more relevant is the fact that this change is quite clearly in the direction of certain general aspirations of contemporary consciousness. Living in the same world, Communists and Christians cannot avoid being faced with the same problems and subjected to the same social pressures. The fact that it is rooted in the contemporary situation makes it easier to believe in the authenticity and stability of the evolution in progress.

It would lead to distortion of these criticisms if we forgot that, in the spirit of those who are making them, they constitute dissent within a movement. The critics declare themselves loyal to the movement and see it as having a highly positive historical value when viewed as a whole. On the doctrinal level it is a question, for them, of internal evolution, not of abandoning the central inspiration of the system. The suppression of integralism would be necessitated, for them, by profound fidelity to the spirit of Marxism. We ask ourselves in the Christian world whether there is any probability that this attempt will be successful.

It may help in tying down the problem to refer to the Catholic Church's experience in the matter. Integralism has existed, and still exists, in the Church, and was considered for a long time to be the expression of Christian orthodoxy. Religious intolerance, the confessionalism of the state and clericalism are among its most significant manifestations. Vatican II represents an historical about-turn on this complex of problems. At least in principle, it marks the end of Catholic integralism.

With regard to the attitude of dialogue, there has been a real 'qualitative leap' in the Catholic world. While remaining faithful to its past, the Church, under the influence of the personalities of John XXIII and Paul VI, as well as through the labours and documents of Vatican II, has affirmed principles, and taken up attitudes, that now make it substantially prepared for dialogue with those genuinely open to it. We note, for example, a sharper sense of the historicity of values and of truth, the proclamation of religious liberty with all its implications, the affirmation of the autonomy of the temporal and the lay in their own spheres, the abandonment of temporal aspirations, recognition of the values present in non-Christian religions and in atheism, etc.

Undoubtedly a profound evolution is still necessary if this new spirit is to be understood in all its theoretical and practical implications, and above all if it is to permeate the life of the Church. The stimulating criticism of our Marxist partners in discussion will certainly help us to accelerate the change. But the movement has definitely been set going.

Now if the Church evolves, stimulated by historical events and by the various ideologies that form outside of it or in opposition to it, this can come about only through the re-discovery and deepening of its original inspiration. Thus it finds that in overcoming integralism and taking up an openly pluralistic stand it is not renouncing anything essential, but rather is fulfilling itself in a more authentic manner. This is not to deny that it must abandon ideas considered for centuries to be essential by many theologians—ideas which had orientated its action for centuries.

The question is whether Marxism is capable of an analogous evolution. With the aim of answering this question I propose to reconstruct Marxism according to the inspiration of Marx and of his most advanced contemporary disciples. This attempt will not be simply historical research, but will include theoretical reflection on the internal requirements of the system.

We must face the various aspects of the problem of values in the light of which we have been describing Marxist in-tegralism, namely, the relationships between base and super-structure, between class and mankind, and between person and institution.

But the fundamental question in the interpretation of

Marxism, the one the answer to which determines all others, seems to be the question of the relationship between the individual and history. If the individual is not autonomous in being and in value, subjectivity will inevitably be absorbed in the objective becoming of history. The class, the party and the state will be regarded as the criteria of value. In short, integralism would be inevitable. Here, in my view, is the real problem to be solved before we can decide how Marxism is to develop in the future. Is it permissible to re-think the system starting from the principle of the relatively autonomous value of the person?

And so we return to the theme of this essay. Humanism is not just the principal object of our dialogue—it is the condition of the possibility of dialogue.

First Antinomy: Individual–History

The most radical obstacle to this reinterpretation comes from dialectical materialism, insofar as the latter treats anthropology as the application to man of a world-view worked out on the basis of nature, and historical laws as particular applications of the laws of nature. In this outlook man's originality, initiative and destiny are seriously compromised. Man is part of a totality to which he is relative, and whose immanent rationality he must ratify. If this is so, then it is difficult to defend the autonomous character of man's being and value. Only by abandoning naturalism can Marxism hope to overcome integralism. But is Marxism not essentially naturalistic?

To overcome naturalism cannot mean, for Marxism, to agree to consider man 'in himself', abstracting from his relationship with nature and with the whole of reality. This dynamic relationship is, in fact, constitutive of man, who creates himself by bringing nature into subjection. Hence there could never be any question of total autonomy for man. But is it possible to reduce man to this relationship? Is he merely a part of the universe?

Marx, on the contrary, had a very sharp sense of man's originality. The constitutive relationship between man and nature, which he describes, is a dialectical one in which each term preserves a certain originality and autonomy. This problem was central for him and nothing could be further from his thought than the idea that it could be solved in the light of certain universal laws established once and for all.

If this is true, the anthropological transposition in question is less revolutionary than it appears to those accustomed to see Marxism through Stalinist eyes, who consider dialectical materialism to be the pivot of the whole system. Marx himself did not see things in this way. The rediscovery of his youthful writings makes the humanism of his central motivation even more evident. Today, Marxism presents the extremely significant phenomenon of a renewed interest in the young Marx and his anthropological problems. Simultaneously, dialectical materialism is receding into second place, if it is not actually abandoned as a general doctrine of being.

The present-day Marxist can attack the problem of man's relationship to society in this context of renewal. The problem of the liberation of the individual and the problem of life and death once more become central concerns, just as they were for young Marx. Certainly, the individual is essentially relative to society; his liberation can be effected only in society and through the mediation of society; the individual cannot solve his own problem except by placing it, theoretically and practically, in the context of the whole of history. But his relativity to history does not suppress his relative autonomy in the spheres of being and value. *Praxis* is directed towards the creation of the objective conditions that will make possible the solution of personal problems. More precisely, it will enable every individual to fulfil himself as an end. In the last analysis, the Communist movement has meaning only in relation to this ideal. The communal ideal is not the sum of personal ideals, but essentially involves the advancement of the individual. What distinguishes Communism from other forms of communal humanism is the universality of its objectives. The liberation of mankind cannot consist in the advancement of an *élite* but must, in principle, reach all men.

On the other hand, even if the objective conditions are created, this will not be enough to supply the solution to personal problems, which must, in the end, be faced separately. Perhaps Marxism will have to admit frankly that some of these questions have no answers and that some of man's aspirations will always remain aspirations.

According to Marx, however, man cannot fulfil himself as an end except by realizing the cause of himself through creative initiative. From this point of view the alienation found in capitalist society arises from the fact that the great majority of men are reduced, historically, to the functional level, the level of objects. They contribute by their labour to the creation of forces which they are then unable to control and which, in fact, recoil against them. Man's domination of nature and the participation of the masses in power ought to effect man's liberation on the objective plane.

It is difficult to understand in any other way the Marxist doctrine of alienation, which is so basic to the humanist outlook, and which Stalinism had obliterated. In its various forms, alienation is always a situation in which the individual cannot realize himself at all levels as the end and the author of history. This is the most radical criticism urged by Marx against the capitalist system; the movement which he launched was inspired by a desire to 'incarnate' this criticism by reversing the situation, and to build a world in which the liberty of each man would guarantee the liberty of all.

Although it is not revolutionary in relation to Marx, this change of outlook is a profound one, nevertheless, with respect to official Soviet Marxism. We must take account of its numerous consequences in regard to the suppression of integralism.

The most important is a deepening of the notion of *praxis*. Even independently of this new outlook, I do not believe, in spite of the many declarations to the contrary that could easily be cited, that *praxis* constitutes the ultimate criterion of value in Marxism. *Praxis* is defined in relation to what it pursues, its ideal, in this case liberty. *Praxis* is successful only insofar as it brings man closer to the ideal. Thus it does not judge the ideal, rather the opposite. The ultimate criterion of value, the key-stone of the whole system, is liberty. But the preceding reflections on the relationship between the individual and history allow us to specify the question further and in a very important direction. Insofar as personal development appears to be an essential component of the ideal, *praxis* will have to be judged in relation to the person.

Another important consequence of these reflections concerns the autonomous value of the present. If the individual is valuable in himself, then *praxis* cannot restrict its viewpoint to the humanity of tomorrow. It must promote the liberation of the men alive today. The horizons of the common good, in whose name the gravest sacrifices may be demanded of the individual, certainly extend beyond the present and reach mankind in the future, but this does not mean that the present may be reduced to a preparation for the future.

SECOND ANTINOMY: BASE-SUPERSTRUCTURE

Can historical materialism admit the autonomous value of the superstructures, especially culture and morality, with respect to the base? Or of subjectivity with respect to objective realities? The denial of this autonomy, along with the monolithic axiology that follows, forms the origin of monolithic social structures.

Our problem directly concerns relationships in the axiological order. Naturally, it can be extended to cover ontological relationships as well. In fact, one cannot affirm the relatively autonomous value of certain activities without allowing a certain autonomy to their being.

On this dual plane the principle of the relative autonomy of the individual supplies us with new elements in the solution.

Ontological Relationships

Historical materialism undoubtedly implies the following affirmations:

(a) Human activities are conditioned by productive relationships. Hence they cannot normally be exercised as a whole unless economic life, in turn, is normal. Conversely, alienations involving the infrastructures are reflected in the whole of human life and give rise to alienations at every level.

(b) The relationship between the base and the other historical factors is such that a correlation can be discovered between economic and historical development. Consequently, the laws of historical development can be formulated scientifically.

As we have seen, this correlation applies to history as a whole and not to particular events. It applies to the masses, not to individuals. It does not call the autonomy of the subjective life of the individual directly into question. But this autonomy would be very precarious if history were rigidly subject to economic laws.

Now insofar as historical materialism is viewed as the application of dialectical materialism to history, historical laws acquire the rigidity of the laws of nature. Above all, dialectical laws seem to be conferred with the absolute character of the laws of nature.

But as soon as relative autonomy is restored to anthropology in relation to the philosophy of nature, and to subjectivity in relation to the objective order, historical laws recover their sociological character. As such, they must be established on the basis of methods proper to sociology, and can aspire only to the degree of necessity belonging to that science, that is to say, to a greater or lesser degree of probability.

This transposition clearly points towards a philosophy of *praxis*. For this reason, historical materialism is a *sine qua non* for the possibility of a scientific study of history, and, consequently, for efficacious action. Thus it can affirm no more and no less than what is postulated by science, under pain of compromising the efficacy of action. Besides, this transposition points towards the affirmation of the historicity of man, whereas dialectical materialism leads anthropology in the direction of naturalism. Finally, and most important, this approach opens the way to giving a determinate function in history to the initiative of the proletariat and of individuals, who thus bear the burden of the destiny of mankind. Man's task is not just to walk in the direction of history but to make history move in a human direction. On the other hand, by viewing historical laws as the application of more universal laws, mankind sees its own area of competence finally reduced to the ratification of the rationality immanent in the process of becoming. Awareness of historical necessity is undoubtedly a component of real liberty, but real liberty cannot be reduced to a simple awareness.

The consequences that flow from these premises are many:

(a) Scientific forecasts of the direction of history cannot claim more than a strong probability. On this basis alone, then, the end of capitalism and the final victory of Communism cannot be considered inevitable. They could be inevitable only in virtue of a postulate in the axiological order. Awareness of the danger of atomic suicide contributes to the extension of this margin of uncertainty.

(b) Economic alienations are not an adequate explanation of human alienations. The Freudian discovery of the unconscious extends considerably the horizon of objective conditions and sources of alienation. Furthermore, Marxism is becoming even more aware, as we have already noted, of the distinct problem-area of subjectivity, the solutions to which cannot be adequately furnished by objective transformations. Consequently, the end of economic alienation is not the end of all alienation. Having demythologized heaven, Marxism proceeds to demythologize earth. If this is so, then the fundamental notion of liberty must be deepened. Indeed, in the totality that constitutes it, the superstructures seem to acquire a degree of relative autonomy.

(c) Progress in the economic sphere is not necessarily the total progress of society, therefore, and does not suffice to set the human conscience moving towards generosity. Human egoism, which is not adequately explained by economic alienation, will not disappear in the city of the future. Some Marxists are warning of the danger of a socialist society preoccupied only with well-being.

(d) The class struggle, which has considerable influence on ideologies, is not sufficient to explain their origin. Thus it is possible to conceive of a plurality of progressive socio-economic ideologies. The coming of Communism does not necessarily involve ideological unity.

(e) The class struggle, which exercises considerable influence on the history of religion, does not suffice to explain its origin. Thus religion can be either reactionary or progressive. Marxists admit the existence of a 'progressive' version of Christianity in the contemporary world. Some deduce from this the idea that socio-economic transformations will not necessarily lead to the disappearance of religion.

Axiological Relationships

If the base determined the superstructure adequately, then the problem of a hierarchy of values would not even be posed. Indeed, on that hypothesis, socio-economic progress would necessarily determine progress as a whole. The primacy of economic values, and the necessity of making them the criterion of value at all levels, would be incontestable and would enable any conflicts that should occur to be resolved. In any case, such conflicts could only be provisional. Morality, the proper function of which is to direct human activity in the light of the totality, would itself be subordinate to the economic sphere. In this consists the monolithic character of Marxist axiology, from which its monolithic social structure is derived.

But if we work to a more 'historical' version of materialism in the sense already indicated, then the problem of possible conflicts between the various spheres, and of setting up a hierarchy among them, becomes more acute. Unity, which can no longer be achieved by the simple subordination of values to economics, must be sought elsewhere. On the other hand, no single sphere of values can pretend to carry out this unifying function. At this point Marxism is obliged to make a choice. Either it consents to become a methodology of political, social and economic action and renounces the power to view reality as a whole, or else it recovers this viewpoint at another level. The second part of the alternative is equivalent to according a certain autonomy to the moral order as total director of action.

Can Marxism acknowledge the autonomy of morality? It certainly cannot concede that morality should be confined to a region other than real life with its political and economic factors. It cannot allow that moral problems have been re-solved simply by the enunciation of certain universal laws, without any study of the concrete possibility of transforming situations in the light of ideals; it cannot allow morality to become a codex of supra-temporal laws foreign to the develop-ing reality of history. But all this does not imply the reduction of morality to any one particular sphere, for example the socio-economic sphere. On the contrary, the concern to project the light of idealism onto each of these areas and to situate them in relation to the whole, forms part of the central inspiration of Marxism. Consequently, it cannot be reduced to any form of utilitarianism or 'economicism' without betraying it. Economic liberation does not consist solely in attaining a higher level of production or a more just distribution of wealth—and thus in satisfying man's economic needs. It essentially implies a transformation of relationships, an ever greater participation of the masses in the control of economic activity and their capacity to overcome individualism in order to orientate their efforts towards the common good. Consequently, if economic progress conditions progress as a whole, it is itself conditioned in turn by this general progress. Economic liberation can be effected only in a world where men are capable of transcending the purely economic point of view. So a system with economic progress as its criterion of value would be in conflict with the central inspiration of Marxism.

Thus in Marxism the point of view of unity, and hence of the totality, is the moral point of view. Those who know the central role played by these themes within Marxism can measure the importance and originality that ought to belong to the moral order. This dimension, too little studied up to now, undoubtedly needs to be further deepened.

Must one conclude that Marxism would stop viewing *praxis* as the criterion of value? Yes and no. Yes, if *praxis* is still defined exclusively in the light of economic progress; no, if the notion of *praxis* as the unified fulness of human activity is restored and if *praxis* is defined in the light of integral liberty. It is certainly a question of efficacy, but of efficacy defined in the most all-inclusive and human manner.

Thus conceived, the liberation of man requires that each of his spheres of activity be situated relative to the whole. But it also requires that each sphere should enjoy whatever autonomy it needs in order to develop. Here, I have in mind, primarily, intellectual research, which cannot be fruitful on the scientific, historical and philosophical levels unless it is genuine. In other words, it must accept in full the methods proper to each individual science, never sacrificing them for the sake of immediate needs. In this sense there is no contradiction between disinterestedness of research and the criterion of *praxis*. This last remark will remind the Marxist intellectual that he is never simply a research worker but always remains, in a certain measure, a militant. Research is his contribution to the construction of the new world, and will be evaluated in the light of the benefit it can bring to the actualization of this historical project. But the autonomy of the various spheres of value cannot be conceived without free confrontation within each of them. Although it is true that ideal liberty and juridical liberty must not be confounded, it remains true that the latter is, to a certain extent, the necessary means to the realization of the former. Indeed the autonomy in question would be a pure abstraction unless it corresponded to a formal and real juridical liberty.

Thus serious historical research is inconceivable as long as history is treated as an instrument in the service of politics. When it is so treated, historians do not enjoy the liberty they need in order to apply the methods of their discipline in full. Serious research is also inconceivable as long as the judgement to be made (concerning the personality of Stalin, for example), must be dictated by the Party Congress, or as long as the interpretation of an historical period can change, in a few years, as a result of considerations that have nothing to do with historical research. If history is not autonomous then it simply is not history. This is a serious consideration for a system which, in principle, is nourished by historical experience and, at least to a certain extent, makes history its criterion of value.

So, too, any real philosophical progress is unthinkable as long as all personal research is conditioned by fidelity to a certain orthodoxy defined by the party. As long as one is not free to think differently, one is not free to think at all. The difficulties facing those Marxist thinkers in socialist countries who tread new ways are well known. Thought is thus condemned to immobility and sterility.

Analogous considerations could be advanced on the question of art. As long as it is viewed solely in the light of politics, its freedom of expression will be limited, many of its sources of inspiration dried up, and its creative possibilities diminished.

In a word, man's artistic dimension will be unable to develop.

The necessity of re-thinking the pragmatic criterion of truth is affirmed, at least implicitly, by those Marxists who recognize a plurality of ideologies capable of committing human action to the ways of progress, and even attribute revolutionary possibilities to religion itself. No ideology could then claim the exclusive title of ideology of the proletariat. Be that as it may, by virtue simply of a new way of conceiving the relationships between *praxis* and ideology, Marxism could assume an attitude of doctrinal esteem for other ideologies that would open the way to the sincere consideration of free confrontation as a mutual enrichment and as an exigency of progress. Axiological pluralism is one of the doctrinal foundations of social pluralism.

Moreover, by recognizing the relative autonomy of the various spheres of value, particularly ideology, Marxism becomes willing, in principle, to meet other elements at a determinate level, elements with which it cannot agree on every point. Better still, it becomes possible to meet them at the level of terrestrial morality. And there is a growing willingness on the part of Marxism to affirm the partial convergence of Christian morality and a renewed Marxist morality.

Nevertheless, having acknowledged the new possibilities in religious ideology and the partial convergence with their morality, Marxists continue, on the whole, to regard religion as an alienation. Now this value-judgement, made in the name of economic liberation, is no longer true of religion in general but only of certain historical forms of it. In fact, many Marxists, while remaining faithful to atheism, have abandoned the thesis that religion is an alienation.

It must be asked what link there is between atheism and Marxism thus renewed. Last year at Salzburg M. Reding expounded his well-known thesis that Marxism is not essentially atheistic, although Marx personally was an atheist. This thesis seems to be valid insofar as Marxism leads back to the principle of historical materialism. From this point of view atheism is based on the contradiction between religion and socio-economic progress. But once it is admitted that religion is not essentially anti-progressive, then it no longer seems possible to claim that religion is an alienation on that basis. Once the specifically Marxist foundations of atheism have been laid bare in this way, it becomes legitimate to ask whether, if we follow this direction, we shall not see Marxism pass from atheism to laicism, to a philosophy of terrestrial reality that abstracts from the problem of God.

Two obstacles seem to be hindering this evolution. First, there is the central concept of liberty, conceived as being incompatible with axiological rivalry between man and God. In this general form, the concept is not exclusive to Marxism. It is found in many forms of atheism. Therefore, it is not necessarily connected with historical materialism. A second obstacle is constituted by the Marxist aspiration to be a total view of reality. This makes it difficult for Marxism to put such a decisive problem as that of God in parentheses. I do not think that these obstacles are insurmountable. Nevertheless, they show us in what depth the system must be re-thought if it is to abandon atheism.

But there is no need to delay further on this topic. However important it may be from other points of view, it affects the possibility of dialogue only insofar as atheism is accompanied by contempt for the religious man or begins to question his liberty.

THIRD ANTINOMY: CLASS-MANKIND

Must Marxism necessarily view the interests of one class, the proletariat, as the exclusive criterion of value? Must it make the interests of a group prevail over those of mankind as a matter of principle? Integralistic Marxism answers in the affirmative.

Whereas in the ideal city there will no longer be classes and values will be universally realized, in the present situation mankind is divided. Within it two classes face each other, the proletariat and the capitalists, the exploited and the exploiters, the slaves and the masters. The struggle between these two classes is the driving force in history (which consequently follows the pattern of antinomy).

This struggle is carried on principally on economic grounds, but it permeates the whole of human existence and acquires, in particular, a moral character. It is in the class struggle that the historical struggle between good and evil, between the 'two cities', takes flesh. Thus the socio-economic struggle is the spinal cord of history. Nothing is foreign to it. There are no neutral men, events, or attitudes, and he who is not with the proletariat is against it. There is no morality, culture, philosophy, art, literature or cinema that can be considered neutral. All values are militant, and unless they militate for progress they favour reaction. Goodness, evil, truth and falsity, at all levels, are to be discerned in this light.

Consequently, neither the individual person nor mankind as a whole, but the proletarian class, is the foundation of values. The historicity of values means that values are defined dialectically, in favour of one social class and in opposition to the other. In fighting for the suppression of classes, the proletariat is fighting for the universality of values. But so far it cannot recognize this universality. Animated by love for the mankind of tomorrow, it cannot yet love present-day mankind. This generates a basically polemical attitude towards 'the others'—they are adversaries and must be fought. In principle they must neither be esteemed nor loved except for the services which they can render to the proletarian cause in a given instance. Class solidarity replaces universal love. Love of the enemy is not virtue but weakness.

However, a personalistic Marxist will place value on these other elements. He conceives the mission of the proletariat only in relation to mankind (this is analogous to the mission of ancient Israel or of the Church). For this reason, a class-based ethic, or, more generally, a class-based axiology, is not purely and simply equivalent to a group ethic. In fact the class can pursue its own interests only insofar as they coincide with those of mankind. There is no question here of a depressed group liberating itself by reversing the situation to its own advantage and becoming the oppressor in turn. It must achieve liberation by building up a community of free men. Thus the class places itself in the service of an ideal that transcends it and must regulate its action. The class-consciousness which must regulate action is not a spontaneous movement directed towards particular interests, therefore, but a reflex attitude corresponding to a universal vocation.

This consideration enables Marxist morality to be distinguished from relativism. It must rediscover, alone, the necessity for a morality centred on the relatively autonomous value of the person. For if it is true that the class prepares for and prefigures the society of tomorrow, it is equally true that a society of free men can be built only on respect for the person.

Furthermore, if man cannot be reduced to his social relationships and if his value is not fully determined by economic infrastructures, then interpersonal relationships cannot be reduced to relationships between classes. Consequently, Marxist morality is not adequately described as a class-based morality. Thus it is possible to fight someone as a member of the ruling class and, at the same time, to love him for his value as a human being. It is possible to prepare for tomorrow's mankind and yet love today's. The universality of love is

correlative to the autonomous value of the person. Class
solidarity and the struggle to which it gives rise are not
necessarily opposed to universal love, but can be considered a
condition of its realization.

Indeed universal respect for the person would remain a
formal and abstract principle unless it committed the men who
believed in it to the policy of ensuring the conditions for its
realization. Now this action will necessarily be dialectical. In
a certain sense, a class struggle conscious of its own universal
vocation not only is compatible with respect for the person
but is demanded by it. It is precisely this dialectical relationship between a particular group and its universal vocation
that generates the dynamism of Marxist morality.

Conversely, the Communist parties and states, insofar as
they enclose themselves in a universal polemic with all who stay
outside them, become a particular group and betray their
universal vocation. In other words, they are unfaithful to
Marxism.

Fourth Antinomy: Person-Institution

Must Marxism assert the primacy of institutions, especially
the state or the party, over the person? Is Marxism essentially
bound up with the dictatorial system? This point is undoubtedly the most decisive in determining the relationship
between Marxism and integralism. Even though on the
doctrinal plane it is subordinate to other questions, it is here,
nevertheless, that doctrine is embodied in social life.

Let us recall rapidly the presuppositions of Marxist political
integralism.

In the city of the future, human relationships will evolve
spontaneously—independently of any institutional structure
or juridical relationship. But Marxism attributes great importance to the role of institutions in the preparatory stage.

They serve to organize the efforts of the proletariat, and finally, to incarnate its values. Where the Communist party has come to power, values become incarnate in the state in this way. Thus the success of the proletarian movement tends to be identified with the success of the party or of socialist states, and this success comes to be the criterion of value, not *de jure* but *de facto*.

Party discipline and civic spirit become a condensed morality because they express dedication to the revolutionary cause in a concrete way. Where it comes to power, the Communist party must gradually lead the whole population to live the ideal of the new man and to effect the transformations, especially in the socio-economic order, that the ideal requires. The actualization of the common good demands the transformation of reigning structures and habits of living, and this can be achieved only at the price of grave personal sacrifice. Asceticism has no value in itself and will disappear in the city of the future. But during the transition stage a highly pressured, austere regime is necessary. Not just groups of volunteers, but the great masses, are called to live in this state of emergency, and not just for a brief period, for example, the duration of a war, but for entire generations. On the other hand, any transforming action meets with vigorous resistance from surviving traces of the *bourgeois* mentality so strongly rooted in the populace.

In this situation, the continuity and effectiveness of action require the socialist political regime to be strong and stable. Where the proletariat has come to power, other parties no longer have any *raison-d'être*. In fact they could only reflect sectional interests in conflict with those of the collectivity. They would polarize survivals of the past into conflict with the demands of the future. Their only effect would be to obstruct the progress of mankind, to retard the rhythm of history. A system is called for, then, in which only the healthy forces in a country can find expression and in which defeatist and reactionary organizations are proscribed. Goodness and truth have all the rights. Evil and error have none. Now the healthy forces in a country—those which endeavour to build up the new man—are crystallized in the Communist party. Consequently, this should be the only party.

By maintaining this point of view in theory or in practice, Marxism adopts, at least implicitly, the following principle: the party and the state must act for the common good of mankind and of the proletariat, even if it cannot count on the free support of the majority. Objective demands must be imposed where they do not spring up spontaneously. This primacy of objectivity determines the primacy of the party over the class, and, within the party, the primacy of the central committee over the rest and of the general secretary over the central committee.

This attitude finds its justification in Marxist integralism. Insofar as the transformation of socio-economic infrastructures is considered of fundamental value, there will be no hesitation in subordinating, and eventually sacrificing, all other values to it. This is all the more true since this sacrifice is only provisional, given that socio-economic liberation will lead to the extinction of all alienation and make the full development of man possible. Values such as political and ideological liberty should be judged from this viewpoint: if they obstruct the fundamental liberation there must be no hesitation in sacrificing them. For, in the end, such juridical liberty would be merely formal and illusory. It would be an alienation. This is how the criterion of *praxis* can justify a dictatorial regime. A monolithic axiology is the basis for monolithic socialism.

Besides, the absolute authority of the party is justified by the fact that the foundation of value is not, in the last analysis, today's mankind but tomorrow's—the mankind of the ideal city. In the present world, authority belongs to the part of humanity that prefigures the future city and is committed to building it up. In other words, authority belongs to the proletariat, and ultimately to the party and its leaders. Any conflicts that occur between the community and the party or state institution are really conflicts between today's mankind and tomorrow's, and they must be resolved in favour of the latter. Thus the ultimate foundation of the primacy of the institution over the person is the supposition that the individual is relative to history.

If, on the other hand, Marxism goes back to its original inspiration, which looked to the person and the community, it comes into obvious conflict with the monolithic state. Man is fulfilled as an end only insofar as he becomes the author of history. Institutions can be guaranteed to be in the service of the community only if the community is really the subject of power. In a monolithic regime, the fate of the entire country is in the hands of a small minority. Individual initiative, even if officially recognized, is in fact non-existent. Are not many elements of the political alienation effectively exposed by Marx in capitalist states to be found again here under new forms?

I have already mentioned other consequences of a mono-lithic political system when dealing with the autonomy of superstructures, and I showed how such a system obstructs personal development and is thereby opposed to the Marxist ideal.

But there is another reason to be found in Marxism for handing over the control of history to popular initiative. The norm of action is the conscience of the working masses, who, in virtue of their harmony with the general direction of history (a kind of connaturality), interpret its requirements in particular situations. Just as the *sensus Ecclesiae* interprets the word of God for the Christian, so the conscience of the community interprets the word of history for the Marxist.

The exercise of authority is legitimate, therefore, insofar as it is faithful to the interests of the proletariat and hence to the meaning of history. This requires permanent contact with the masses. In order to guarantee this fidelity to the people, both party and state must have a predominantly democratic structure. If, on the one hand, effective action demands rigid discipline in the carrying out of decisions once they have been made, it is no less essential, on the other hand, that these decisions should in fact be the outcome of extensive democratic consultation and open debate at all levels. If the masses must follow their leaders in a docile manner, this is only because they have elected them, and have thus ensured that they embody the general will. Moreover, decisions should be made collegially. Collegialdirection makes a strong contribution to the suppression of individualism, since an elected college will reflect the conscience of the people more easily than will an individual. In this light, authoritarian forms of government and the cult of personality would be deviations from Marxist doctrine.

Consequently, those present-day Marxists who look towards social pluralism can and must return to Marx's original inspiration, which was personalistic and based on the community, as well as to his ideal of liberty and his demand for fidelity to the masses.

This pluralism is being affirmed with increasing clarity by Western Marxists in regard to the autonomy of the various institutions connected with the party and the state. It is also being affirmed at every level of human activity in regard to the pluralism of ideas and of organisms designed to express these ideas, especially political parties. Among the most significant of these general theses are the following: the autonomy of culture and ideological pluralism; religious liberty; the laicity of the state (including the rejection of the idea of an official ideology and particularly of state atheism); recognition of the right of opposition and of the possibility of a change of majority.

But the logic of this reasoning must be pushed further. If it is true that different ideologies can successfully inspire revolutionary *praxis*, must not the same be affirmed *a fortiori* in the case of methodology? If this is so, then no institution can consider itself the sole interpreter of the welfare of mankind, and no political party can hold the exclusive title of conscience of the proletariat. Undoubtedly the necessity of organized and unified action from the workers at the political level can be derived from Marxist principles, but once again this unity of action is truly efficacious (according to the genuine sense of the term) only if it is accomplished in an environment of mutual respect for liberty.

So a system can really call itself Marxist only if it is freely chosen by the masses. A system rejected by the masses could not be Marxist. Marxism must be able to run the risk of liberty.

Even from the Marxist point of view there is a real risk. If it is true (as many contemporary Marxists acknowledge it to be) that the evolution of mankind in the direction of Communism is not inevitable, then a Communist party must be prepared to accept the possibility of remaining indefinitely a minority, or of becoming a minority again after having held power.

As long as a system does not dare to run this risk, it does not show itself sure of popular backing. The psychological basis of integralism is insecurity.

The Marxist will be faithful to his vocation as liberator as soon as he is willing to allow a confrontation of free men with free men on a worldwide scale. Marxism will have proved its superiority as soon as it is freely chosen by the masses who have experienced it. The time has come to offer an adult Marxism to an adult humanity.

CONCLUSION

In conclusion, our answer to the problem which we posed at the beginning is quite clear. Marxism can overcome integralism through an internal development. In other words, integralism is not of its essence. But the development calls for a profound change of outlook in relation to the naturalistic collectivistic version spread by Soviet Communism and those inspired by it. In the first place it implies a rediscovery of the relatively autonomous, unconditional value of the person as the end and the author of history, and, as such, the solid foundation for the universality of values. Marxism will overcome integralism by overcoming objectivism. It will become pluralistic by becoming humanistic. This is the same as saying that Marx's thought authorizes quite a radical critique of the systems inspired by it.

But if this personalistic dimension is truly Marx's original intuition, the question arises as to how it was possible for a Marxism to emerge that presented a very different face to the world. The integralistic development in Marxism seems due to various reasons, some of them doctrinal, others (perhaps the more influential) of an historical nature.

On the doctrinal level, Marx was led in his mature works to stress his own original contributions rather than the themes which he had in common with some of his contemporaries— themes that greatly concerned him in his youth. His attention came to dwell more and more on the objective, social, political and economic aspects of human existence and less on the problems of subjectivity. The demands of his polemic against individualism and abstract moralism, as well as the interpretations of his disciples and his adversaries, helped greatly to spread this image of Marxism. Engels's extension of the dialectic into the world of nature, and above all, the reduction of historical laws to applications of the laws of nature, gave firm foundations to this degeneration into objectivism.

On the other hand, the political and economic difficulties encountered at the national and international levels demanded emergency measures by the new regimes if the encircling capitalism was to be resisted. Meanwhile, Communism in power has never ceased to consider itself in a state of emergency and, as a result, to impose a military discipline. The measures adopted by all states in time of war, such as dictatorship, intolerance, a radically polemical attitude towards others, austerity, the subordination of particular to collective interests, etc., are naturally to be found in socialist states. Consequently, even doctrine has been marked by this militant character.

Finally, on the doctrinal as on the practical plane, one must not omit as causes of integralism the massive presence of anti-Communist integralisms of lay inspiration (for example, Nazi-fascism), or of religious inspiration. While we denounce Marxist integralism, we must remember, not only that a Christian integralism has existed and still exists, but that it has contributed to the generation, and still contributes to the maintenance, of Marxist integralism. We have no right to criticize Marxist integralism without criticizing Christian integralism on the same grounds. In fact, possibly the most substantial contribution we can make to the suppression of Marxist integralism is to set to work suppressing our own by ensuring that the spirit of the Council documents penetrates ever deeper into minds and into realities.

The 'model' which I have proposed, and which owes its inspiration to Marx and his most advanced disciples, is of a Marxism structurally open to dialogue. But have Marx's essential intuitions been respected? If they have, then is it legitimate to criticize in his name systems that derive from him? These are the questions I am putting to my Marxist opposite numbers.

If their answer to these two questions must be substantially positive, and if this image of Marxism must sooner or later become general, this would mean a clear advance and would open up new horizons of doctrinal dialogue. But the problem of our relationship would not thereby be resolved. Indeed it would be quite unrealistic, and therefore quite alien to Marxism, to believe that it is only a philosophy and that the problems posed by it will have been solved by the simple fact that a doctrinal solution to them has been found. Our awareness of the decisive importance of historical conditions in this matter will enable us to measure the limitations of our competence as intellectuals in the task of building the city of the future.

Nevertheless, the elaboration of a doctrine open to dialogue must have the effect of reciprocal involvement for Christian and Marxist intellectuals—involvement in making dialogue descend progressively from the heaven of ideas to the earth of institutions and lived relationships. Here, as elsewhere, one cannot be content with contemplating the world—one must transform it.

In conclusion, there is a Marxism that is open to dialogue, the Marxism of men. And there is a Marxism that is closed to dialogue, the Marxism of institutions. Our hope, and the hope of the world, is that in this dramatic tension between man and institution, the final victory will belong to man.

CHAPTER IV

Peace and Revolution

THE PROBLEM

Peace, a problem of our time

The problem of peace is undoubtedly the most urgent problem raised by reflection anchored in history.

The exceptional gravity of this problem in our time derives primarily from the unprecedented horrors of modern warfare, from the anguished feeling that the energies created by man's genius are ending up by escaping his control, from the threat to the very survival of civilization and humanity represented by atomic armaments, and from the realization that the irreversible could happen even by mistake.

Modern warfare is the culmination of alienation. It is the supreme example of a situation in which man is no longer in control, in which his power over himself is utterly taken from him. 'But we should not let false hope deceive us. For enmities and hatred must be put away and firm, honest agreements concerning world peace reached in the future. Otherwise, for all its marvellous knowledge, humanity, which is already in the middle of a grave crisis, will perhaps be brought to that mournful hour in which it will experience no peace other than the dreadful peace of death' (*Gaudium et Spes* 82, 4; referred to hereafter as GS). Today, the problem of survival comes hand in hand with that of building up a new world. A growing awareness of the dignity of every person and race is giving rise to revolt against the presence of immense needs, hunger, poverty, ignorance and alienations that characterize the world situation. On the other hand, the same awareness reveals the need of working to transform the situation through vigorous action on a worldwide scale. The necessity for a new world is today clearer than ever, and, thanks to technology and social action, it is a concrete possibility. Man is discovering in himself hitherto undreamt-of powers and possibilities.

Alongside such an anguishing situation, alongside such wonderful possibilities appears the spectre of war, adding to the sum-total of evil in the world and squandering the energies that could fight it. The transformation of the world is held up by actual and prospective wars, by those being fought and by those in preparation. This, then, is the most distressing problem of our time. Will the immense power which man is discovering in himself serve in the end to build up the world or to destroy it? Are we heading towards a new birth or towards atomic suicide? We have reached an 'ontological' turning-point in history: mankind must choose between being and non-being.

A problem of these dimensions can be faced and resolved only through worldwide collaboration, and the problem of peace coincides in large measure with that of the possibility of such collaboration. But here we face serious, one is tempted to say insurmountable, difficulties. Collaboration depends on wanting the same thing. An appeal for collaboration issued to all men of 'good will' runs the risk of remaining mere wishful thinking, because good will is an empty form that can be filled out with the most diverse and opposite contents. Every peace-plan involves the identification of the causes of war, a model of future society and a method of action. Now one cannot commit oneself to put a plan into action without fighting those who oppose it and seek peace by other means.

The task of building up peace, considered in the abstract, demands that men work together, whereas, considered in the concrete, it seems to demand that they oppose one another. If peace can be achieved only through war, there will never be peace. Are we trapped, then, in a vicious circle?

The Problem of Peace and the Relationships between Marxists and Christians

The urgency and the difficulty of collaboration towards peace are particularly serious when the parties in question are Marxists and Christians—two communities that represent, under profoundly different forms, great historical forces and great idealistic aspirations.

Although the relationship between these movements is regulated by very complex historical factors, it is paradoxical, nevertheless. We are dealing here with men who, by reason of their original inspiration, pursue ideals of world peace, but who, in fact, are often in conflict with one another. In fact, they contribute towards making the struggle more absolute, providing it with ideal justifications and attributing to it the grandeur of a holy war.

Indeed, if Christian peace and Marxist peace have only the name in common, as many assert, what sense is there in thinking about collaboration towards peace? If Marxists and Christians dream of radically different worlds, how could they unite in order to 'build up the world'? The Council, nevertheless, explicitly calls on Christians to collaborate with all men, including non-believers, in 'building up the world' (GS 57. 1; 21, 6; 92, 5), and establishing 'true peace' (78, 4; 90, 2). Is this collaboration possible?

The problem arises just as much for socialist countries as for others. Indeed, it is very important that it should be seen from the beginning in this reciprocal aspect. All of us, Christians and Marxists, are exposed to the temptation of tackling the question pragmatically, of appealing to certain principles when they favour our position and of forgetting them when they do not. Thus Christians would like to be able to collaborate on an equal footing with Communists in countries where Communists are in power, but they sometimes question the legitimacy of such collaboration in the West, and, in fact, think it normal that Communist parties should be outlawed. On the other hand, Communists seek to collaborate with Christians on an equal footing in Western countries, but where they are in power they discriminate against them.

Peace obviously cannot be reduced to a doctrinal problem. The objective and subjective dynamism of humanity is totally involved in it, and historical forces normally exercise a greater influence on it than do ideas.

It seems to me, nevertheless, that even philosophical reflection has its part to play in real change. If philosophy must be considered as the mere reflection of economic structures and consequently of a conflict of interests, then it is certain that no autonomous function can be attributed to it in the solution of real problems and in the evolution of the world. But while we admit the conditioning of ideas by history, we, Christians and Marxists alike, think that the infrastructures do not explain them adequately, and, consequently, that it cannot be denied that culture has a relatively autonomous function in history. Historical materialism and historical idealism must be mutually integrated.

This conviction is all the more important since it is impossible to believe in human initiative without believing in a certain autonomy of thought. Indeed, there is no initiative unless there is planning for the future, unless thought is transformed into a scheme of action. Man is not a creator unless, in a certain measure, his thought is. The ideal significance of human existence is also in question. It is the autonomy of intellect that makes it possible for the ideal to arise in history. Initiative and ideal are correlative terms.

What is the function of thought, then, in the movement of men towards peace? It consists, first and foremost, in a lucid awareness of the situation and its deep roots. War cannot be seriously combated unless we penetrate to its causes. But the analysis and critique of the situation must be clarified by a vision of the ideal. How can one commit oneself to the ideal of peace without giving a precise meaning to the word, without being inspired by an historical plan, a plan for the future? If there is some risk of the contemplation of the ideal remaining sterile by abstracting from the concrete conditions of its realization, it is no less true that action aimed at peace and conducted entirely at a technical level, would be extremely impoverished, and, in the last analysis, ineffective.

In order to avoid the danger of technocracy, therefore, it is the duty of intellectuals to make men constantly aware of the ideal aspect of their life and struggle. Moreover, Christians and Marxists have a common conviction: human life and history cannot be orientated solely by the search for immediate welfare, but must be inspired by a great ideal. This appeal, launched into the deafening noise of industrial civilization, is a message of salvation. It is by deepening its meaning that Christians and Marxists can probably come to a greater understanding and perhaps, in some measure, to the discovery of a common mission. We can understand others only by beginning with their ideal, with what they aspire to. We are too much given to the practice of opposing our own ideals to the realities of others. If we have a feeling of mutual misunderstanding, it may well be because we really do misunderstand each other. A complex of historical circumstances has prevented us from realizing our ideal in full and from understanding that of the other side. Their accusations are certainly difficult to understand, and a climate of distrust is created between us, even though we are all working for the liberation of mankind. The first and most urgent step in re-establishing human relations between us must be a mutual effort to transcend the deficiencies of our historical achievements and to aim at the ideal which is the wellspring of our initiative.

But is an ideal convergence between Christians and atheists, above all between Christians and Marxists, possible? Must it not be said that since we start off from profoundly different systems of thought we will have radically different meanings for the terms 'peace', 'liberty', 'justice', 'solidarity', 'fraternity', and 'democracy'? Is it not true that the diversity of the intellectual universe within which we move will lead to radical ambiguity in every attempt at dialogue, and every plan for collaboration?

Christians and Marxists alike often come to the conclusion that the peace to which they aspire will be reached only in opposition to the 'others'. They think collaboration is possible only when the others have renounced their position. Now it is inconceivable that collaboration should be effected in this way without a lack of coherence and dignity.

Our contribution, as intellectuals, to building peace lies, therefore, in trying to understand others by considering their historical ideal, and in searching for conditions for any possible genuine collaboration while remaining faithful to our respective convictions.

Perhaps it would be useful at this point to state that by studying the conditions of the possibility of collaboration between Marxists and Christians at a philosophical level, it is not my intention to usurp the place of politicians. They must judge the expediency of such collaboration in any given situation. Nor do I wish to usurp the place of local hierarchies, which, while they respect the autonomy of the laity in its own sphere, may see fit to make pronouncements on the religious and moral implications of a political alliance in a particular historical context. Our reflection is made solely at the level of the doctrinal basis for such practical steps.

This project is at once much less and much more ambitious than that of politicians who seek concrete agreements—for example, on the non-proliferation of nuclear armaments, on disarmament, on the cessation of atomic experiments, or on the cessation of hostilities. It is less ambitious because it remains at the level of doctrines and converging ideals. Precisely on this account, however, it is more ambitious, too, because, not content with agreement on various details, it investigates the possibility of a common vision of peace, which would give greater profundity and stability to any agreement of a practical order.

The effort to understand is made particularly difficult insofar as it is a question of bringing two 'faiths' face to face. It seems impossible, in fact, for either to understand the other or to welcome his criticism without being unfaithful to his own ideals. In reality, a faith is all the richer to the extent that it is capable of opening itself to the ideal values of others. The more capable it is of constant self-criticism, the more alive it is.

As far as I am concerned, it is important to distinguish Christianity as an ideal from psychological and sociological manifestations of Christianity; from actual Christian life as it faces up to daily and scientific experience, often contrasting with the gospel.

Although by the power of the Holy Spirit the Church has remained the faithful spouse of her Lord and has never ceased to be the sign of salvation on earth, still she is very well aware that among her members, both clerical and lay, some have been unfaithful to the Spirit of God during the course of many centuries. In the present age, too, it does not escape the Church how great a distance lies between the message she offers and the human failings of those to whom the gospel is entrusted.

Whatever be the judgement of history on these defects, we ought to be conscious of them, and struggle against them energetically, lest they inflict harm on the spread of the gospel (GS 43, 6).

The distance referred to here concerns the faithful not only in their personal lives, but also in their social relationships and consequently in their effect on history.

On the same doctrinal level, all assertions by Christians do not necessarily express essential Christian tenets. In fact, there is plenty of room within Christianity for opposing views on a great diversity of theoretical and practical problems. The contemporary Church is more open than ever before to this pluralism, and is becoming particularly sensitive to the evolution of doctrine, above all in the political, economic and social fields.

Often enough the Christian view of things will itself suggest some specific solution in certain circumstances. Yet it happens rather frequently, and legitimately, that with equal sincerity some of the faithful will disagree with others on a given matter. Even against the intentions of their proponents, however, solutions proposed on one side or another may be easily confused by many people with the gospel message. Hence it is necessary for people to remember that no one is allowed in the aforementioned situations to appropriate the Church's authority for his opinion (GS 43, 3).

In reality it has not always been so. The apologetic, protective attitude, which was especially characteristic of the Counter-Reformation period, promoted in our theologians a tendency to minimize the role of liberty and research and to emphasize that of infallibility. This tendency showed itself in political, social and economic matters too, and was often responsible for theories being presented as the 'social doctrine of the Church' which would be difficult to trace to the gospel, and which, in fact, merely reflected cultural frameworks of the time. Religious reflection can tend, and in practice often has tended, towards the defence of the established order.

It is becoming increasingly clear—and this process is hastened by sometimes dramatic historical experiences—that this monolithicism can deform the authentic face of the Church and identify it with states of affairs and ideologies of doubtful merit. The contemporary Church is so conscious of the seriousness of these deformations that it sees fit to proclaim the responsibility of believers for the genesis of atheism: 'To the extent that they neglect their own training in the faith, or teach erroneous doctrine, or are deficient in their religious, moral, or social life, they must be said to conceal rather than reveal the authentic face of God and religion' (GS 19).

It is our very loyalty to the gospel that must lead us to search out and frankly denounce those attitudes in present and past Christian communities which may have contributed towards the consolidation of an unjust social order instead of opposing it. It is this same loyalty to the gospel that prompts us to distinguish, on the doctrinal level, what constitutes the essence of the message from positions which the believer has the right to dispute and reject even though they may be widely held by Christians.

These considerations open up infinite horizons of research, enrichment and dialogue to Christian reflection. 'The Church also realizes that in working out her relationship with the world she always has great need of the ripening which comes with the experience of the centuries' (GS 43, 6). 'The Church requires special help, particularly in our day, when things are changing very rapidly and the ways of thinking are exceedingly various. She must rely on those who live in the world, are versed in different institutions and specialties, and grasp their innermost significance in the eyes of both believers and unbelievers. . . Indeed, the Church admits that she has greatly profited and still profits from the antagonism of those who oppose or persecute her' (44, 2–3).

The question is whether analogous considerations should not apply with regard to Marxism. A distinction appears to be necessary between doctrinal and historical Marxism. One must, at the very least, admit that the Marxist movement has had to come to terms with historical circumstances on matters of primary importance, with results often far removed from what Marx had in mind. Will criticism of historical Marxism not be a condition of loyalty to ideal Marxism? It seems to me that the meaning of Marxism is distorted when it is turned into a canonization of history, an identification pure and simple of the real with the ideal. Moreover, on the doctrinal level, Marxism is progressively passing out of its dogmatic stage and adopting an attitude of research. Now there is no true research without self-criticism and a guiding ideal as perspective.

Besides, is it not true that Marxist doctrine has been presented, for a long time back, both by its protagonists and by its adversaries, under monolithic forms which have contributed to the misunderstanding of its basic inspiration? If many Marxists frankly condemn these distortions today, is it any wonder that they have provoked radical criticism in Christian circles?

I think that if we face our problems in this spirit of reciprocal honesty and openness our dialogue has a good chance of success, in the short or in the long term. The following is our working hypothesis: there is a real possibility that we can meet each other without being unfaithful to our fundamental options. The questions and criticisms that we exchange should contribute to this honesty and to this encounter.

Review of the position so far

The criticisms of each other made by Marxists and Christians have as their respective targets certain images of Christianity and Marxism which might usefully be presented schematically, since this will enable us to pinpoint the problem more accurately. Then we must question these interpretations, or better, integrate them. It cannot be denied, nevertheless, that history provides a certain justification for such impoverished reconstructions both of Christianity and of Marxism.

For Christianity, the roots of war must be sought essentially in the subjective order, in the realm of interior imbalance which is the result of original sin and which, in consequence, will never disappear in this life. As regards the objective situation, this is good in itself and willed by God, although the egoism of men has produced injustice.

The ideal of peace outlined by Christianity is based on personal conversion therefore, and has an essentially moral and religious content. The prospect of a new world concerns, above all, the world beyond. Certainly, objective transformations are praiseworthy, too, but they are reforms within a system considered to be satisfactory and final. In particular, private ownership of the means of production is a natural right, and, consequently, every reform must be compatible with that system. One must not think, therefore, in terms of setting up a new order on earth or of planning a revolution. Reforms will come about through evolution.

Action aimed at furthering this evolution will be essentially moral and religious. It will seek to be effective only in respect of needs in these areas. It will particularly avoid every form of subversion or violent overturning of the established order. In Julius Stahl's formula, 'All revolutions are against the will of God'.

For Marxists, on the other hand, the causes of war are to be sought essentially in the objective situation of mankind, above all in the economic sphere, particularly in the system of private ownership of the means of production. This system legalizes the enslavement of men and of peoples by one another. War is the natural result of imperialism, the monopolistic stage of capitalism. The most powerful trusts try to solve the problem of commercial outlets by supplying war materials to the state and by conquering new markets. The master-slave dialectic applies not only to relationships between men, but also to relationships between peoples, above all in the case of colonial or neo-colonial regimes. At the same time, this state of alienation provokes wars of liberation. Peace can be re-established, therefore, only through a radical revolutionary transformation of the economic system, that is, through a change-over from private to collective ownership of the means of production. The new infrastructures will create a new moral climate. Relationships between men will develop in an atmosphere of liberty and fraternity.

The overturning of the established order will necessarily involve warfare, violence and the dictatorship of the proletariat. Every method which helps to bring about revolution is good. Consequently, Marxists reproach the Church for giving a merely moralistic, ineffective solution to the problem of peace, a solution which distracts attention from the real problems, and favours passivity and immobilism. The Church is blamed for canonizing the capitalist system along with all the alienations that it generates. Behind a screen of indifference it takes the side of the rich against the poor. On the problem of violence it adopts an ambiguous attitude, approving of violence, or rather of war, for the defence of the established order, but condemning it when it aims to overthrow unjust structures through revolution or a war of liberation. It admits the possibility of a just war but not that of a just revolution. In condemning the violence of the poor, the Church ends by favouring that of the rich.

But Christians, for their part, will reproach Marxists with detracting from the problem of war by ignoring its subjective components, and with making the requirements of effectiveness and economic progress prevail over the requirements of the moral order. They will reproach them, above all, for giving preference to violent and dictatorial methods.

The heart of the problem is this, then: in order to ensure peace, must revolution be repressed or must it be brought about? If peace is the tranquillity of order, is it a question of preserving an existing order or of establishing a new one? Is there a radical divergence between the Marxist and Christian positions on the relationship between peace and revolution? In answering these questions, whether in relation to Marxism or to Christianity, we shall have to use again the fundamental distinction between the integralistic and humanistic models. Integralisms can never meet, on the problem of peace or on any other problem. I see the possibility of research in common as dependent on a humanistic re-interpretation of both Christianity and Marxism.[1]

[1]My inspiration in this presentation of Christian humanism comes mainly from the documents of Vatican II and from Pope Paul's latest encyclical, *Populorum Progressio*. May I be permitted also to refer to my own article ' L'Église Face à l'Humanisme Athée' which will be published in *Constitution Pastorale sur l'Église dans le Monde de ce Temps, Série Vatican II, Textes et Commentaires des Décrets Conciliaires*, edited by Y. Congar, O.P., Paris, *Editions de Cerf*. I will limit myself to these more recent documents in order not to prolong this report excessively. But it would be easy to show that, although they reveal a new sensitivity, they are firmly rooted in the most ancient Christian tradition.

My views are often very close to those of Emmanuel Mounier, especially in his *Révolution personnaliste et communautaire*, Paris, 1935; *De la Propriété Capitaliste à la Propriété Humaine*, 1936; *Feu la Chrétienté*, 1950; *Les Certitudes Difficiles*, 1951. The problem of the theology of revolution greatly occupied the World Conference of the World Council of Churches dealing with the subject, see *Église et Société* (Geneva, 12–26 July, 1966), the proceedings of which constitute a very important contribution to the

THE CAUSES OF WAR

The question of the causes of war is one of the most dramatic aspects of the problem of evil. Indeed, it would be difficult to imagine a more massive concentration of physical amd moral evils. In this respect, the Marxist and Christian solutions seem to be irreconcilable. But are they really so if one makes an effort to leave current formulas behind and to return to the inspiration at the source of each system?

The Christian world, on the one hand, is becoming increasingly aware of the objective, and especially the economic circumstances of human existence and of war.

> Never has the human race enjoyed such an abundance of wealth, resources and economic power. Yet a huge proportion of the world's citizens is still tormented by hunger and poverty, while countless numbers suffer from total illiteracy. Never before today has man been so keenly aware of freedom, yet at the same time, new forms of social and psychological slavery make their appearance. Although the world of today has a very vivid sense of its

---

clarifying of the problem. I have had access to cyclostyled copies of these proceedings and I should like to mention, in particular, the contributions of the Metropolitan Nicodemus, the Archpriest Borovoy, Richard Schaull, Max Kohnstamm, and Heinz-Dietrich Wendland.

With regard to Marxist humanism: inspired by Marx and his most advanced contemporary disciples, I have presented it synthetically in the report 'Marxism and Integralism'. The soundness of this interpretation has been confirmed by numerous reactions in Marxist circles. My essential theses at the historical level coincide with those of R. Garaudy in his latest work *Le Marxisme du XX Siècle*, Paris 1967, a book in tune with history and a major contribution to the progress of dialogue.

With regard to Soviet thought, the proceedings of the Twenty-second Congress of the Communist Party of the Soviet Union,especially the programme laid out by it, represent an important development.

unity and of how one man depends on another in needful solidarity, it is most grievously torn into opposing camps by conflicting forces. For political, social, economic, racial and ideological disputes still continue bitterly, and with them the peril of a war which would reduce everything to ashes (GS 4, 4).

While an enormous mass of people still lack the absolute necessities of life, some, even in less advanced countries, live sumptuously or squander wealth. Luxury and misery rub shoulders. While the few enjoy very great freedom of choice, the many are deprived of almost all possibility of acting on their own initiative and responsibility, and often subsist in living and working conditions unworthy of human beings. . . The contrast between the economically more advanced countries and other countries is becoming more serious day by day, and the very peace of the world can be jeopardized in consequence (GS 63, 3-4).

If peace is to be established, the primary requisite is to eradicate the causes of dissension between men. Wars thrive on these, especially on injustice. Many of these causes stem from excessive economic inequalities and from excessive slowness in applying needed remedies (GS 83).

Paul VI, having taken up and developed this analysis, writes: 'There are certainly situations whose injustice cries to heaven' (*Populorum Progressio* 30; referred to hereafter as PP), and which risk provoking 'the judgement of God and the wrath of the poor' (49). 'The Church shudders at this cry of anguish and calls each one to give a loving response of charity to his brothers' cry for help' (3).

The conciliar and pontifical texts do not go into the details of this economic interpretation of the causes of war. One can deduce from them, however, that the subjective explanation is inadequate and must be complemented by an analysis of the objective situation, especially in its economic aspects. This must take into account, not just objective requirements, but liberty, too. Even if it is not stated that imperialism is a cause of war, there is nothing to prevent the Christian, acting on his own responsibility, from interpreting it in this way. But can the Christian condemn the system of private ownership of the means of production as one of the fundamental causes of war? If he has in mind the system in its present state, then he certainly can. But if, on the other hand, he is considering the system of private ownership in itself, then the question becomes more delicate. We shall take it up again shortly.

The Christian, nevertheless, will decline to see in economic laws an adequate explanation of war; he will consider it necessary to take other subjective and objective factors into account. 'Other causes spring from a quest for power and from contempt for personal rights. If we are looking for deeper explanations, we can find them in human jealousy, distrust, pride, and other egotistic passions' (GS 83).

The way that structures tend towards egotism requires a more profound explanation than any that can be given at the economic level. Christianity finds it in the original condition of man as marked by sin. 'Insofar as men are sinful, the threat of war hangs over them, and hang over them it will until the return of Christ. But to the extent that men vanquish sin by a union of love, they will vanquish violence as well, and make these words come true: "They shall beat their swords into plowshares and their spears into pruning hooks; one nation shall not raise the sword against another, nor shall they train for war again" (*Is.* 2:4)' (GS 78, 6).

On the other hand, we know that we still have much to learn from theological reflection about the exact significance of original sin. But, prescinding from these discussions, when Christian tradition proclaims a state of fundamental imbalance in the human condition, this is an historical experience to be reckoned among the broadest and most profound.

As we shall see shortly, it is essential that this explanation should not introduce fatalism into the consideration of evil and of war, or deprive human initiative of its drive and its terrestrial hope.

Is there something in this point of view that is absolutely incompatible with Marxist principles? The placing of a question-mark over internationalism—with the revival of nationalism in socialist countries, and, above all, with the conflict between Russia and China—forces the most sensitive Marxists to revise their idea of the causes of war. Moreover, the increasing awareness in humanistic Marxism of the autonomy of superstructures draws attention to a complex of problems to which economic transformations alone, however much advanced, will never provide the answers.

Undoubtedly Marxists, by virtue of their atheism, will refuse to see subjective disorder as a state of sin, much less as the consequence of a personal act which dragged down the whole of humanity in its fall. But is it really inconceivable that they should be able to admit the presence in the human condition of an original imbalance with deeper and more permanent roots than those which they have considered up to now?

Marxists and Christians can agree, it seems, on the need for an objective, and, above all, an economic explanation. They agree that the inequalities to be overcome are not merely those dividing individuals and social classes, but also those which divide countries and continents. Action aimed at suppressing the causes of war must operate, therefore, on the objective sphere (and above all, the economic sphere) and, at the same time, on the subjective and especially the ethical level It must affect both national and international issues.

Thus we are led on to analyze the ideal of peace to be pursued. This further reflection will enable us to deepen our critique of alienation, a critique that should be carried out with reference to a clearly defined historical project.

THE IDEAL OF PEACE

Peace and Revolution: the Marxist Position

A plan of the city of the future is central to Marxism. In fact, Marxism offers itself as a message of hope dominated by an ideal of the new man. By an analysis of this ideal one can discover the profound inspiration of the doctrine and of the movement. The new man is the complete man, the developed man; he has satisfied his really genuine desires. He can come to be only within a new mankind. The evolution of the ideal man coincides with the construction of the ideal city. Liberty and unity are the themes which will enable this goal to be fully realized. In the city of the future the liberty of all will be conditional on the liberty of each. All dominion of man over man will be outlawed. Man will have acquired such mastery over nature and over history that he will allow them to orientate his destiny. In a communal manner, every man will fulfil himself as the end, author and guide of his own action.

The concept of liberty is wedded, in Marxism as in Hegelianism, to that of unity. The liberation of man is his unification. The end of enslavement coincides with the suppression of dualism and conflict between man and his ideal, man and nature, man and society. Man discovers interior unity and peace when he achieves unity with the world, which he masters through work, and unity with the community, of which he becomes a part through the medium of collaboration and fraternity. The ideal for man is this reconciliation with himself which involves the reconciliation of the universe.

Liberty, unity and peace are historical tasks, therefore, which mankind is called upon to carry out gradually. The whole of history thus becomes a movement of liberation, unification and pacification.

With regard to the existing condition of mankind, this project represents a radical breakthrough. It is not a perfecting of the existing order, but the establishment of a new order involving the whole of personal and social life, political, economic and social structures, and the very principles that regulate them. It is a question, then, of an ideal revolution in the most complete sense.

This revolution has no longer simply the aim of toppling one group from power in order to replace it with another, or of making the interests of one class prevail over those of another. The intention is to strike at the very system in which the liberty of some can be the product only of the oppression of others, in which some cannot fulfil themselves subjectively unless others are reduced to the status of objects. Although it concerns the whole of human existence, personal and social, the proletarian revolution attributes fundamental importance to the overthrow of the capitalistic structures which lie at the origin of alienation.

But it would be a radical distortion of the meaning of Marxism to reduce its ideal to the institution of a new economic system. In fact, one of its fundamental insights is into the necessity of placing the economic aspect in the context of the total human reality. This certainly means that one cannot plan a human revolution without taking the economic basis into account; but it also means that one can tackle economic problems only by viewing them in a wider context. The

Marxist attitude to economics can be understood only by transcending the narrow economic viewpoint.

Economic liberation is not just freedom from want; nor is it the general raising of living standards as a result of increased production and a revision of the distribution of wealth. All this is essential, but in itself gives rise only to a welfare civilization. The Marxist ideal implies essentially a moral element, that of liberty defined as the active participation of men in the orientation of economic affairs and of the whole of history. In short, revolution consists in the passage from a society based on slavery and the desire for power to a society based on love and liberty.

In comparing Communism and capitalism, therefore, the capacity to increase the rhythm of production and the level of welfare must not be taken as the exclusive criterion. If in underdeveloped countries, which must attend to primary needs, the emphasis on productivity prevails over other considerations, in those countries, on the other hand, where the primary needs have been catered for, the need for social responsibility, respect for human dignity, and so on, will emerge more and more clearly.

These reflections on the integral significance of a proletarian revolution that is at once personalistic and communal, ethical and economic, are indispensable in arriving at the exact meaning of the concepts of *praxis* and effectiveness, and in superseding current pragmatic interpretations.

It is in this perspective that we must face the problem of systems of ownership. Collective ownership of the means of production is not an end in itself. For Marxism, it is a necessary condition for social life centred on liberty and fraternity. Thus collective ownership and Marxist economics may not be identified without more ado as one and the same thing. Marxist economics represents a form of collective ownership, the purpose of which is to allow the most extensive participation of the masses in economic power; it is a form of collective ownership in the service of liberty. But we must return to this problem later.

It is on the requirements of this historical ideal that Marx and many of his disciples base their atheism. For him, the development of man comes only with the denial of God and the disappearance of religion. Here again we find the conflict between religion and revolution, the essential terms of which have already been defined. The religious problem itself, which is provoked by economic alienation, will have no *raison d'être* in the city of the future. Total peace will coincide with total atheism.

A growing number of contemporary Marxists, however, are being led to ask themselves whether this opposition must be considered absolute, or whether it may not be tied to a certain type of religion and of Christianity that is susceptible of evolution, if, indeed, it has not already been left behind by vast sections of the Christian world. I have in mind, in particular, the Tenth Congress of the Italian Communist Party, during which it was declared that the religious conscience can become a source of revolutionary commitment. If this interpretation of religion is to be affirmed, will not the Marxist ideal cease to be essentially atheistic and become simply lay?

Peace and Revolution: the Christian Position

Whatever Communists may think, it is natural for Christians themselves to ask whether these idealistic aspirations are, of their nature, incompatible with religious commitment. Must one really choose between religion and revolution?

There undoubtedly exist theoretical and practical versions of Christianity which seem to demand such a choice. In these, religion seems to be identified with an immobilistic conception of the world and of society, and consequently of peace. Radical transformations of reality are postulated, but solely at the level of the individual, while the reigning social order becomes more or less sacred. But our chief interest in these formulations derives not so much from the political, economic and social spheres as from the monolithic way in which they are linked up with religious motivation. So we can appreciate the force of certain Marxist criticisms. The Council felt it had a duty to proclaim explicitly the responsibility of Christians in the genesis of atheism. Is it not true that the divorce between Christianity and the modern world derives largely from this supposed incompatibility of Christianity and revolution?

The Christian conscience, however, is finding it increasingly difficult to recognize itself in such formulations. It feels the need to make the central commandment of love explicit in a dynamic plan for the future of the world.

An authentic Christian attitude, in fact, must involve revolt against the current condition of the world and awareness of the need for radical changes; it must involve 'conscientious objection' to a whole system of life and of society. I have stressed the vigour with which the Council denounced the multiple alienations rooted in the structures of our age at the individual level and at the level of whole peoples. How could it have failed to do so if it is true that 'The joys and the hopes, the griefs and the anxieties of the men of this age, especially those who are poor or in any way afflicted, these too are the joys and hopes, the griefs and anxieties of the followers of Christ. Indeed, nothing genuinely human fails to raise an echo in their hearts' (GS 1)?

Now this participation in the sufferings of men, this solidarity with the poor, must be translated into the will to transform. One can no longer love one's neighbour without loving mankind. And one cannot love mankind without working to transform it. The Church knows that, if it is not to remain at the level of generality, it must become involved in fighting the causes of poverty and tackling the objective conditions that give rise to it. As the Council puts it: 'Vigorous efforts must be made . . . to remove as quickly as possible the immense economic inequalities which now exist. In many cases, these are worsening and are connected with individual and group discrimination' (GS 66, 1).

'An improvement in attitudes and widespread changes in society will have to take place if these objectives are to be gained. God's Spirit, who with a marvellous providence directs the unfolding of time and renews the face of the earth, is not absent from this development. The ferment of the gospel, too, has aroused and continues to arouse in man's heart the irresistible requirements of his dignity' (GS 26, 4).

For Paul VI, the dispute, besides involving the moral deficiencies of those mutilated by atheism, also involves 'oppressive social structures, whether due to the abuses of ownership or to the abuses of power, to the exploitation of workers or to unjust transactions' (PP 21). 'Development demands bold transformations, innovations that go deep. Urgent reforms should be undertaken without delay' (PP 32). 'It is not just a matter of eliminating hunger, nor even of reducing poverty. The struggle against destitution, though urgent and necessary, is not enough. It is a question, rather, of building a world where every man, no matter what his race, religion or nationality, can live a fully human life, freed from servitude imposed on him by other men or by natural forces over which he has not sufficient control; a world where freedom is not an empty word and where the poor man Lazarus can sit down at the same table with the rich man' (PP 47). The Pope prefers to reserve the term 'revolution' for violent insurrection, which he does not condemn indiscriminately in any case (PP 31). But this detail of terminology should not veil the revolutionary import of what he is saying, properly understood. The Christian revolution is first of all an interior conversion, a profound change of mind, an encounter with a new set of values centred indissolubly on the love of God and of men. If the love of God is genuine, it does not draw one away from the love of men, but leads to a religious giving of oneself to them. One can be converted to God only by being converted to men, above all to those most in need. The word of God is heard through the cry of the world's wretchedness.

But the Christian realizes that the driving force of history is the egoism of individuals and groups, become incarnate in objective structures. This fact is all the more scandalous when it is found in countries where Christians form a majority.[2] Any appeal for love which does not postulate the transformation of the world is, therefore, wishful thinking. The revolution will be authentic only if it aspires to flow over into objective reality, to bend the laws of history. Thus the Christian conscience discovers the historical dynamism latent in the commandment of love, 'the basic law of human perfection and hence of the transformation of the world' (GS 38, 1). The spirit of revolution takes its place, therefore, alongside the commandment of love, at the very heart of Christianity.

The love of man requires the creation of the objective conditions for his development in the religious and secular spheres. 'Hence, the norm of human activity is this: that in accord with the divine plan and will, it should harmonize with the genuine good of the human race, and allow men as

[2]'Some nations with a majority of citizens who are counted as Christians have an abundance of this world's goods, while others are deprived of the necessities of life and are tormented with hunger, disease, and every kind of misery. This situation must not be allowed to continue, to the scandal of humanity. For the spirit of poverty and of charity is the glory and authentication of the Church of Christ' (GS 88, 1).

individuals and as members of society to pursue their total vocation and fulfil it' (GS 35, 2).

But man must be viewed as an 'historical' reality rather than simply as a 'natural' reality. The evolution of conscience is an essential factor in the concrete determination of the conditions for his complete fulfilment. For this reason, the commandment of love, though absolute, is itself historical, and one cannot limit oneself to scanning the biblical texts in order to grasp all its requirements for today's world.

In the present stage of the evolution of conscience, liberty has taken on an essential role. Man must fulfil himself as subject, that is, as end, author and controller of his action, of institutions and of history. 'Throughout the world there is a similar growth in the combined sense of independence and responsibility. Such a development is of paramount importance for the spiritual and moral maturity of the human race. This truth grows clearer if we consider how the world is becoming unified and how we have the duty to build a better world based upon truth and justice. Thus we are witnesses of the birth of a new humanism, one in which man is defined first of all by his responsibility toward his brothers and toward history' (GS 55, 1).[3]

[3]'A sense of the dignity of the human person has been impressing itself more and more deeply on the consciousness of contemporary man. And the demand is increasingly made that men should act on their own judgment, enjoying and making use of a responsible freedom, not driven by coercion but motivated by a sense of duty' (*Dignitatis Humanae*, I).

'And man is only truly man in as far as, master of his own acts and judge of their worth, he is author of his own advancement, in keeping with the nature which was given to him by his Creator and whose possibilities and exigencies he himself freely assumes' (PP 34). 'World unity, ever more effective, should allow all people to become the artisans of their destiny. . . . The younger or weaker nations ask to assume their active part in the construction of a better world, one which shows deeper respect for the rights and the vocation of the individual. This is a legitimate appeal; everyone should hear it and respond to it' (PP 65).

The contemporary religious conscience, adopting these requirements, affirms that the organization of the world in terms of man is postulated by the affirmation of God: there is a theocentrism that does not exclude anthropocentrism, but essentially implies it.

Consequently, a revolution inspired by love should be a movement of personal and social liberation. For today's Christian, the central commandment of love becomes the commandment of the liberation of man, of the struggle against all alienation. The synthesis of the commandments of the love of God and the love of man becomes the synthesis of religion and liberation, of religion and revolution. It is the task of our time to bring into the open all the social and global implications of this challenge.

'If we call ourselves revolutionaries and do not will all of this, we lie. But if we will all of this and do not wish to be called revolutionaries, what does it matter? By revolution I mean a complex of transformations far-reaching enough to destroy the real evils of a society that has arrived at a dead end; rapid enough to deny these evils the time in which to poison the land with their decomposition; measured enough to allow time to mature what can mature with time alone'.[4]

There is no reason, therefore, to consider the revolutionary ideal as essentially tied to atheism. The making explicit of the anthropocentric component of Christianity offers to atheism the possibility of working out a common historical project with all who, regardless of their religious perspective, are concerned with the liberation of man.

Peace and the Economic System: the Christian Position

The confrontation between Marxist and Christian ideals has still to pass through a decisive phase, namely, the economic

[4]E. Mounier, *Les Certitudes Difficiles*, Paris, Seuil, 1951.

phase. Indeed, Marxists and Christians alike think that the total liberty of man must involve economic liberty. Whereas for the Marxist, however, economic liberty presupposes collective ownership of the means of production, it would seem that, for the Christian, liberty demands the system of private ownership.

Is this opposition as irreducible as it sounds? Is there something at the heart of the Christian message that necessitates the rejection of the very principle of collective ownership? Must the idea of Christian socialism be considered contradictory? Is the link between Christianity and the private-ownership system an essential one, or must it be considered 'historical' and hence susceptible of evolution at the practical and doctrinal levels?

Before going more deeply into this divergence, I should like to underline the importance of the convergence which accompanies it and provides its foundation. An ownership system should place economic goods in the service of all men and under the active control of a majority. It should eliminate not only inequality of distribution but all dominion of man over his fellows.

'The fundamental purpose of this productivity must not be the mere multiplication of products. It must not be profit or domination. Rather, it must be the service of man, and indeed of the whole man, viewed in terms of his material needs and the demands of his intellectual, moral, spiritual, and religious life. And when we say man, we mean every man whatsoever and every group of men, of whatever race and from whatever part of the world' (GS 64).

'Whatever the forms of ownership may be, as adapted to the legitimate institutions of people according to diverse and changeable circumstances, attention must always be paid to the universal purpose for which created goods are meant. In using them, therefore, a man should regard his lawful possessions

not merely as his own but also as common property in the
sense that they should accrue to the benefit not only of himself
but of others' (GS 69, 1).

It is not enough that economic affairs be controlled to the
advantage of all; it is also necessary that men should be in a
position to exercise initiative, that they should be subjects
rather than mere objects.

> Economic development must be kept under the control
> of mankind. It must not be left to the sole judgment of a
> few men or groups possessing excessive economic power,
> or of the political community alone, or of certain,
> especially powerful nations. It is proper, on the contrary,
> that at every level the largest possible number of people
> have an active share in directing that development. When
> it is a question of international developments, all nations
> should so participate. It is also necessary for the spontaneous
> activities of individuals and of independent groups to be
> co-ordinated with the efforts of public authorities. These
> activities and these efforts should be aptly and harmo-
> niously interwoven (GS 65, 1).

These principles are among the most traditional in Christian
social thinking. But their implications, and, above all, their
incompatibility with liberal economics have only gradually
become manifest.

It is in the light of this that the critique must be undertaken
of any system of ownership, private or collective, which places
productive goods in the service of, or under the exclusive
control of, a restricted group of private individuals or of
politicians.

Deriving from this in particular is the thesis that 'Private
property does not constitute for anyone an absolute and
unconditioned right. No one is justified in keeping for his
exclusive use what he does not need, when others lack

necessities' (PP 23). Consequently, property, of its nature, is never merely private, since its finality is essentially communal.

But these principles will remain abstract and inoperative unless given flesh in structures. Harmony of individual and communal needs cannot result from the spontaneous play of economic laws. Specifically, it requires massive intervention by the state as the expression of the interests of the community. 'Because of the increased complexity of modern circumstances, government is more often required to intervene in social and economic affairs, by way of bringing about conditions more likely to help citizens and groups freely attain to complete human fulfilment with greater effect. The proper relationship between socialization on the one hand and personal independence and development on the other can be variously interpreted according to the locales in question and the degree of progress achieved by a given people' (GS 75, 3).[5]

'Individual initiative alone and the mere free play of competition could never assure successful development. . . . It pertains to the public authorities to choose, even to lay down the objectives to be pursued, the ends to be achieved, and the means for attaining these, and it is for them to stimulate all the forces engaged in this common activity' (PP 33).

'One must recognize that it is the fundamental principle of liberalism, as the rule for commercial exchange, which is questioned here' (PP 58).[6] On the other hand, Paul VI

---

[5]'Growth must not be allowed merely to follow a kind of automatic course resulting from the economic activity of individuals. Nor must it be entrusted solely to the authority of government. Hence, theories which obstruct the necessary reforms in the name of a false liberty must be branded as erroneous. The same is true of those theories which subordinate the basic rights of individual persons and groups to the collective organization of production' (GS 65, 2).

[6]'But it is unfortunate that on these new conditions of society a system has been constructed which considers profit as the supreme law of economics, and private ownership of the means of production as an absolute

denounces 'the danger of complete collectivisation or of
arbitrary planning, which, by denying liberty, would prevent
the exercise of the fundamental rights of the human person'
(PP 33). This intervention does not consist only in economic
planning, but can go as far as appropriation: 'The right of
private control, however, is not opposed to the right inherent
in various forms of public ownership. Still, goods can be
transferred to the public domain only by the competent
authority, according to the demands and within the limits of
the common good, and with fair compensation. It is a further
right of public authority to guard against any misuse of
private property which injures the common good' (GS 71, 4).
The encyclical *Mater et Magistra* had already established that
'State and public ownership of property is very much on the
increase today. This is explained by the exigencies of the
common good, which demand that public authority broaden
its sphere of activity'.[7] But to what extent is this movement

right that has no limits and carries no corresponding social obligation. This
unchecked liberalism leads to dictatorship rightly denounced by Pius XI
as producing "the international imperialism of money". One cannot condemn
such abuses too strongly by solemnly recalling once again that economy
is at the service of man. . . . It is true that a type of capitalism has been the
source of excessive suffering, injustices and fratricidal conflicts whose
effects still persist' (PP 26).

[7] *Mater et Magistra*, no. 117.

'During the last two centuries, the whole trend of economics and of
society has been incessantly and increasingly to reduce the field of application of the idea of individual ownership of goods (productive goods in
any case), the idea that physical dominion over a thing mediates one's
will over it.

This sphere is restricted to the artisan, to the small property and to petty
agricultural or horticultural profiteering at the family level; to durable
equipment, to household goods and to human dwellings. Anything over
and above this falls, or is tending more and more to fall, under the scope
of regulations that transcend the person' (L. Jansse, *La Propriété*, Paris,
Les Éditions Ouvrières, Economie et Humanisme, 1953, 226–227).

legitimate? How far can appropriation by the state be pushed? *Mater et Magistra* restates the principle enunciated in *Quadragesimo Anno:* public ownership of productive goods is justified 'especially those which carry with them a power too great to be left to private individuals without injury to the community at large'.[8]

There will be a great diversity of concrete applications of this principle, since the exigencies of the common good can be interpreted in various ways. But the principle as such allows of great advances along the road to nationalization if the community democratically decides to follow it.

Thus the right of private property is further delimited, since it concerns only those productive goods which do not give excessive economic power to a private individual.

There is another important point to be made, I think. The increasingly fundamental role played by technologists in the regulation of modern enterprise calls for a distinction between ownership and control over goods (as made in several places by the Council: cf. GS 71, 1, 2, 3). This control seems to be derived more and more from labour. The Council first affirms that 'Human labour which is expended in the production and exchange of goods or in the performance of economic services is superior to the other elements of economic life. For the latter have only the nature of tools' (GS 67, 1). It then looks forward to 'the active participation of everyone in the running of an enterprise' (GS 68, 1). The right of participation in the power to make decisions is becoming increasingly bound up with labour, and the owner who, as such, decides the fate of goods, is less and less in evidence.[9]

[8] *Mater et Magistra,* no. 116.
[9] 'The significance attributed to ownership by Christian social doctrine has been constantly diminishing, in conformity with modern reality. In the productive sector, where there is a preponderance of large enterprises, "the role played by the owners of capital in very large productive enter-

It must be pointed out, finally, that private ownership is opposed to public ownership but not to social or communal ownership. The right to private ownership of productive goods can also be understood, therefore, in the sense of participation in social ownership, which constitutes a further limitation of private individual ownership and of the corresponding right.

How, then, are private ownership and individual liberty related? According to *Gaudium et Spes*, 'Ownership and other forms of private control over material goods contribute to the expression of personality. Moreover, they furnish men with an occasion for exercising their role in society and in the economy. Hence it is very important to facilitate the access of both individuals and communities to some control over material goods' (71, 1). 'Private ownership or some other kind of dominion over material goods provides everyone with 'a wholly necessary area of independence' (71, 2). Thus there is no explicit mention of productive goods, and besides, private ownership is subsumed under the broader and more fundamental concept of 'control over goods'.

The Council, faced with an extremely complex problem,

---

prises has been separated more and more from the role of management" (*Mater et Magistra*, no. 104). This means that the exercise of economic responsibility is increasingly less tied to ownership. The large enterprise, on the successful functioning of which thousands of families depend, is no longer directed by the owner, but by experts. This shows that the old opposition between capital and labour has changed its character too. . . . All these changes and problems demand new thinking on social doctrine. . . .

As labour gradually gains in importance, ownership as the economic basis of existence is losing ground. . . . This increase in the significance of labour is not a neutral phenomenon. On the contrary, it is of its nature a moral phenomenon, because it brings economies more into conformity with the essential values of man and of society' (Theodor Mulder, S.J., 'La Vita Economico-Sociale', from *Le Idee Centrali del Capitolo*, in *La Chiesa nel Mondo di Oggi*, Florence, Vallechi, 1966, 435, 452).

preferred to take up a markedly prudent position, leaving
the possibilities wide open, as shown in formulations like
'ut, sive singulorum sive communitatum . . . ad quoddam
bonorum exteriorum dominium accessio foveatur'.

It is well, too, to note that no distinction was made
between ownership of productive and consumer goods.[10]
The notion of property, which has already become
'analogous', not to say 'equivocal', continually creates
difficulties in the social doctrine of the Church. It seems
urgent, therefore, as suggested, in fact, by one of the
preparatory texts, to replace it with the notion of
'availability of goods', or 'control over goods'. In this
way, the analysis would be much more relevant in a
period which, to use the expression of *Mater et Magistra*,
is one of 'socialization'.

The word 'ownership' no longer expresses with sufficient
precision the diversity of rights over the means and
instruments of production, over collective social organizations, over social security services, over perishable and
durable, domestic and personal goods. . . .[11]

In a commentary on *Gaudium et Spes*[12] we read: 'The section
devoted to ownership is undoubtedly the most novel in this
chapter, and it marks important doctrinal progress on several
points. . . . There is a clear detachment from Roman law, which
influenced certain formulations in the past'.[13] In particular,

[10]Louis Joseph Lebret, 'La Vita Economica e Sociale', in *La Chiesa nel
Mondo Contemporaneo*, Brescia, Queriniana, 1966, 220.
[11]*Ibid.* 228.
[12]*Concile Oecuménique Vatican II, Documents Conciliaires, III, Éditions du
Centurion*, Paris 1966, Part II, ch. 2. The introductions to *Gaudium et Spes* are
by Mgr. Vilnet, Mgr. René Piérard, Mgr. Gabriel Matagrin, Mgr. Marius
Mazier, Mgr. Alfred Ancel and Charles Ehlinger.
[13]*Ibid.* 177.

'it is constantly asserted that the values of personal liberty, responsibility and security can be guaranteed by means other than private ownership; there are other forms of personal power over goods, other sources of security'.[14]

Father Jarlot, commenting on the same texts, writes:

> Some new progress will be noted in this passage. The living space of a family no longer consists principally, as it did for Pius XII, in landed property, nor, as in the case of John XXIII, in the addition of artisan enterprises and some personal securities. But mention is made of a sufficiency of goods and, more exactly, of ownership or some other form of dominion over material goods. This indicates an evolution of thought. The scope of indispensable personal and domestic autonomy is no longer tied to the juridical formula of private ownership as defined by nineteenth-century civil law. The property-liberty duality established by the eighteenth-century physiocrats and protagonists of natural law, and taken up again by the encyclopaedists and by the revolution, has been abandoned. It is now asserted that in order to guarantee the necessary autonomy of person and family some kind of dominion over material goods is sufficient. Moreover, the forms of such dominion or ownership are varied today and are becoming increasingly diversified. In this kind of perspective, discussion about the origin of private appropriation of goods (as to whether it is a secondary natural right or a right derived from *ius gentium*) becomes a school dispute and belongs to the past. The Constitution *Gaudium et Spes* does not disinter it.[15]

[14]*Ibid.* 178.

[15]Georges Jarlot, 'La Dottrina della Proprietà Privata da Pio XII alla "Populorum Progressio" ', *La Civiltà Cattolica*, 20 May 1967, 353-354.

It seems, indeed, that to call for private ownership of productive goods in order to protect individual liberty would be to ask both too much and too little. Too much, if it were meant that every man, in order to be free, must possess productive goods or have the concrete possibility of possessing them, since, if it is evident that the exercise of liberty demands the ownership of certain consumer goods, it would be difficult to prove that it demands ownership of productive goods.

But if, in speaking of private ownership of productive goods, one has in mind a right which, being exercised by a minority of private individuals, represents a defence of liberty by ensuring that there will be no preponderance of public power, this would seem to ask too little. In fact, from the moment when the right of appropriating the great centres of economic power and of directing activity as a whole is granted to the state, the private ownership of any productive goods ceases to constitute a sufficient defence of individual liberty. The latter must be ensured by means of control by the whole community over the public authorities and by means of the participation of workers in decision-making power at all levels. As long as decision-making power coincided with ownership, private ownership could have seemed to be an essential condition for the exercise of liberty. It seems today that decision-making power does not coincide with ownership, or rather, that it is becoming increasingly separate from it, and is becoming associated with labour and professional competence, on the one hand, and with exigencies in the political order on the other. Thus the problem has shifted. In this new context, it is a question of seeking the economic system that will simultaneously ensure the universal distribution of goods and communal participation, especially by the workers, in economic and historical decisions. Thus the role of private ownership appears to be subordinate. All the limitations imposed on it by the need to solve the essential problems are legitimate.

In a word, Christian thought, while it affirms the natural right of private ownership of productive goods,[16] is placing more and more limits on it. It recognizes the universal purposes of wealth, the right of all to participate in economic initiative, the need for forceful state intervention, the legitimacy of public ownership of the principal means of production, the primary role of labour in economic affairs, the importance of social forms of ownership, and, finally, it relegates ownership to a category of 'dominion over goods', a concept which more adequately expresses the importance of the natural rights of the person.

In speaking of natural right, I should like to say that this right is not conferred by the state but derives from the

[16]This, at any rate, is the most widely found doctrine among Christians. Nevertheless, Father Diez-Alegria, Professor of the Social Doctrine of the Church at the Gregorian University, questions this thesis on the basis of an analysis of the Constitution *Gaudium et Spes* placed in the context of Christian tradition. 'As far as I am concerned', he writes, 'the confrontation of par. 2. no. 71 of *Gaudium et Spes* and the texts referred to in the footnotes demonstrate that *Gaudium et Spes* follows the line of the preceding documents. Its special contribution consists in the generalization of the affirmation of the necessity of private ownership, or if one wishes, in rendering more general this concept of private ownership whose necessity is affirmed. The fact that reference is not made to productive as distinct from consumer goods is due to this development of the concept of ownership, necessary if it is to remain possible to assert that ownership is positively and absolutely demanded by natural law (by the objective moral needs of the human community). In these circumstances, the affirmation in *Gaudium et Spes* of the necessity of private ownership or some other kind of dominion over material goods does not include in its general terms, positively or necessarily, the affirmation of the absolute and unconditioned necessity of the system of private ownership of the means of production',('El Concilio Vaticano II y el Problema de la Propriedad Privada' to be published in *Actitudes Cristianas ante los Problemas Sociales*, Barcelona, Estela, the author of which has kindly let me read the manuscript. This, to my knowledge, is the most profound commentary available on the treatment of the problem of ownership in *Gaudium et Spes*).

exigencies of the person himself. In this regard, one sometimes hears reference to the priority of the person over society. The expression is not a very happy one, since it tends to give the impression that the social order has an accidental character —as though the social order were a qualification of the person conceived in fundamentally individualistic terms. Now, on the ontological and axiological levels, man is essentially and simultaneously individual and communal. His being, his knowledge and his destiny can be realized only in the community and by means of the community.

Nevertheless, man is not completely explained by this relationship. He cannot be adequately defined as a pattern of relationships. More precisely, his relationship with the community is not merely that of part to whole, but that of one whole to another, and his relationship to social structures, including the state, is that of end to a system of means. This means that the person has rights which are not conferred on him by the state, but which the state ought to make it possible for him to exercise. It means that the initiative belonging to the state in economic affairs belongs to it solely in the measure in which it truly represents the interests and will of the community.

Peace and the Economic System: the Marxist Position

How does this conception of economics stand with regard to Marxism? It certainly conflicts with a totalitarian and monolithic Marxism in which the individual is essentially and completely relative in his being, his end and his initiative to the collectivity. In this context, in fact, the participation of the individual in control over goods is never a right but is, at best, a concession by the state. The radical opposition lies here, in the right of participation in the dominion over goods which accompanies economic initiative.

Nevertheless, I think that this view contrasts with the original inspiration of doctrinal Marxism, according to which the whole economic system is orientated towards allowing the participation of the individual in the historical initiative of the community. The abolition of private ownership means, essentially, the suppression of the great centres of private economic power and the accompanying institutionalized egoism. As regards the state, its sole *raison d'être* is to render possible the development of the individual in the community, so that the state itself will disappear when it has carried out its function. In fact, we might well ask whether Marxism has not undervalued the role of the state and of its links with the essential requirements of social life. In any case, Marxism is definitively orientated, not towards public ownership, but towards communal ownership. Public ownership, like the state itself, is a transitional phenomenon.

In these conditions the right of the person over goods is not conceded by the state but recognized by it. State intervention in economic matters is legitimate only insofar as it is required by the universal purpose of wealth. Thus the small private property can be, and in fact is allowed by systems inspired by Marxism.

Unfortunately, the historical incarnations of Marxism, in the economic field as elsewhere, are much closer to the integralistic than to the humanistic model, although nowadays a certain evolution towards a wider and more independent participation of the workers in decision-making power and in profit may be discerned. But I shall return again to the historical aspect of the problem.

Staying with the problem at a doctrinal level, it seems to me that quite extensive possibilities of dialogue are opened up. The theme of private ownership will no longer be so very central, because it will have to be subordinated to the wider context of economic and historical initiative. Dialogue implies

evolution on both sides. Just as Christians are becoming more
and more aware of the need to ensure the social orientation of
economic affairs, so Marxists are called upon to leave behind
the idea of integralistic action by the state and to restore the
creative value of autonomous initiative. In the search for these
new syntheses each side will have to face rather serious
difficulties. They will be honest enough to admit that their
respective doctrines and experiences do not so far furnish a
solution. It is a question, therefore, of continuing the search
and (why not?) of searching together.

ACTION TOWARDS PEACE

If Christians and Marxists can come together on an historical
project, will they not inevitably come into conflict when the
question arises of choosing the means of action? Has the
Christian's task anything in common with Marxist *praxis*?
As regards revolution, the Marxist does not simply aim at the
establishment of a new order: he offers a method of bringing it
about. Even if an encounter between Marxist and Christian
thinking is possible at the level of ideals, do they not necessarily part company on the question of methods? Can the
Christian adopt revolutionary methods? What is in question
here, primarily, is the problem of violence. It must be faced
in the light of a more general problem, that of the relationship
between morality and effectiveness, and, more radically, of the
relationship between the value of the individual and the value
of the community. Are the Christian and Marxist views on
this matter quite incompatible? Any comparison is made
particularly difficult by relevant differences at the heart of
Marxism and of Christianity. On the other hand, this internal
pluralism demands avoidance of monolithic formulae and of
any over-facile elimination of divergences.

The Christian Position

Within Christianity attitudes vary from the proclamation of holy war to the absolute condemnation of violence. Besides, there is a marked difference of perspective between the Old and New Testaments in this matter. It is principally to the Old Testament that the theorists of holy war owe their inspiration, whereas apostles of non-violence lean heavily on the New Testament.

The history of the problem has also been influenced by the integralistic mentality and by its accompanying political and social conservatism. Recourse to violence and war was much more easily justified when it was a question of defending the established 'order', or the 'rights' of God or of the Church, of fighting infidels or heretics, and even of spreading the faith, than when it was a question of overthrowing a regime (especially if it supported the Church). This means that the evolution of doctrine on the problem of violence is a consequence not solely of the new dimensions of modern warfare, but also of the advance of a personalistic and communitarian mentality in the Church.

The solution which I am outlining here cannot be considered universal, therefore, in the Christian world. On the other hand, while it is Christian, it is not specifically so, and I think it should be capable of gaining the approval of a great part of the Marxist world. I intend to tackle the problem of violence, not in all its aspects, but from the specific viewpoint of revolutionary action.

My position can be summed up in two theses: (1) a decided preference for non-violent action, with acceptance of its inevitable slowness; (2) the legitimacy of violence as an extreme solution for the prevention of violent action with irreparable consequences.

First, a decided preference for non-violent action, with acceptance of its inevitable slowness: 'We cannot fail to praise those who renounce the use of violence in the vindication of their rights and who resort to methods of defence which are otherwise available to weaker parties too' (GS 78, 5). Before justifying this choice, it will be essential to establish its significance. I am speaking here, not simply of non-violence, but of non-violent action. What I am advocating is not a passive, resigned, quietistic attitude, but a dynamic attitude, the aim of which is to act on the person as such, on his very conscience, and to provoke a change of mind, or 'conversion' within him. The new mentality, centred on love and on liberty, must penetrate community and individual alike. The new education which it demands devolves especially on the young generation, which is more in tune with the new expectations of the time and with the new calls on man's spirit.[17]

Although it attributes a decisive function to interior conversion, non-violent action seeks, nevertheless, to be objectively effective. It is not just a protest: it is a real movement. The concept of man which inspires it is not disembodied and a certain historical materialism is not alien to its spiritualism. Love must not merely flow from man to man: it must permeate structures (where it finds incarnate the mentality which it is fighting), whether on the political, the economic or the social level, and it must also create new ones which will effectively promote liberty and secure, in form and in reality, government for the people and of the people. In order to promote liberty effectively, the authorities must be in a position to 'choose, even to lay down the objectives to be pursued, the ends to be achieved, and the means for attaining these' (PP 33). Thus non-violent action does not exclude coercion;

[17]'Hence arises a surpassing need for renewed education of attitudes and for new inspiration in the area of public opinion. Those who are dedicated to the work of education, particularly of the young, or who mould public opinion, should regard as their most weighty task the effort to instruct all in fresh sentiments of peace' (GS 82).

rather, it requires it, as long as individuals and communities move spontaneously in the direction of egoism. A liberal system is such only when the liberty of each is limited by that of others. Properly understood, this means that limitations should be imposed by the liberty of the great majority on that of a small minority. To be effective, this action must be cosmic. 'Today', writes Paul VI, 'the principal fact that we must all recognize is that the social question has become world-wide' (PP 3). 'There can be no progress towards the complete development of man without the simultaneous development of all humanity in the spirit of solidarity' (PP 43). Non-violent action aspires, therefore, to create a universalistic mentality and to launch a world-wide movement capable of bending the very laws of history. Its object is to make of love an historical force. For the achievement of this objective, international collaboration, however important, is inadequate as long as it does not fit into the framework of a world-wide community with effective authority at its head. 'This organization', says Paul VI in his speech to the United Nations, 'represents the necessary road of modern civilization and world peace'.[18] 'This international collaboration on a world-wide scale requires institutions that will prepare, co-ordinate and direct it, until finally there is established an order of justice which is universally recognized' (PP 78). 'Who does not see the necessity of thus establishing progressively a world authority, capable of acting effectively in the juridical and political sectors?'[19] Just as injustice in inter-personal relations can be dealt with only through the intervention of public authorities, so injustice in international relations can be suppressed only through the organic and

[18]*Discorso di Paolo VI all'ONU, Documenti del Concilio Vaticano II*, Ed. Dehoniane, Bologna 1967, 99.

[19]*Ibid.*, repeated in *Populorum Progressio*.

courageous action of an international authority which is the real expression of the interests of the whole of humanity. In order to be effective, this authority must be able to 'choose, even to lay down the objectives to be pursued, the ends to be achieved, and the means for attaining these', and must be able, in this way, to render operative the principle that economic benefits exist to serve everyone.

Finally, if it is to be effective, action, on a local, national, or international level, must be dialectical. The rejection of violence does not mean the rejection of resistance. Non-violent action must not be confused with an immobilistic conception of 'social peace', or with a pretended inter-classism which is really a camouflaged form of classism. There is a classism animated by hate and a classism animated by love. Resistance will be carried on, as far as possible, within the limits of legality, but it can cross these limits when laws are unjust or inadequate, thus exposing itself to condemnation by 'moderates'. If a law is unjust then disobedience is a duty. Christianity, itself born illegitimately, cannot abandon its mission of resistance and simply conform to the established order. As far as 'peaceful coexistence' is concerned, even if it involves condemning war as a method for bringing about a new world-wide equilibrium, it cannot mean the pure and simple acceptance of an existing equilibrium.

Therefore, non-violent action is revolutionary action. It involves worldwide resistance to the present system based on egoism and the desire for power and adopts in face of it an attitude involving resistance and discontinuity.

One can follow two quite different paths in order to justify this methodological choice. The first is based on reducing the importance of effectiveness by referring it to the total context; the second is based on a new concept of effectiveness. The first argument affirms the transcendence of love and the moral and religious grandeur of sacrifice, which enables a man willingly to become a victim so as to avoid creating victims himself. It pushes his giving to the point where he prefers the lives of others, even of the violent, to his own and to those of persons dear to him. This argument seems inconclusive to me, for reasons which will appear later.

The more valid argument, as far as I am concerned, is that which sees in non-violent action unique possibilities for revolutionary effectiveness. Indeed, total effectiveness bears upon both structures and consciences, transforms them permanently, and bases its stability on the consensus of the masses rather than on that substitute for violence called dictatorship.

Now violence, even if it achieves its immediate end of toppling the old structures, lacks revolutionary effectiveness, in the last analysis. It occasions the destruction of material and moral energy, destruction that is unforeseeable in the disordered chain of its development. Revolutionary forces, even if they succeed, will be absorbed for a long time in the urgent task of reconstruction, instead of being available for the task of organizing new structures.

But above all, the ineffectiveness of violence derives from the fact that it cannot decide how consciences will evolve. Moreover, because of man's instincts, because of hate, rivalry and the disorders which it provokes, violence becomes an obstacle in the way of evolution towards love and liberty. The stability of the system established by its means could be guaranteed, for a very long time, at least, only through dictatorship.

Violent action adopts the very methods which it seeks to destroy. It adheres in practice to the principle of the victory of the strongest. It adopts the rules of the game instead of transforming them. It risks merely reversing roles, therefore, without suppressing the state of alienation. It inevitably bears with it the seeds of counter-revolution.

Hence the internal contradiction of 'holy wars', which propose to advance ideal values by means which are constitutionally unsuited to the purpose. The very idea of a just war seems to me to reflect less and less anything concrete and realizable in our time. Modern war, as seen in progress and in preparation, is the most serious obstacle to revolution.

Must all forms of violence be condemned, therefore, without further ado? That of the master who oppresses and of the slave who rebels? That which strikes the innocent and that which defends him? The war of aggression or colonization, and the war of liberation?

Here is a question of making a judgement about non-violence as an absolute principle. In my view, absolute non-violence, however inspired, by a lay or by a religious outlook, is a heroic vocation, the traumatic, testimonial function of which is extremely important in the world today and especially in the revolutionary movement. It is a prophetic vocation, proclaiming the central commandment of love in a disturbing way, and anticipating the new humanity which it is helping to build.

For these reasons it resembles the religious vocation. Like it, however, it cannot be considered universal. In the present situation of mankind there are still cases in which recourse to violence is the sole means possible of preventing violence which would have irreparable consequences. It is not always possible to wait. The universal adoption of a non-violent attitude in this kind of situation would mean, in practice, giving free play to disordered violence. Heroic love can certainly go as far as self-sacrifice in order to avoid sacrificing an assassin, but when it is a question of others, who can say that the life of the malefactor should be preferred to that of the innocent? There is violence, then, which is postulated by love, violence which is postulated by non-violence.

How is this kind of situation identified in practice? At what moment is it legitimate to assert that violence has become the only way out? This concrete decision is a very difficult one and is subject to relativity. Starting out from the same principles and using the same data, different decisions may be reached about the approach that should be adopted in a concrete situation. The relativity of situational judgement, with all its accompanying risks, is part of the human condition.

Therefore, I do not place all forms of violence on the same level. I do not indiscriminately condemn recourse to violence. I do not say that a revolution inspired by Christian principles absolutely excludes recourse to violence. 'But it is one thing to undertake military action for the just defence of the people, and something else again to seek the subjugation of other nations' (GS 79, 4). 'As long as man remains the weak, unstable and even wicked being that he shows himself to be, defensive arms will unfortunately be necessary.'[20]

In regard to revolutionary insurrection, Paul VI, though he vigorously denounces the destruction to which it gives rise, does not absolutely exclude it. In fact, he makes an exception in the case of 'long-standing tyranny which would do great damage to fundamental personal rights and dangerous harm to the common good of the country' (PP 31). It is understood, however, that it is a question of something tolerated, of a last resort. Even when revolution makes use of violence, it succeeds only in spite of it. Violence never makes a revolution, although it may condition it at times.

For the sake of mankind's future, then, it is urgent that the distinction of revolution from violence should penetrate men's consciences.

The same principles that underlie a decided preference for non-violent action also underlie a preference for a substantially and formally democratic system. An authentic revolution is

[20]*Ibid.* 103.

one that is brought about and stabilized in a context of liberty. Of course, the same principles that justify recourse to violence in a state of emergency can justify, in this case and provisionally, recourse to dictatorial methods. But a dictatorship is not revolutionary unless it is definitely orientated towards the creation of conditions for democracy.

The Marxist Position

Could Marxism recognize itself in a doctrine such as I have outlined? Marx certainly attributed a decisive importance to violence in the gestation of a new society, and, in general, Communist revolutions have undoubtedly chosen this method.

After Marx, however, two new orders of facts were forced on the attention of Marxists as of others. On the one hand, violence has reached such atrocious and destructive forms that it is difficult to view them as instruments of progress or of liberation. There is no reason to suppose that the desire for peace on the part of Marxists is less sincere than ours. On the other hand, the spread of the democratic system and mentality, the evolution of a world conscience, and the opportunities for influencing public opinion which have been opened up by mass communications all open new paths to revolutionary action.

> These changes, which have left their mark on every country and on every social class, together with the fighting experience of the fraternity of Communist parties, were synthesized in the progress report of N. Krushchev at the Tenth Congress of the Communist Party of the Soviet Union. Congress deduced from it that, in the present circumstances, it would be possible for some countries to pass to socialism without armed insurrection or civil war. This conclusion was sub-

sequently confirmed in the documents of the conferences of representatives of Communist and workers' parties (in 1957 and 1960), and was thus adopted by the whole World Communist Movement.[21]

Moreover,

A peaceful changeover to socialism has great advantages. It enables a profound transformation of social life to be brought about with the minimum of sacrifice from the workers, with the minimum destruction of productive sources in society, and the minimum disruption of production. The peaceful conquest of power corresponds better to the world-view of the working class. The great humanistic ideals of the proletariat exclude unjustified violence, since the force of historical truth, of which the working class is the bearer, is such that the proletariat can depend entirely on the support of the vast majority of the people.[22]

But is it possible to justify preference for this type of action from Marxist doctrine itself? Let us recall, to begin with, that the Marxist ideal is of a new world from which every form of violence and coercion must be banished, even to the point where the state itself would be suppressed. As far as methods are concerned, the distinction to which I have already referred more than once, between the two models of Marxism, remains fundamental. For integralistic Marxism, since conscience is determined by structures, a revolution of objective conditions would necessarily involve a moral revolution. The essential thing is to act on structures by

[21]*Les Principes du Marxisme-Léninisme*, Moscow, Éd. du Progrès, II ed., (no date given; 1961?), 499.

[22]*Ibid.* 497. Cf. all of Ch. 20, *Différentes Formes du Passage à la révolution socialiste*, 473–503.

the most rapid means: effectiveness and revolution are defined solely in economic and objective terms. Consequently, recourse to violence becomes the normal method of revolution. Slow democratic methods will be used only if one has not enough power to do otherwise.

According to humanistic Marxism, on the contrary, conscience enjoys a certain autonomy, and, in consequence, revolutionary action ought to be able to act simultaneously on structures and on consciences. While aware that the transformation of subjective attitudes is largely conditioned by that of structures, Marxism realizes, too, that objective action alone is insufficient to constitute a true revolution. If nonviolent action reveals itself, therefore, as more effective in the complete sense, Marxism must be led by the internal logic of the matter to give preference to it.

The problem of dictatorship must be approached along the same lines. First of all, there is something equivocal about the concept of the dictatorship of the proletariat which must be rejected. By dictatorship is generally meant the power exercised by one man or by a small minority over the great majority in a country. But the dictatorship of the proletariat, as proclaimed by Marx and Lenin, is the absolute power of the majority over the minority. It is dictatorship, but in another sense, since it discriminates against the old propertied class in order to avoid a new reversal of the situation in favour of that class. Moreover, this system of discrimination is provisional, being destined to disappear along with division into classes and the mentality that accompanies that division.

Humanistic Marxism could admit dictatorship in the narrow sense as a solution in an emergency, almost by the same right as it could admit violence. Like violence, however, dictatorship is essentially insufficient to bring about the proletarian revolution. As long as dictatorship remains, the revolution has not yet succeeded. To believe in revolution is to believe

in the possibility of doing without violence, and dictatorship
in the strict sense, brings it about.

A Historical Perspective

If the foregoing reflections are valid, a certain convergence
of Marxist and Christian positions is possible in the working
out of a historical project in the secular sphere. In my view,
the most serious obstacles come, not from doctrinal questions,
but from relationships between communities and institutions
in their historical reality. Having set our ideals face to face, it
remains for each of us to acknowledge frankly at what points
we find a discrepancy between them and reality. This stage
of dialogue is all the more important insofar as history constitutes the testing ground of every plan for a new society.
History is the laboratory of the science of the future. As far as
I am concerned, once we have revealed the revolutionary
implications of the commandment of love for the secular
sphere, we must realize that the activity or passivity of
Christians often involves flagrant contradiction of this programme. I am aware of the scandal (GS 88, 1) of the ineffectiveness of our presence in the world, of the indifference
of too many of our number to the anguish of the poor, of the
support given by some of our number to oppressive regimes.
The Council (GS 19, 3), as already mentioned, finds in the
deficiencies of the religious, moral and social life of Christians
one of the sources of atheism. If social revolutions have often
had an anti-religious character, we cannot throw all the
responsibility for this on to the shoulders of the revolutionaries.
The history of the persecutions begins a long time before the
persecutions themselves took place.

One must take this opportunity of recalling the moving
testimony of Cardinal Beran during the Council:

In my country, the Church seems to be expiating today, the faults and sins committed at one time, in its name, against religious liberty, as, for example, in the fifteenth-century burning at the stake of the priest John Huss, and in the seventeenth century, with the forced return of a great part of the Bohemian people to the Catholic faith, on the principle 'cuius regio illius et religio'. This recourse to the secular arm, the intention or pretence of which was the service of the Catholic Church, has, in reality, left a wound in the hearts of the people. This traumatic action has obstructed religious progress. It has furnished, and still furnishes the enemies of the Church with a convenient argument with which to attack it.

The growing consciousness of the social demands of the Christian calling should be much more evidently expressed at the level of action. Much remains to be done before we can dissociate ourselves unequivocally from 'oppressive social structures, whether due to the abuses of ownership or to the abuses of power, to the exploitation of workers or to unjust transactions' (PP 21). It remains for us to carry out 'bold transformations, innovations that go deep' (PP 32), if we are to support our message with the testimony of history. Marxist criticism has stimulated us and will continue to stimulate us in the search for this more profound fidelity to our vocation (see GS 44, 2–3).

May I be allowed, in turn, to make a constructive critique of Marxism. This will not consist of 'objections' brought against our 'adversaries', but of problems whose gravity we appreciate and to which we would like to devote common research.

According to Marxist doctrine, the advent of Communist society should be preceded by a period of socialism. The Twenty-second Congress of the Soviet Communist Party adopted the thesis that socialism has already been brought about in the Soviet Union, which is now heading towards Communism.[23]

I should like to know what my opposite numbers think of this important statement. The revolution has not as its sole purpose the establishment of a new economic system. It involves the creation of a new man, characterized on the moral level by an attitude of responsibility and historical initiative, and on the level of structures by effective participation in power. In view of this, is it true to say that the socialist society already exists? Frankly, this kind of statement reveals a profound delusion, since the idea of socialism which we get from a reading of Marx, Engels and Lenin is much richer.

For my part, I wish to 'submit the following working hypothesis for discussion: to socialism and Communism, the stages initially foreseen by Marx, history has added a third stage, which we might call 'collectivism'. During this stage government exists, in principle, to serve the people. Political, economic and ideological monolithicism are considered essential to it. Strictly speaking, one cannot yet speak of dictatorship of the proletariat under this system, since that would involve the dominion of the proletarian masses over the *bourgeois* minority, whereas circumstances up to now have led to the concentration of power in the hands of a restricted group. This system has made achievements possible in certain sectors which would, perhaps, have been impossible with other methods. Nevertheless, it involves very serious risks, as the Stalinist experience so tragically proved. Even at best, this system, by reserving decision-making to a small minority, prolongs a structural situation of alienation,

[23]'Programma del partito Comunista dell'Unione Sovietica', in *XXII Congresso del PCUS, Atti e Risoluzioni*, Rome, Editori Riuniti, 1962, 785–909. Cf. all of this volume and especially Krushchev's report on the plan for a programme, 143–266.

which is the very thing that socialism aimed to suppress. If this is true, then the present problem is how to pass from collectivism to strict socialism as characterized by the people's active participation in power, and, consequently, by pluralism. Would this passage not perhaps have the nature of a 'qualitative leap'? In the last analysis, would it not have the qualities of non-violent revolution? It would mean a profound transformation at the level of structures and mentality and would involve a certain discontinuity with the past. It would mean taking the values of the first revolution and integrating them dialectically into a broader synthesis. This qualitative leap would be the signal, not for class warfare, but for the war between conservatives and innovators which is at present threatening to convulse the world of Marxism. The class struggle is not the only driving force in history, and the dialectic can take various forms. The temptation to treat the established order as something sacred always threatens those in power, including revolutionaries. A Christian dictatorship is tempted to see the existing state of affairs as the expression of the will of God, and a Marxist dictatorship is tempted to see it as the will of the people. God and the people remain relatively silent, however, and many things can be attributed to them.

In a word, I wish to reprove a great many Marxists, not for wishing to carry out a revolution, but for concluding too hastily that it has already succeeded; not, in other words, for being revolutionaries, but for not being revolutionary enough. No revolution launched in the name of liberty is complete until it has established a regime of liberty.

I should like to add a few words on an aspect of the question that is particularly offensive to the religious conscience, namely, atheistic monolithicism. From a general point of view, monolithicism, whether religious or atheistic, is an obstacle to the development of secular values and exercises a counter-revolutionary influence. Christian monolithicism pursues a policy of 'Christian civilization', characterized by the institutional subordination of the secular to the religious sphere, and by a tight bond between political and religious unity. The Christian state under an authoritarian regime is the best incarnation of these aspirations. Again, the confessional party is not considered simply as a fact justified by history, but as an ideal. In these politico-religious unities, the action of socially more advanced Christians is often neutralized or retarded by the massive presence of conservative elements. Religious monolithicism becomes a counter-revolutionary factor, a source of alienation. Nevertheless, Christian and Marxist monolithicisms assist each other. This is one of the most dramatic aspects of our relationships. The left has become atheistic because believers belonged socially to the right and seemed to be obliged so to belong by virtue of their social principles. Today, many Christians belong to the right because the left is atheistic and seems to be obliged to be so by virtue of *its* social principles. It seems to me that our Marxist friends should put the following question frankly to themselves: what is the present contribution of atheism, particularly state atheism, to the cause of revolution and of peace? In fact, the established link between socialism and atheism prevents many believers from collaborating in the building up of socialism and even from looking dispassionately at the problems it raises. Atheism offers conservative minds a basis for total condemnation of Communism. The religious polemic distracts attention from the urgency of the political and social struggle, gives rise to divisions among the workers, and, for that very reason, becomes an obstacle in the path of revolution. There is a contradiction, I think, between the call 'workers of the world, unite' and the desire to raise the banner of atheism. Unity will not be achieved under this banner. I certainly do not question the right of anyone to be an atheist and to propagate his convictions, but I am asking whether it is permissible on the doctrinal plane, or constructive on the practical plane, to associate atheism so strictly with the revolutionary ideal.

Besides, the problem of religious liberty is only one aspect of the broader problem of pluralism, and, in the last analysis, of the problem of the people's effective participation in power. The liberty of thought which we ask for ourselves we also ask equally for all. We are not defending the rights of the Church; we are defending the rights of man.

There are, of course, very serious difficulties involved in the participation of the masses in power at the national or international level. These arise in every revolutionary policy, not just in socialism, because they are rooted in the human condition. Mention must here be made of the technical difficulties arising out of the participation of the masses in political and economic power in the present state of civilization, where important decisions require an increasingly high degree of specialization. On the other hand, there is also that attachment to power which sometimes leads authorities to avoid genuinely free consultations with the people, where this could threaten their position or place the system itself in jeopardy. But it is perhaps the antinomy between liberty and revolutionary effectiveness, between subjective and objective needs, that raises the most delicate problems. It is actually a question of keeping a moral tension alive in the multitudes over a period of time, of leading them to accept freely a certain austerity and to resist the attractions of immediate welfare in order to help the country over more immediate hurdles, or to help underdeveloped regions, or to prepare for the humanity of tomorrow. This is all the more true insofar as it is not enough simply to bring about a revolution: efforts must be made to make its conquests irreversible. In such circumstances, members of the *avant-garde* will often be divided into those conscious of the urgency of the task and those conscious of the time it takes for the collective conscience to mature. They may be tempted to impose with violence or coercion an ideal for which they cannot gain free acceptance.

Deeper reflection on these difficulties can lead to questioning the very possibility of a new order, and to consideration of the whole project as utopian. 'Will the world ever change the individualistic, warlike mentality that has been manifest in such a great part of history up to now?' Paul VI asked in his address to the United Nations. 'It is difficult to foresee this, but it is easy to affirm the necessity of resolutely setting out along the road to a new peaceful history, fully and truly human—that promised by God to men of good will'.[24]

The question comes up again in his latest encyclical: 'Some would consider such hopes utopian. It may be that these persons are not realistic enough, and that they have not perceived the dynamism of a world which desires to live more fraternally—a world which, in spite of its ignorance, its mistakes and even its sins, its relapses into barbarism and its wanderings far from the road of salvation, is, even unawares, taking slow but sure steps towards its Creator. This road towards a greater humanity requires effort and sacrifice; but suffering itself, accepted for the love of our brethren, favours the progress of the entire human family' (PP 79).

It is a question of having trust in man; of taking risks in the belief that he is capable of initiative and moral maturation. The chance is worth taking.

As for us Christians, we believe that this immense project is at once our work and the work of God. The creative power of man is for us the most illuminating sign of God's creative power. The mysterious operative presence of love in history does not in any way detract from our responsibility, but gives us a new reason for hope. We believe in the revolutionary

[24]*Discorso di Paolo VI all'ONU, op. cit.,* 102–103.

power of grace and of the spiritual movement launched into the world by the life, death and resurrection of Christ. 'To those, therefore, who believe in divine love, he (the Word of God) gives assurance that the way of love lies open to all men and that the effort to establish a universal brotherhood is not a hopeless one' (GS 38, 1).

Nevertheless, though the ideal must be pursued unceasingly, everything would lead one to believe that its realization on earth will be only partial. Can such a profound aspiration of man, such a great movement in history, be largely doomed to frustration? Would such a prospect really be worthy of man?

Will our Marxist friends allow us to share with them, before concluding, our firm hope? We believe that the historical labours of man and of God are all the greater insofar as they are destined to last for ever, insofar as they are animated by the certitude that, at the end of the weary road, the eternal and universal community will be reunited in the fullness of the new humanity.

We do not know the time for the consummation of the earth and of humanity. Nor do we know how all things will be transformed. As deformed by sin, the shape of this world will pass away. But we are taught that God is preparing a new dwelling place and a new earth where justice will abide, and whose blessedness will answer and surpass all the longings for peace which spring up in the human heart.

Then, with death overcome, the sons of God will be raised up in Christ. What was sown in weakness and corruption will be clothed with incorruptibility. While charity and its fruits endure, all that creation which God made on man's account will be unchained from the bondage of vanity (GS 39).

It is the same conviction as that expressed in a picturesque manner by the Apocalypse: 'Then I saw a new heaven and a new earth. . . and I heard a great voice from the throne saying, "Behold the dwelling of God is with men. . . He will wipe away every tear from their eyes, and death shall be no more, neither shall there be mourning nor crying nor pain any more, for the former things have passed away." And he who sat upon the throne said, "Behold I make all things new." Also he said, "Write this, for these words are trustworthy and true" ' (21, 1–5).

Conclusion

The question which I have tried to answer is the following: Is collaboration possible between Marxists and Christians in building up peace, provided, naturally, that each side restricts itself to acting in a manner faithful to its own historical ideal? The Council issued an invitation to believers and non-believers without exception to act together in a 'gigantic task' (GS 93, 1), that of the 'construction of the world' (GS 57, 1; 21, 6; 92, 5) and the 'establishment of true peace' (GS 78, 4; 90, 2). Can it be concretely applied in this case? It was not my intention to pronounce on the expediency or otherwise of this or that political alliance, but to study the doctrinal implications of the question.

The difficulties in the way of this collaboration are of a theoretical and an historical order. I am principally concerned with the former, though, to my mind, the latter are the more serious. I believe that the nucleus of this problem is to be found in the problem of the relationship between peace and revolution.

My conclusion is that the strictly doctrinal difficulties, though real, are not insuperable. The differences between the two systems, radical as they are, do not exclude the possibility of broad and deep convergence at the level of ideals, convergence that could lay the foundation for a programme of common action.

In searching for this convergence, we must not forget that Christianity and Marxism present, and will do so increasingly, a certain internal pluralism. The distinction between the 'integralistic' and 'humanistic' models is of capital importance. Dialogue is possible only on a base line of humanism. More precisely, the possibility of dialogue is conditional on the recognition of the relative autonomy of secular values in relation to religious options, positive or negative. The convergence which I have tried to bring to light is not necessarily reflected in the thought of all Christians and Marxists, therefore, but can be found in large sections of both worlds. By affirming that the doctrinal difficulties are not insuperable, I do not mean that they have already been overcome. For many Christians and Marxists, in fact, they have not. In my judgement, however, deeper reflection on the original inspiration of the two systems and on the significance of the evolution in progress will solve the problem.

Because of its specific mission, Christianity shows more evidence of pluralism. While Marxism presents fairly definite technical solutions in the political, economic and social fields, the Church offers ethical principles that are capable of development and of many different applications, and these must be made by Christians acting on their own responsibility.

The points of convergence which I believe can be identified are the following:

1. The problem of war can be resolved only by striking at its deepest roots, which are at once objective and subjective,

national and international. The objective roots lie principally in the economic order, and place a universal question-mark over structures themselves.

2. Peace consists in the tranquillity of order; of a new order, however, not the existing order. This new order must be established though the consolidated action of men on a worldwide scale. In this sense, peace comes about through revolution. Contemporary man's consciousness of the grandeur and urgency of this historical task is a sign of his maturity. It may mean the coming of a new epoch.

3. The complete revolution produces a new humanity. So the transformation involved in it should be at once objective and subjective. It includes an interior conversion, a new ideal perspective, and a new attitude towards man, based on love and liberty. But there will be no cultural revolution without a structural revolution, and no new humanity without a new economy, without the incarnation of the new ideals in new structures.

4. The economic system, particularly as regards ownership, must, therefore, be transformed through the vigorous intervention of public authorities, national and international, and must be orientated to the service of all men, while under the effective control of the greatest possible number. This presupposes that the machinery of the state really expresses the interests and will of the community, and that the workers are participating in decision-making at all levels, and, consequently, in the economic and historical initiative of the nation. The ruling principle in the new regime will be the primary value of work in relation to all other economic factors.

5. Genuine revolutionary action will be action capable of these profound objective and subjective transformations. Although recourse to violence can sometimes be justified as an extreme solution to prevent violence, the method most appropriate to revolutionary requirements is non-violent action. Although

dictatorship can be justified as an emergency and only provisional solution, a revolution cannot be considered a success until its stability is based on the free support of the masses.

This dissociation of violence from revolution is of the greatest importance for the future of mankind. Thus revolution becomes an act of faith in man, and accepts the risks involved.

6. Private ownership of the means of production can, or rather, must be suppressed insofar as it gives a preponderance of the life of the country to private individuals, contrary to the needs of the common good. The concrete application of this principle will be very diverse, since the exigencies of the common good can be judged in various ways. As far as Christians are concerned, they must formulate these judgements on their own responsibility, without wishing to tie Christianity to a definite model of society. The principle, as such, allows much advance along the path of nationalization, if the community democratically decides to follow this path, respecting the fundamental rights of the person. These rights exclude, among other things, the replacement of private capitalism by state capitalism.

7. The future of mankind for a long time to come will be marked by the competitive coexistence of East and West, of capitalism and socialism. But there is no conclusive reason for making this competition coincide with that between faith and atheism, which belong to another order.

8. Consequently, a revolutionary ideal is identical neither with a religious viewpoint nor with an atheistic viewpoint. In order to put it into practice, believers and non-believers must be able to carry on the fight as equals, without discrimination. 'According to the almost unanimous opinion of believers and unbelievers alike, all things on earth should be related to man as their centre and crown' (GS 12, 1). It is inexact, therefore, to say, as is often said in order to put a hasty end

to any wish for dialogue, that atheism and Christianity, materialism and spiritualism, have nothing in common. Undoubtedly, the meaning of secular life is deeply marked by a total perspective, be it religious or atheistic, which embraces the whole of existence. But this kind of divergence, however decisive, does not essentially imply a difference of political, social, or economic outlook. The Christian obviously cannot collaborate with atheists in carrying out an historical project insofar as that project is atheistic, nor could an atheist collaborate with believers in carrying out such a plan insofar as it is religious. But each can collaborate in carrying out a plan that is simply human, and capable of being integrated into different doctrinal contexts.

9. This principle becomes operative only when the laicity of the state, with all its consequences, is acknowledged. The state must respect all ideologies and favour none with privileges. By virtue of its proper mission, it is neither Christian nor atheistic, but simply human. Believers and non-believers alike should be able to feel that they are citizens of it in the full sense.

These questions, which, for many of us, Christians and Marxists alike, have been solved at the level of doctrine, constitute grave difficulties, nevertheless, at the level of history. At this level Marxists are asking Christians to detach themselves, not only in theory, but also in practice, from capitalism. Christians are asking Marxists to detach socialism from dictatorial methods. At present the debate is centred on the question of whether it is possible for these steps, which look very like revolutions, to be taken at all.

The spirit of honesty demanded that we take account of the problems which remain to be solved even as we were considering those which had been solved or were in the course of solution. It demanded that we appreciate the realities that divide us just when we were discovering the ideal that unites us.

But is the ideal not perhaps that within us that is most real, the source of everything we have achieved? And, once discovered, must it not be translated, sooner or later, into common action for the transformation of the world?